Enlightenment
Unfolds

TRANSLATORS

Tenshin Reb Anderson
Edward Brown
Norman Fischer
Gil Fronsdal
Blanche Hartman
Jane Hirshfield
Taigen Daniel Leighton
Rebecca Mayeno
Susan Moon
Alan Senauke
Kazuaki Tanahashi
Katherine Thanas
Mel Weitsman
Michael Wenger

CONTRIBUTING TRANSLATORS

Robert Aitken
John Daido Loori
Tensho David Schneider
Brian Unger
Dan Welch
Philip Whalen

Enlightenment Unfolds

The Essential
Teachings of
Zen Master Dōgen

EDITED BY

KAZUAKI TANAHASHI

SHAMBHALA
Boston & London
1999

Shambhala Publications, Inc.
Horticultural Hall
300 Massachusetts Avenue
Boston, MA 02115
http://www.shambhala.com

© 1999 by San Francisco Zen Center

9 8 7 6 5 4 3 2 1

First Edition
Printed in the United States of America
⊗ This edition is printed on acid-free paper that meets the
American National Standards Institute Z39.48 Standard.
Distributed in the United States by Random House, Inc., and
in Canada by Random House of Canada Ltd

Library of Congress Cataloging-in-Publication Data
Dōgen, 1200–1253.
    Enlightenment unfolds: the essential teachings
of Zen Master Dogen/edited by Kazuaki Takahashi.
        p. cm.
    Includes bibliographical references.
    ISBN 1-57062-305-8 (cloth)
    1. Sōtōshū—Doctrines—Early works to 1800.
I. Takahashi, Kazuaki, 1933– . II. Title.
BQ9449.D652D6 1998   98-39897
294.3'420427—dc21   CIP

In deep gratitude to
Zen Master Shunryū Suzuki
who taught in San Francisco
from 1959 to 1971

Contents

Preface and Acknowledgments   ix
Notes to the Reader   xiii
Introduction   xv
Texts and Translation Credits   xlv

EMERGENCE OF THE TRUE DHARMA EYE, 1223–1235   1

   Journal of My Study in China   3
   Poems   28
   On a Portrait of Myself   29
   Record of Bringing Master Myōzen's Relics   30
   Recommending Zazen to All People   32
   Actualizing the Fundamental Point   35
   Cases for Study   40

RAISING SAGES, 1235–1246   45

   Donation Request for a Monks' Hall
     at the Kannon-dōri Monastery   47
   Formal Talk upon Establishing the Kōshō Monastery   49
   Informal Talks   50
   Valley Sounds, Mountain Colors   59
   The Time-Being   69
   The Power of the Robe   77
   Encouraging Words   102
   Miracles   104

Continuous Practice, Fascicle One   114
Continuous Practice, Fascicle Two   137
Within a Dream Expressing the Dream   165
Undivided Activity   173

GREAT AWAKENED ONES, 1243–1246   177

Intimate Language   179
Insentient Beings Speak Dharma   185
Turning the Dharma Wheel   196
In Honor of Master Rujing   199
On Carving the Buddha Image for the Daibutsu Monastery   200
Space   201
Formal Talk on the First Day of the Practice Period   205
Given to Hironaga Hatano   206

ETERNAL PEACE, 1246–1253   207

Formal Talk   209
Guidelines for Officers of the Eihei Monastery   210
Auspicious Beginning of Spring   255
Original Face   256
Transmission Outside Scripture   256
Formal Talk upon Returning from Kamakura   257
Omens of the Sixteen Arhats   259
On a Portrait of Myself   260
Three Auspicious Signs at the Eihei Monastery   261
Identifying with Cause and Effect   263
Eight Awakenings of Great Beings   270
Final Instructions   275
Poem   278
Death Poem   279

Selected Bibliography   280
Glossary of Terms   283
Glossary of Names   292

Preface and Acknowledgments

A PROFOUND THINKER and imaginative writer of medieval Japan, the monk Dōgen remains an extraordinary source of inspiration for readers of our time. The dramatic increase of translations and criticisms of his works published in the English language in the last two decades reflects a sudden recognition in the Western world of the greatness of this literary giant. Although Dōgen's work has been studied mainly by Buddhist practitioners, the interest seems to extend further to circles of scholars and artists as well as peace and environmental workers.

We present this selection of Dōgen's writings in chronological order. We hope the texts in this book illustrate Dōgen as a whole person—not only as a seeker, traveler, teacher, and priest who brought Zen from China to Japan, but as a poet, thinker, scholar, administrator, and woodcarver. The text consists of formal and informal talks, essays, monastic rules, journals, poems, and notes, including Dōgen's words as recorded by his disciples. Some were originally written in Chinese, others in Japanese.

This book is intended to be accessible to readers who are not familiar with Zen texts as well as to those who are. We have tried to make our translation as clear and readable as possible, while maintaining the original images and tone. At times we have added some interpretive words to explicate implied meanings behind the lines. Brackets indicate our own explanations. Full texts are presented unless otherwise indicated in the Texts and Translation Credits.

Dōgen's writings are full of technical terms, both Buddhist and non-Buddhist, and also of paradox and ambiguity. We chose, however, not to give multiple meanings of lines, or sources of quotations and references. Instead of referring to earlier masters with respectful titles, as Dōgen does, we usually use their best-known names (such as Bodhidharma instead of the First Ancestor or Great Master). Likewise, where more than one name of a person is given, we have put the best-known name first. We divided the texts into sections, with ornamental symbols in between, so that shifts in topics are easily seen.

A follow-up to *Moon in a Dewdrop: Writings of Zen Master Dōgen* (North Point Press, 1985), the present translation project of *Enlightenment Unfolds* has been sponsored by the San Francisco Zen Center. My cotranslators are all long-term practitioners of Zen in Dōgen's lineage. Some of them are teachers at the Zen Center and some are celebrated for their own literary work. The cotranslator's name on each text is shown in the section Texts and Translation Credits. We reprinted some pieces from *Moon in a Dewdrop* and credited my collaborators on these works as contributing translators on the frontispiece. We also credited Abbot John Daido Loori of Zen Mountain Monastery, Mt. Tremper, New York, as this book includes an excerpt from the translation he and I did of Dōgen's three hundred *kōans*.

I would like to express my deep gratitude to all my cotranslators. Studying thoroughly and translating Dōgen's texts with special friends has given me unspeakable joy. The earliest translation in this book was done with Robert Aitken Rōshi at the Diamond Sangha in Honolulu in 1965. Some other translations were done after 1977, when Richard Baker Rōshi, the abbot at San Francisco Zen Center at that time, invited me to work there as a scholar in residence, which I did for seven years. The translation work continued after I became a freelancer, and intensified in 1995 when the Zen Center approved the two-year project for creating this book. I appreciate the staff and leaders of the Zen Center community for their continuous friendship and support. My special thanks go to Michael Wenger, former president and current dean of Buddhist Studies of the Zen Center, for initiating and overseeing the project, and to Barbara Kohn, the current president.

Among my collaborators, Susan Moon has provided invaluable guidance by reading the entire manuscript and offering detailed editorial suggestions. Taigen Daniel Leighton has defined some words in the Glossary of Terms and created the Selected Bibliography. As we listed published books only, those who are interested in academic articles may refer to the bibliography in *Dōgen's Pure Standards for the Zen Community*, which he coauthored with Shōhaku Okumura. I would like to thank Abbot Mel Weitsman of the Berkeley Zen Center for meeting with me almost every week these several years, including the time when he was busy as coabbot of San Francisco Zen Center. Katherine Thanas, the dharma teacher at Santa Cruz and Monterey Bay Zen centers, often drove a long way to meet with me in my garage office in Berkeley. Rebecca Mayeno read aloud a number of translated texts to me while I reviewed the original. Her editorial suggestions are also appreciated. Dr. Gil Fronsdal provided his expert advice on some passages of my introduction. My partners have worked with me so many times for so many hours just for the love of Dōgen.

Those who have participated in translation sessions and helped improve the texts include Victoria Austin, Gaelyn Godwin, Michael Katz, Robert Lytle, and Meiya Wender. Basya Petnick and Robert Lytle have done some typing, and Victoria Austin did some research for us. Andy Ferguson, compiler of "Map of the Zen Ancestors," was kind enough to check the accuracy of the Chinese spellings and dates in the Glossary of Names. Also helpful was the discussion among scores of participants who attended the review meetings which took place in San Francisco, Berkeley, and Green Gulch in the spring of 1997. Linda Hess has responded to my frequent questions about English expressions. I would like to take this opportunity to thank the readers of *Moon in a Dewdrop*, as the enormous appreciation from many of them has allowed us to take on this current project. "The Teachings of Zen Master Dōgen," the audio cassettes of Gary Snyder's reading of the selections from that book, has added a new dimension to the literary heritage of Dōgen.

Michael Katz represented us in concluding a contract with Shambhala Publications. We are very happy that Peter Turner from Shambhala Publications encouraged us to make a proposal and accepted it. His editorial suggestions have helped improve many aspects of this book. I would also like to thank his colleagues David O'Neal, for overseeing the final stage of editing, and Brian Boland for directing the design process of the book. Jisho Warner has contributed to this book with her thorough and expert copyediting. Katharine Thanas, Linda Groteleuschen, and Michael Wenger helped in the process of proofreading.

We owe much gratitude to a number of Japanese scholars who have published accurate texts, detailed annotations, and historical examinations. The books we most frequently consulted are listed in the Selected Bibliography. Among those that are not listed, *Zengaku Daijiten* or *Comprehensive Dictionary of Zen Studies* has always been helpful. I have had the pleasure of working with Dr. Carl Bielefeldt and Dr. Griffith Foulk in the Sōtō Text Translation Project organized by the Sōtō School Headquarters in Tokyo. My conversations with these experts have put me in touch with current scholarship in Dōgen studies.

Jokingly, I sometimes ask my partners, "Are you ready to go back to the thirteenth century?" After being immersed in the dense world of Dōgen, we would reenter the present century, with the sense of having lived a very long time. Now it is time for me to wish the reader a marvelous journey.

Kazuaki Tanahashi

Notes to the Reader

Transliteration. Chinese terms are represented by the pinyin system, which is an official way of transliteration in the People's Republic of China. Sanskrit words are simplified and their diacritical marks are omitted, except for macrons.

Names. The abbots of Zen monasteries are often called by the name of the mountain, monastery, or region where they resided. Monasteries are also sometimes represented by the name of the mountain they were on.

Dates. This book follows the lunar calendar, used traditionally in East Asia. The first to third months correspond to spring, and the other seasons follow in three-month periods. The fifteenth day of the month is the day of the full moon. An extra month was occasionally added to make up a year.

Time. According to the traditional East Asian system, the daytime from sunrise to sunset is divided into six hours. The nighttime has six hours in the same manner. Hence the length of each hour changes daily.

Age. A person is one year old at birth and gains a year on every New Year's Day.

Years. A partial year is counted as a full year.

Introduction

Aspiration for Enlightenment

The founder of an early Zen* monastic community in Japan, Eihei Dōgen wrote extensively for the benefit of his students. Originals and hand-written copies of his writings were scattered in the course of time in temples all over Japan. But thanks to traditional and contemporary scholarship, a critical edition that compares variants in all available versions of Dōgen's texts has been published and is available for study.[1] Now the life of this thirteenth-century monk can be reconstructed with amazing detail, mainly using information from his own work. This book consists of some of the writings that reflect the progression of his life. In the following account I will try to let Dōgen speak as much as possible to describe his own life. When necessary, however, I will use information from the three main early biographies, all of which were written more than a century after Dōgen's death.[2]

We have no accounts by Dōgen himself about his family and personal history before he became a monk. He simply says, "When I was young, I loved studying literature that was not directly connected to Buddhism."[3]

According to the early biographies, Dōgen was born in 1200 CE, near the capital city of Kyōto. He was a member of a noble family and was believed to be an illegitimate son of an influential figure in the imperial court who died when Dōgen was an infant. He lost his mother when he was eight. Possibly referring to this early misfortune, Dōgen himself says, "Realizing the impermanence of life, I began to arouse the way-seeking mind."[4] At thirteen, he visited the monk Ryōkan who had a hut at the foot of Mt. Hiei, east of Kyōto, and entered the monkhood. In the following year he was formally ordained by Kōen, the head priest of the Tendai School. Probably Kōen was the one who named this novice Buppō Dōgen, meaning Buddha Dharma, Way, Source.

At that time Tendai and Shingon were the two most influential schools of Buddhism in Japan. The Shingon School exclusively practiced esoteric teachings—the secretly transmitted teachings of Tantric Buddhism—with emphasis on prayer rituals dedicated to guardian deities of supernormal appearance. Tendai, the Japanese form of the Chinese Tiantai School, was the most comprehensive school of Buddhism and included both esoteric and exoteric (non-Tantric) practices. Thousands of monks lived in huts and monasteries on Mt. Hiei, the Tendai center, where a wide range of practices and academic studies of Buddhism were conducted.

It was a dark and confusing time for Buddhists. All the high positions of the Tendai establishment were occupied by people from aristocratic families. Temples were competing with one another to gain imperial patronage, offering a variety of magical prayers. Mt. Hiei housed one of the strongest of the various armies of monk soldiers who frequently engaged in battle, often burning other monasteries. The Tendai armed forces were noted for their frequent demonstrations in Kyōto and for forcing their demands upon the imperial government.

According to Buddhist texts, the period of five hundred years after the time of Shākyamuni Buddha is the Age of True Dharma, which is followed by another five hundred years of the Age of Imitation Dharma. Then the Age of Declining Dharma emerges. Many Japanese Buddhists believed that this last period—of no true practice* or enlightenment*—had started in 1052. People attributed calamities such as famines, epidemics, social disorder, and wars to the decline of dharma. The wish for attaining rebirth in the Pure Land prevailed among those who felt that it was hopeless to attain enlightenment in the present world. Monk Hōnen emphasized an exclusive, intense practice of chanting the name of the Buddha of the Pure Land, Amitābha, and found a multitude of dedicated followers. Threatened by the popularity of this new spiritual movement, the Tendai community put constant pressure on the imperial government and finally had Hōnen and his noted disciple Shinran expelled from Kyōto in 1207.

Dōgen left Mt. Hiei after receiving basic training as a monk and studying the scriptures. Later he reflects, "After the thought of enlightenment arose, I began to search for dharma, visiting teachers at various places in our country."⁵ We don't know whom he visited, except Kōin, who was abbot of the Onjō Monastery, a noted Tendai center of esoteric practices, and a dedicated follower of Hōnen. Dōgen reflects later, "The late Bishop Kōin said, 'The mind of the way is acquired after understanding that one thought embraces all existence in the three thousand realms.' "⁶ Dōgen summarizes the first four years of his pursuit: "I had some understanding of the principle of cause and effect; however I was not able to clarify the real source of buddha, dharma, and *sangha*.* I only saw the outer forms—the marks and names."⁷

Dōgen continues, "Later I entered the chamber of Eisai, Zen Master Senkō, and for the first time heard the teaching of the Linji School." Myōan Eisai, who had visited China twice and received dharma transmission* from Xuan Huaichang, was among the first to teach Zen in Japan. But because the Tendai establishment was oppressing new movements of Buddhism, he had to teach conventional practices along with Zen. It was around 1214 when Dōgen visited Eisai at the Kennin Monastery in Kyōto, one of the three monasteries Eisai had founded. Eisai was seventy-four years old and he died the following year.

In 1217 Dōgen became a disciple of Butsuju Myōzen, Eisai's successor as abbot of the Kennin Monastery. We can assume that Dōgen was trained by Myōzen in *kōan**studies, which was the principal method of training in the Linji School. Kōans are exemplary stories of ancient masters pointing to realization, which are investigated by students under the personal guidance of their teacher and which may lead to direct experience of the nondual aspect of all things beyond intellect. In 1221 Dōgen received a certificate of full accomplishment from Myōzen.

Meanwhile, Dōgen was affected by the tragic bloodshed that took the lives of some court nobles related to his family: In 1221, after a long-standing power struggle between the Kyōto palace and the warrior government in Kamakura, Former Emperor Gotoba attempted to regain imperial rule. He ordered the monk-warriors of Mt. Hiei and other monasteries to attack the armies of the Kamakura administration. Quickly defeated in battle, the leading courtiers involved in the rebel plot were executed in Kyōto, and Gotoba and two other former emperors were exiled to remote areas.

Myōzen was respected in Kyōto and even gave the bodhisattva precepts* to Former Emperor Gotakakura, but he was aware of the need to deepen his studies. As China was the only place where he could study authentic Zen, he wanted to follow Eisai's example of traveling to the Middle Kingdom. A young but outstanding student at the Kennin Monastery, Dōgen was allowed to accompany Myōzen.

Due to difficulties in navigation, trade ships between China and Japan sailed infrequently, sometimes at intervals of several years. As Myōzen's company was getting ready to leave, his first teacher Myōyū became quite ill and asked him to stay. Myōzen gathered his students and asked for their opinions. All of them, including Dōgen, suggested that Myōzen stay. But Myōzen responded, "Although it would go against the wish of my teacher, if I can fulfill my wish to go to China and unfold enlightenment, this may help many people to realize the way."[8] Thus, leaving the care of Myōyū to other students, Myōzen went ahead and obtained a travel permit from the Kamakura government. This permit was endorsed by the imperial office.

Search in China

Myōzen's company, including Dōgen and two other disciples, left Japan from the Port of Hakata on Kyūshū Island in the second month of 1223. Two months later the boat arrived at the main trading port of Qingyuan, Zhejiang Province. Reflecting on this, Dōgen writes, "After a voyage of many miles during which I entrusted my phantom body to the billowing waves, finally I have arrived."⁹

Dōgen's first encounter with Chinese Zen happened in the following month, while he was still on board waiting for permission to enter a monastery. Myōzen, acknowledged as Eisai's dharma heir, had already left the boat and been admitted to the monastery. An old monk who was the head cook of a nearby monastery came on board to buy dried mushrooms. After some conversation Dōgen said, "Reverend Head Cook,* why don't you concentrate on zazen* practice and on the study of the ancient masters' words, rather than troubling yourself by holding the position of head cook and just working?" The old monk laughed and replied, "Good man from a foreign country, you do not yet understand practice or know the meaning of the words of ancient masters." Dōgen was surprised and ashamed.¹⁰

China's highest ranking Zen monasteries, known as the Five Mountains, were located in Zhejiang Province, where Dōgen arrived. He entered one of them, the Jingde Monastery on Mt. Tiantong, also known as Mt. Taibo. Soon he noticed monks around him holding up their folded dharma robes, setting them on their heads, and chanting a verse silently with palms together, "How great! The robe of liberation . . ." Seeing this solemn ritual for the first time, he made a vow to himself: "However unsuited I might be, I will become an authentic heir of the buddha-dharma, receive correct transmission of the true dharma, and with compassion show the buddha ancestors' correctly transmitted dharma robes to those in my land."¹¹

The abbot of the Jingde Monastery was Wuji Liaopai, a dharma descendant of Dahui Zonggao, the most influential advocate of kōan studies in the Linji School. While studying in Liaopai's community for a year and a half, Dōgen familiarized himself with formal monastic practices. Then he started visiting other monasteries in search of a true master.

In early 1225 Dōgen went to meet Abbot Yuanzi of the Wannian Monastery on Mt. Tiantai, who showed Dōgen his document of dharma heritage and said, "Following a dharma admonition of

buddha ancestors, I have not shown this even to a close disciple or
a long-term attendant monk.* But I had a dream five days ago that
an old monk gave me a branch of plum blossoms and said, 'If a true
man comes who has disembarked from a boat, do not withhold
these flowers.' So I have taken this document out for you. Do you
wish to inherit dharma from me? I would not withhold it if so."[12]
Dōgen had learned the significance of documents of heritage in the
Chinese Buddhist tradition, as the proof of the completion in studies and succession of the dharma lineage. They were often kept
strictly confidential, but Dōgen had managed to see some and made
careful studies of them. Moved by Yuanzi's offer to transmit
dharma to him, Dōgen bowed and burned incense, but he did not
accept.

The more closely he saw what was happening in monasteries in
the heartland of Chinese Zen, the more he was disappointed. He
comments in his journal: "Nowadays elders of different monasteries
say that only direct experience without discrimination—to hear the
unhearable and to see the unseeable—is the way of buddha ancestors. So they hold up a fist or a whisk, or they shout and beat people
with sticks. This kind of teaching doesn't do anything to awaken
students. Furthermore, these teachers don't allow students to inquire about the essentials of the Buddha's guidance and they discourage practices that aim to bear fruit in a future birth.* Are these
teachers really teaching the way of buddha ancestors?" [13]

Dōgen also saw corruption in monastic practices. Even documents of dharma heritage that were supposed to be valued with
utmost respect were given to those who were not qualified. Monks
tended to try to get credentials from famous masters who had given
dharma heritage to retainers of the king. When monks were old,
some of them bribed public officials in order to get a temple and
hold the abbot's seat.

In 1225 Dōgen heard that Rujing, who had been abbot* of the
Qingliang and Jingci monasteries, had just become abbot of the
Jingde Monastery on Mt. Tiantong, where Dōgen had first stayed.
Rujing was a monk from the Caodong School, in which "just sit-
ting," rather than kōan studies, was emphasized. He was known as

a strict and genuine teacher, not easily admitting monks into his community and often expelling those who did not train seriously. Dōgen returned to Mt. Tiantong. While he participated in the practice of the monastery as one of the many monks, he wrote to Rujing explaining why he had come from Japan and requesting the status of a student who could enter the abbot's room to receive personal guidance. This letter impressed Rujing, who must have heard from officers of the monastery that Dōgen was a remarkable student. Rujing wrote back and granted his request, saying, "Yes, you can come informally to ask questions any time, day or night, from now on. Do not worry about formality; we can be like father and son."[14]

On the first day of the fifth month of 1225, Dōgen entered the abbot's room and met Rujing for the first time. On this occasion Rujing affirmed his recognition of Dōgen and said, "The dharma gate of face-to-face transmission from buddha to buddha, ancestor to ancestor, is realized now."[15]

This exhilarating time for Dōgen was also a time of great loss. Myōzen died from an illness on the twenty-seventh day of the same month. He had been Dōgen's teacher for eight years, as well as a traveling companion and fellow seeker.

Expressing his doubt to Rujing about the current trend of Zen teachers who emphasize "transmission outside scriptures" and discourage students from studying the Buddha's teaching, Dōgen asked for Rujing's comment. Rujing said, "The great road of buddha ancestors is not concerned with inside or outside. . . . We have been followers of the Buddha for a long time. How can we hold views that are outside the way of the Buddha? To teach students the power of the present moment as the only moment is a skillful teaching of buddha ancestors. But this doesn't mean that there is no future result from practice."[16] Thus, Rujing demonstrated that he was an ideal teacher for Dōgen, who was seeking Zen that fully embodied the teaching of the Buddha described in the scriptures.

While receiving rigorous training from Rujing, Dōgen asked him further questions in a respectful but challenging way, showing his sincerity as well as his brilliance. Rujing was confident of himself as an authentic carrier of the Zen tradition, and Dōgen sought to experience the heart of his teaching. The culmination of his practice came one day in zazen when he heard Rujing speak in the monks' hall.* Reflecting on this experience, Dōgen says, "Upon hearing Rujing's words 'dropping off,' I attained the buddha way."[17] In the fall of 1227, after completing his study and receiving a document of heritage from Rujing, Dōgen ended his four-year visit to China. He went back to Japan to teach people in his own country.

Hope for a Rising Tide

In the tenth month of 1227, soon after returning to the community of the Kennin Monastery in Kyōto, Dōgen recorded that he had brought home Myōzen's relics.[18] In the same year he wrote a short manifesto called "Recommending Zazen to All People," in an elaborate, formal style of Chinese.[19] It was his declaration establishing a new form of Buddhist practice in Japan, based on his understanding of the traditional Zen teaching he had studied in Song China. Dōgen was twenty-eight years old.

In the following year, Monk Jiyuan from Mt. Tiantong traveled to Japan to inform Dōgen of Rujing's death. In 1230, under pressure from the Tendai establishment, Dōgen was forced out of Kyōto. In this year of extraordinary, nationwide famine that filled many cities with the dead, he settled in a small temple in Fukakusa, a village in the vicinity of Kyōto. In this quiet environment, he wrote dharma essays in Japanese. In the following year he summarized his teaching in a fairly extensive discourse called, "On the Endeavor of the Way," later collected in *The Treasury of the True Dharma Eye*, in which he says, "I came back to Japan with the hope of spreading the teaching and awakening sentient beings*—a heavy burden on my shoulders. However, I put aside the intention of having the teaching prevail everywhere until the occasion of a rising tide. Yet there may be true students who are not concerned with fame and gain and who allow their thought of enlightenment to guide them. They may be confused by incapable teachers and ob-

structed from the correct understanding. . . . Because I feel concerned for them, I would like to present the standards of Zen
monasteries that I personally saw and heard in Great Song as well as
the profound principle that has been transmitted by my teacher."[20]

In this essay he emphasized that the understanding of buddha-
dharma is possible for both men and women, noble and lowly, laity
and home-leavers.* Disagreeing with the widespread view of the
need for an expedient practice in the Age of Declining Dharma, he
says, "The genuine teaching of the Mahāyāna does not divide time
into the three Ages of True, Imitation, and Declining Dharma. It
says that all those who practice will attain the way."[21]

In the spring of 1233 Dōgen established a small practice place
called the Kannondōri Kōshō Hōrin-ji (Avalokiteshvara's Guiding
Power, Raising Sages, Treasure Forest Monastery) in Fukakusa. In
the eighth month of the same year he wrote "Actualizing the Fundamental Point," and gave it to lay student Kōshū Yō.[22] In the following year monk Ejō, a student of the Zen teacher Ekan, joined
Dōgen's community. Ejō was two years older than Dōgen.

Dōgen had been selecting ancient Zen stories from various Chinese texts to be the core of his lifetime teaching. This selection
became a book of three hundred cases, titled *The Treasury of the
True Dharma Eye*.[23] Its preface is dated 1235. (Nowadays this text is
called *The Chinese-language Version Treasury of the True Dharma Eye*
to distinguish it from his major work of the same title.)

In the twelfth month of that year he wrote a fund-raising letter
for the construction of the monks' residential training hall of the
Kōshō Hōrin Monastery.[24] The construction was completed in the
tenth month of the following year. Two months later Ejō was ap-
pointed head monk and was asked to give a dharma talk.[25] In 1237
Dōgen wrote "Instructions for the Head Cook."[26] In 1240 he wrote
"Mountains and Waters Sutra,"[27] "The Time Being,"[28] "The
Power of the Robe,"[29] and "Valley Sounds, Mountain Colors."[30]

In 1241 Monk Ekan, the main teacher of the Japanese Daruma
(Bodhidharma) School, joined Dōgen's community. This Zen
school had been founded by Nōnin over half a century before.
Ekan, a student of Kakuan and a dharma brother of Ejō, brought

along many students, including Gikai, Giin, and Gien. In this year
Dōgen gave over fifty formal talks. The next five years were Dōgen's most prolific time of writing. In 1241 he wrote ten fascicles
of *The Treasury of the True Dharma Eye*, including "Document of
Heritage,"[31] "Buddha Nature,"[32] and "Miracles."[33] His writings in
1242 included "Going beyond Buddha,"[34] "Continuous Practice,"[35]
"Body and Mind Study of the Way,"[36] and "Within a Dream, Expressing the Dream."[37]

In the twelfth month of 1242, he presented the short text "Con-
certed Activity"[38] at the home of Lord Yoshishige Hatano, a high
official in the office of the governor of Kyōto appointed by the
Kamakura government. It was probably about this time that Hatano
asked Dōgen to establish a full-scale training monastery in Hatano's
home province, Echizen.

Community in the Mountains

In the middle of 1243 Dōgen moved to a village deep in the mountains of Shibi County, Echizen, a province on the Japan Sea, north-
east of Kyōto. He took Ejō and his other main students with him,
leaving the leadership at the Kōshō Monastery to Senne. Dōgen
continued his writing spurt with new portions of *The Treasury of the
True Dharma Eye* delivered as talks to his community at a hut near
Yamashi Peak and at the Yoshimine Monastery. Sometimes he
talked at both places on the same day.

As plans for building the Daibutsu (Great Awakened One)
Monastery progressed, Dōgen's dream of establishing the first full-
scale Zen monastery in Japan slowly became a reality. Its construction was started in the seventh month of 1244. The dharma hall was
completed in the ninth month, and the monks' hall in the tenth
month. Dōgen appointed Gikai head cook. To facilitate full-scale
practice at the new monastery, in 1245 he wrote, "Method of the
Practice of the Way,"[39] a detailed guideline for monastic life. This
was when his writing of philosophical essays started to slow down.

It was customary for the abbot of a monastery to call himself after the name of the monastery or the mountain where he resided. Thus Dōgen called himself Daibutsu or Great Buddha at that time. But he must have felt that calling himself in this way was rather awkward. This may be one of the reasons why he decided to change the name of the monastery. On the fifteenth day of the sixth month of 1246 Dōgen renamed it Eihei, the Japanese sounds that correspond to the Chinese Yongping, an allusion to the time Buddhism was first brought to China, in the tenth year of the Yongping Era—67 CE. In his formal talk he said, "In the heavens above and on the earth below, this very place is Eihei (Eternal Peace)."[40] He presented over seventy formal talks to his community in that year.

Soon he completed "Guidelines for Officers of the Eihei Monastery."[41] Dōgen's life was more and more focused on training a limited number of monks who would transmit dharma to future generations. In "Home-leaving," a fascicle of *The Treasury of the True Dharma Eye*, delivered to his community in the ninth month of the same year, he said emphatically, "You should clearly know that the attainment of the way by all buddhas and ancestors is no other than leaving your household and receiving the precepts. The life vein of all buddhas and ancestors is no other than leaving the household and receiving the precepts. . . . The unsurpassable enlightenment is fulfilled upon leaving the household and receiving the precepts. It is not fulfilled until the day of leaving the household."[42]

Meanwhile he occasionally received lay visitors from Kyōto or nearby towns and talked to them about dharma. In 1247 he made a departure from his monastery for an exceptionally long journey eastward to Kamakura at the request of Regent Tokiyori Hōjō, who, as head of the warrior government, was the ruler of the nation. Dōgen was housed at the residence of a lay person, probably his major supporter Yoshishige Hatano, during his six-month stay in Kamakura.

According to the biographies, Dōgen gave the precepts to a number of people including Tokiyori. Tokiyori asked Dōgen to stay longer and to open a monastery in Kamakura, but Dōgen declined. Aside from the ten poems Dōgen gave Tokiyori's wife, practically no writings of Dōgen remain from this period.[43] It seems that his visit to Kamakura was disappointing because of the lack of opportunity to explore dharma in depth with his students. Returning to the Eihei Monastery in the third month of 1248, he gave a formal talk and said, "I was away over half a year, a lonely moon in a great void."[44]

Toward the Ultimate Simplicity

During the five years between 1248 and 1252, Dōgen gave more than fifty formal talks each year. He wrote further guidelines on monastic activities. Although he did not write any new fascicles of *The Treasury of the True Dharma Eye*, he presented the fascicle "Face Washing,"[45] first written in 1239, to his community for the third time. By giving detailed instructions on formal ways of cleansing, he emphasized the importance of cleanliness both inside and out.

In 1252 Dōgen revised "Actualizing the Fundamental Point," one of his earliest pieces in *The Treasury of the True Dharma Eye*.[46] In the fall of 1252 he became sick. In the first month of 1253, Dōgen wrote "Eight Awakenings of Great Beings."[47] This was the last piece in *The Treasury of the True Dharma Eye* and consisted largely of a full quotation of Shākyamuni's admonitions from the *Buddha's Final Will Sūtra*. Dōgen wrote this piece in a very simple style with little trace of the brilliance he had demonstrated in his prime. In the same year the monk Nichiren started teaching the intense solo practice of chanting the name of *The Lotus Sūtra*.

In the fourth month of 1253, Dōgen asked the senior student Gikai about the last days of Ekan. The first Zen teacher of Ejō and Gikai, Ekan had joined Dōgen's community twelve years before and had served as head monk of the Eihei Monastery, but he had died in 1251. Gikai said that Ekan had died with great regret as Dōgen had not given him the opportunity of seeing a document of dharma heritage. Dōgen was sorry for Ekan and asked Gikai to dedicate to Ekan whatever merit Gikai acquired when he was given the opportunity to see Dōgen's document of dharma heritage.[48] Although Dōgen himself had seen and received documents of heritage in China, he had made it extremely difficult to receive or even to see such a document. Perhaps he wanted to make sure that only fully mature students would be allowed to examine certificates of teachers' highest approval.

In the seventh month of the same year, 1253, Dōgen became sick again and knew that his current life was coming to an end. He said to Gikai, "Even though there are ten million things that I have not clarified concerning the buddha-dharma, still I have the joy of not having formed mistaken views and having genuinely maintained correct faith in the true dharma."[49] In the same month Dōgen gave Ejō a robe he had sewn, appointing him abbot of the Eihei Monastery.

On the fifth day of the eighth month, acceding to Lord Hatano's repeated request, Dōgen left for Kyōto for medical treatment. He was accompanied by Ejō and other students. He asked Gikai to run the monastery while they were away.

On the fifteenth day of the eighth month, under a harvest moon, he wrote a poem:

In autumn
even though I may
see it again,
how can I sleep
with the moon this evening?[50]

On the twentieth day of the eighth month of 1253, Dōgen died in Kyōto at the home of lay student Kakunen.

Circle of the Way

The "way" is a common image in many religious traditions for the process of spiritual pursuit. It often implies that a seeker is bound to toil on a long path, wandering about and overcoming numerous obstacles before arriving at the final destination. There is a huge distance between the starting point and the goal. In the context of the Mahāyāna or Great Vehicle teaching—a developed form of Buddhism that spread through North and East Asia—this process represents the journey a seeker, or bodhisattva,* takes to become a fully awakened one, a buddha. The time span between the initial practice and the achieved goal—enlightenment—is described in scriptures as "hundreds and thousands of eons."

Dōgen accepts this image of a linear process of seeking. But he also talks about the way as a circle. For him, each moment of practice encompasses enlightenment, and each moment of enlightenment encompasses practice. In other words, practice and enlighten-ment—process and goal—are inseparable. The circle of practice is complete even at the beginning. This circle of practice-enlighten-ment is renewed moment after moment.

At the moment you begin taking a step you have arrived, and you keep arriving each moment thereafter. In this view you don't journey toward enlightenment, but you let enlightenment unfold. In Dōgen's words, "You experience immeasurable hundreds of eons in one day."[51] The "circle of the way" is a translation of the Japa-nese word *dōkan*, literally meaning "way ring." Although this word, which Dōgen coined, appears only four times in his writing, it may be taken to represent the heart of his teaching.

This circle of practice-enlightenment describes not only the journey of one individual, but also the process and goal of the entire collection of practitioners of the way throughout past, present, and future. Dōgen says, "On the great road of buddha ancestors there is always unsurpassable practice, continuous and sustained. It forms the circle of the way and is never cut off. Between aspiration, prac-tice, enlightenment, and nirvāna,* there is not a moment's gap; con-tinuous practice is the circle of the way. This being so, continuous practice is unstained, not forced by you or others. The power of this continuous practice confirms you as well as others. It means your practice affects the entire earth and the entire sky in the ten directions. Although not noticed by others or by yourself, it is so."[52]

Thus the practice of all awakened ones actualizes the practice of each one of us. And the practice of each one of us actualizes the practice of all awakened ones. The practice of each one of us, however humble and immature it may be, is seen as something powerful and indispensable for the entire community of awakened ones. Our life at each moment may be seen likewise in the context of all life.

Dōgen usually describes "life" as "birth," for Buddhism sees one's life as a continuous occurrence of birth and death moment by moment. He says: "Birth is just like riding in a boat. You raise the sails and row with the pole. Although you row, the boat gives you a ride, and without the boat no one could ride. But you ride in the boat and your riding makes the boat what it is. Investigate such a moment."[53] Dōgen's understanding of the interconnectedness of all things at each moment sheds light on the absolute value of the present moment.

Treasury of the True Dharma Eye

Dōgen calls the path of practice-enlightenment "the buddha way." It is the path of all awakened ones of past, present, and future. He cautions against calling his own community part of the Caodong School, the Zen School, or even the Buddha Mind School. For him this teaching is the universal road of all awakened ones.

The path may be wide and limitless in theory but narrow in practice. Dōgen calls it "the great road of buddha ancestors," the "ancestors" being those who hold the lineage of a certain teaching. In the Zen tradition this lineage is restricted to dharma descendants of Shākyamuni Buddha and Bodhidharma, the First Ancestor in China, and no other teachers are called ancestors.

Following the Zen tradition, Dōgen attributes the authenticity of this lineage to the legend about the great assembly of beings at Vulture Peak where Mahākāshyapa alone smiled when Shākyamuni Buddha held up a flower. The Buddha said, "I have the treasury of the true dharma eye, the wondrous heart of nirvāna. Now I entrust it to you."[54] Dōgen affirms that this treasury has been transmitted from teacher to disciple, face to face, throughout generations.

The heart of this teaching is zazen, or meditation in a sitting posture, from which all understanding derives. Dōgen offers a highly defined way of doing zazen, as well as guidelines for activities in the monastic community. Details of what and how to eat, and what and how to wear, are all presented as indispensable aspects of the life of the awakened ones.

Dōgen constantly talks about true dharma, genuine teaching, correct lineage, and correct ways. He often uses the word *zheng* in Chinese or *shō* in Japanese many times in one sentence. This is the word that means "genuine," "true," or "correct." Establishing authenticity in understanding and in the daily activities of a monastic community was one of Dōgen's primary concerns as a thinker and teacher.

Wondrous Heart of Nirvāna

Enlightenment in the Buddhist context is represented by the Sanskrit word *bodhi*,* which essentially means "awakening." A buddha, or one who embodies bodhi, is an awakened or enlightened one. In the Zen tradition Shākyamuni, the original teacher of Buddhism, is the main figure called the Buddha.

A buddha can be understood as someone who experiences nirvāna and fully shares the experience with others. "Nirvāna," another Sanskrit word, originally means "putting out fire," which points to a state where there is freedom from burning desire or anxiety, or from the enslavement of passion.

According to a common Asian view that originated in ancient India, one is bound to the everlasting cycle of birth and death in various realms, including those of deities, of humans, of animals, and hell. In Buddhism nirvāna is where the chain of such transmigration is cut off and one is free from suffering. That is why the word *nirvāna* is also used as a euphemism for "death."

Nirvāna is often described in Buddhist scriptures as "the other shore." One crosses the ocean of birth and death toward the shore of total freedom. In Mahāyāna teaching bringing others across the ocean of suffering to the shore of enlightenment is considered to be as important as or even more important than bringing oneself over. Those who vow to dedicate their lives to this act of "ferrying" others are called bodhisattvas, or beings who are dedicated to bodhi. In some schools of Mahāyāna, Zen in particular, there is a strong emphasis on the immediacy of enlightenment, indicating that the ocean of birth and death is itself nirvāna.

As quoted earlier in this introduction, Dōgen says, "Between aspiration, practice, enlightenment, and nirvāna, there is not a moment's gap." Thus, nirvāna is one of the four elements in a practitioner's spiritual activity. For Dōgen, nirvāna is inseparable from enlightenment, and it is inseparable from one's practice at each moment. In other words, there is no authentic practice that lacks enlightenment or nirvāna.

While Dōgen discusses aspiration, practice, and enlightenment in detail, he does not explain the last element, nirvāna, which seems to be an invisible element in his teaching. It is as though he talks about the experience of nirvāna without using this word.

Nirvāna is regarded as the realm of nonduality, where there is no distinction between large and small, long and short, right and wrong, appearing and disappearing, self and other. It may be called reality itself, or the absolute place beyond time and space. This is a realm that cannot be grasped objectively. The intuitive awareness or transcendental wisdom that goes beyond dualistic, analytical thinking and leads us into this realm is called *prajñā* * in Sanskrit.

Dōgen calls this place of inner freedom the buddha realm. It is where one is many, part is whole, a moment is timeless, and mortality is immortality. To experience this beyondness in the midst of the passage of time, change, and decay is a miracle. For Dōgen, this miracle can happen each moment, as each moment of duality is inseparable from a moment of nonduality.

Duality and nonduality, change and no-change, relative and absolute, coexist and interact with each other. Dōgen calls the experience of this dynamic "actualizing the fundamental point." It is an immediate but subtle and mysterious unfolding of nirvāna within a life of change and decay. Dōgen suggests that we can realize this dynamic of "not one, not two" by going into and maintaining the

deep consciousness that is experienced both in zazen and in daily
activities conducted in a meditative state of body and mind.

Enlightenment as a Breakthrough Experience

Enlightenment is commonly seen as a spiritual breakthrough experience. Scriptures say that Shākyamuni Buddha, upon seeing the
morning star after days of rigorous meditation, suddenly realized
that mountains, rivers, grass, and trees had all attained buddhahood.
When a monk was sweeping his hermitage yard, a pebble hit a bamboo stalk and made a cracking sound, and he was awakened. As in
these examples, a dramatic shift of consciousness occurs after a
seeker goes through a period of intense pursuit and has an unexpected transformative experience. The breakthrough may not only
be an in-depth understanding of reality, but a physical experience—
such as an extraordinary vision, release of tension, and feeling of
exuberance.

In the Zen tradition many stories of this sort are studied as
exemplary cases of great enlightenment. In the Linji School and its
Japanese form, the Rinzai School, such enlightenment stories are
used systematically as kōans to help students break through the
conventional thinking that is confined by the barrier of dualism.

Dōgen himself often quotes enlightenment stories of earlier
masters and comments on them. Kōans were certainly important
elements for his teaching. But Dōgen's journal of studies with Rujing does not mention any occasion when Rujing gave him a kōan
to work on, nor do any of Dōgen's writings suggest that he himself
used this method for guiding his own students. Unlike teachers of
the Linji way, Dōgen did not seem to use kōans as tasks for students
to work on and pass, one after another. In fact he often used the
word *kōan* to mean reality itself, translated here as "fundamental
point."

Here lies the paradox of enlightenment. On the one hand, when
one practices the way of awakening, there is already enlightenment
moment after moment. On the other hand, one has to endeavor

long and hard to achieve a breakthrough. Dōgen says, "There are those who continue realizing beyond realization."[55] Thus, enlightenment unfolds itself, but the unfolding is fully grasped by one's body and mind only when one has a breakthrough. In other words, unfolded enlightenment is initially subconscious awakening, which is spontaneously merged with conscious awakening at the moment of breakthrough.

The kōan studies of the Linji-Rinzai line are an excellent method for working consciously toward breakthrough. By contrast, Dōgen's training method was to keep students from striving toward breakthrough. Although he fully understood the value of breakthroughs and used breakthrough stories of his ancestors for teaching, he himself emphasized "just sitting," with complete nonattachment to the goal of attainment. But isn't freedom from attachment an essential element for achieving breakthroughs?

Cause and Effect Revisited

The experience of nonduality is the basis for the Buddhist teaching of compassion. When one does not abide in the distinction between self and other, between humans and nonhumans, and between sentient beings and insentient beings, there is identification with and love for all beings. Thus, the wisdom of nonduality, prajñā, is inseparable from compassion.

An action that embodies compassion is wholesome and one that does not is unwholesome. Any action, small or large, affects self and other. Cause brings forth effect. Thus, the dualistic perspective of Buddhist ethics—good and bad, right and wrong—is based on nondualism.

Here emerges a fundamental dilemma of Buddhism. If one focuses merely on prajñā, one may say that there is no good and bad, and one may become indifferent and possibly destructive. On the other hand, if one only thinks of cause and effect, one may not be able to understand prajñā. The legendary dialogue of Bodhidharma

with Emperor Wu of southern China is revered in the Zen tradition
exactly because it illustrates this dilemma in a dramatic way:

> The Emperor said, "Ever since I ascended the throne, I have
> built temples, copied sūtras, approved the ordination of more
> monks than I can count. What is the merit of having done all
> this?"
> Bodhidharma said, "There is no merit."
> The Emperor said, "Why is that so?"
> Bodhidharma said, "These are minor achievements of hu-
> mans and *devas*,* which become the causes of desire. They are like
> shadows of forms and are not real."
> The Emperor said, "What is real merit?"
> Bodhidharma said, "When pure wisdom is complete, the es-
> sence is empty and serene. Such merit cannot be attained through
> worldly actions."
> The Emperor said, "What is the foremost sacred truth?"
> Bodhidharma said, "Vast emptiness, nothing sacred."
> The Emperor said, "Who is it that faces me?"
> Bodhidharma said, "I don't know."
> The Emperor did not understand.[56]

Thus the primary concern of the Zen practitioner has been described as the experience of "the pure wisdom" that sees reality as
"empty and serene." This experience was regarded as the source of
all scriptural teachings. Often Chinese Zen Buddhists talked about
the transmission of teachings "outside scriptures." Are living buddhas, or those who are awakened, free from ethics? Are they free
from cause and effect?

The Zen answer to this question may be found in the parable
of Baizhang and an earlier Zen teacher, who was reborn as a wild
fox because of his belief that he was free from cause and effect.[57]
This story clearly illustrates that practitioners of the "pure wisdom"
of nonduality have no license to abandon ethics. It is not a coinci-
dence that Baizhang, a great master of eighth- and ninth-century
China, was credited with establishing guidelines for monastic communities.

Mahāyāna Buddhism calls for the six completions as the essential elements for arriving at nirvāna. They are: giving, ethical conduct, perseverance, enthusiasm, meditation, and prajñā. The first five may be seen as elements for sustaining compassion in prajñā. Thus, keeping and transmitting the precepts are the core of Zen teaching.

Soon after beginning to study with Rujing in China, Dōgen expressed his concern about the widespread tendency to overemphasize the "here and now" and disregard the future effect of practice. Rujing agreed with Dōgen about his concern and said, "To deny that there are future births is nihilism; buddha ancestors do not hold to the nihilistic views of those who are outside the way. If there is no future there is no present. This present birth definitely exists. How could it be that the next birth doesn't also exist?"[58]

Dōgen's own understanding on this issue is clear in his fascicle "Identifying with Cause and Effect" in *The Treasury of the True Dharma Eye*, where he says, "Thus, the significance of studying cause and realizing effect is clear. This is the way of buddhas and ancestors. . . . Those of you who have pure aspiration for enlightenment and want to study buddha-dharma for the sake of buddha-dharma should clarify causation as past sages did. Those who reject this teaching are outside the way."[59] Thus, Dōgen makes it clear that authentic Zen practice is not divorced from the teachings expressed in scriptures. For him deep trust in and identification with causation should be the foundation for practice of the way.

Bilingual Zen

Dōgen used the Chinese language for writing formal addresses such as recommendations for zazen and formal lectures, as well as for most of the monastic guidelines, poems, and his own study journals. It was natural for him to write in Chinese, as he had received the major part of his Zen training in China, and his formal lectures and poems followed the tradition of Chinese Zen masters. Writing in Chinese was also appropriate for addressing the larger Buddhist community, as most scholarship in Japan at that time relied on this language, although the texts were read in a special Sino-Japanese way due to the differences in sound and grammar between the two languages.

Dōgen's early informal talks were recorded by Ejō in Japanese, but his later informal talks were recorded by Gikai in Chinese. Dōgen wrote some Japanese traditional-style *waka* poems, written in thirty-one syllables. He used Japanese for writing his lifework, the ninety-five fascicles of *The Treasury of the True Dharma Eye*, except that he kept quotations from sūtras and Zen texts in Chinese, for he almost exclusively used Chinese books as research materials.

Thousands of ideograms are used in the Chinese writing system. Each ideogram represents a word and embodies a wide range of meaning and connotation derived from the long social and literary tradition of China. Parts of speech are quite flexible in this language; the same word can function as a noun, verb, or adjective. There is no conjugation by cases or inflection by number, and subjects and objects are often implied. Word order often indicates syntax, but there can always be exceptions. Thus, because of its richness of meaning and ambiguity, the Chinese language was instrumental in the development of highly intuitive thinking in the Zen tradition, both for earlier masters and for Dōgen himself.

In the Japanese writing system Chinese ideograms are used particularly for major parts of speech such as nouns, stems of verbs and adjectives. Japanese phonetic letters are added to indicate conjugations as well as conjunctions and connecting words somewhat analogous to prepositions in English. The Japanese language shares with the Chinese language the richness of ideograms and ambiguity of expression. The poetic ambiguity in Japanese writing has to do with its tendency to imply subjects and with its usual absence of plural forms. On the other hand, parts of speech are clearly defined in a Japanese sentence, and all words in a sentence, including those that are implied, have well-defined functions as the subject, object, predicate, or modifier. Thus, writing prose in Japanese is grammatically demanding. Much of the acuteness of Dōgen's writings is the result of expressing vastly intuitive thoughts through the logical structure of the Japanese language.

Words beyond Words

In Zen teaching awakening is regarded as something beyond intellectual studies, or beyond understanding what has been said in the past. It ought to be a direct experience, which is personal, intuitive, and fresh. The dilemma is that the experience of awakening needs to be approved by an authentic master, and to be transmitted to the next generation without distortion.

Dōgen wrote his essays to convey to students his understanding of what he regarded as most essential and authentic in Buddhist teaching. He focused on the theoretical aspects of the teaching, while constantly reminding students that awakening is beyond thought. In some of his essays and monastic guidelines he gave detailed instructions on the practical aspects of zazen and communal activities, often with philosophical interpretations and poetic expressions. Dōgen regarded all daily activities, such as washing the body, wearing robes, cooking, or engaging in administrative work, as sacred.

It is clear that Dōgen's thinking and understanding deepened as he wrote his essays and read them to his community. He made a careful revision of his texts with the help of his senior student Ejō. Either he or Ejō calligraphed the final version of the texts. The fascicle "Actualizing the Fundamental Point" was revised nineteen years after it was first written.

Extensively quoting stories and poems from the Chinese Zen tradition, Dōgen often comments on each line of these ancient dialogues, and makes a detailed examination of the meaning behind the words. He does not hesitate to criticize great masters like Linji and Yunmen, while revering their teachings in other passages. But he places ultimate value in the accounts of the earliest Chinese masters such as Bodhidharma and the Sixth Ancestor, Huineng, as well as later "ancestors" in his lineage.

Dōgen introduces the full range of traditional Zen rhetoric on the paradox of awakening beyond thought. The rhetoric includes nonverbal expressions such as silence, shouting, beating, and gestures, which have been recorded in words. It also includes repetitious statements, turning around the word order, non sequiturs, tautology, and seemingly mundane talks. The use of absurd images and upside-down language is also common. Sacrilegious and violent words that are intended to crush stereotypical thinking are not uncommon in the Zen heritage. These Zen expressions are called "turning words,"* as they can turn students around from limited views. Dōgen would call it "intimate language," as it bypasses the intellect and directly touches upon the matter of duality and nonduality.

The Zen tradition sometimes loads a word with positive, negative, concrete, and transcendental meanings, thus making its semantics ambiguous or enigmatic. A well-known example of that is Zhaozhou's *wu* (*mu* in Japanese, originally meaning "no" or "not") in response to the question of whether a dog has buddha-nature. Following and extending this tradition, Dōgen uses some words in opposite meanings. By the word "self," he sometimes means a confined ego and sometimes the universal reality that is based on selflessness. "To be hindered" can also mean "to be fully immersed."

Commenting on earlier Zen masters' words, Dōgen develops his own thinking and finds a way to expand the meaning of their words to elaborate his understanding of the ultimate value of each moment. A remarkable example of this may be found in his interpretation of Yaoshan's words, "For the time being, stand on a high mountain." From here Dōgen starts his explication that time is no other than being, and presents the concept of "the time-being," or existence, as time. Another example of expanding the meaning of the original words is his reading of a line of *The Mahā Pari-nirvāna Sūtra*, "All beings have buddha-nature," as "All beings completely are buddha-nature."

In the Chinese Zen tradition there are a number of stories in which a teacher of scriptures gives up lecturing and starts practicing

Zen, or of Zen teachers who make paradoxical comments on passages of scriptures. There are almost no cases in which Zen teachers make extensive efforts to examine the meaning of scriptural phrases. But Dōgen does a thorough investigation of phrases from a number of sūtras, which makes him unique as a Zen teacher. His writings in *The Treasury of the True Dharma Eye* provide syntheses of these two traditional aspects: studies of scripture that contain vast systematic expressions of the Buddhist teaching, and Zen, which emphasizes direct experience of the essence of the Buddhist teaching.

Heritage of Dōgen

Dōgen spent most of his later life training a small number of students in a remote countryside monastery. The audience for his writing was quite limited, as he used customary Zen language, which often consisted of colloquial Chinese expressions unfamiliar to most Buddhists in his country. The theme of his writing was a specific practice, centered around "just sitting" in the monastic environment. None of his prose or poetry was published during his lifetime.

He produced a dharma heir, Ejō, a fully dedicated practitioner of the way, and several mature students to whom Ejō gave dharma transmission for Dōgen after his death. Dōgen's dharma descendants eventually formed the Sōtō School—the Japanese form of the Caodong School—which is now the largest Buddhist organization in Japan. The other major school of Japanese Zen is the Rinzai School, which regards Eisai as its founder.

Dōgen is known as one of the reformers of Buddhism in the Kamakura Period (1192–1333). Other prominent reformers during this period include Hōnen, Shinran, and Nichiren. The communities they started are now called respectively the Jōdo (Pure Land) School, the Jōdoshin (True Pure Land) School, and the Nichiren School. The members of the schools formed in the Kamakura Period outnumber by far the members of the organizations that started earlier.

While Dōgen's dharma descendants increased, gaining popular support and building temples all over, most of his writings were quickly forgotten. No one wrote a substantial commentary on his essays between the fourteenth and seventeenth centuries. Ryōkan, a mendicant monk of the eighteenth to nineteenth centuries, now famous for his calligraphy and poetry, wrote a poem about reading the *Record of Eihei Dōgen:*

For five hundred years it's been covered with dust,
just because no one has had an eye for recognizing dharma.
For whom was all his eloquence expounded?
Longing for ancient times and grieving for the present, my
   heart is exhausted.[60]

There was a movement in the Sōtō community after the seventeenth century, however, for restoring the founder's spirit. The movement included extensive studies of his writings, along with the emergence of commentaries on Dōgen's writings by several monk scholars, which resulted in the publication of *The Treasury of the True Dharma Eye* by the Eihei Monastery in 1816.

Studies about Dōgen remained in the domain of Sōtō sectarian scholarship until the 1920s, when Japanese scholars of Western philosophy started to realize the importance of Dōgen's thinking. That was when Tetsurō Watsuji's *Shamon Dōgen* (Monk Dōgen) awakened interest in Dōgen's work among intellectuals.

In the 1960s Dōgen began to be recognized as one of the greatest essayists in the history of Japanese literature. His writings were included in various collections of classical literature. Six modern Japanese translations of the entire *Treasury of the True Dharma Eye* have been published, making much of Dōgen's thought available to Japanese readers.

As Zen meditation began to spread to the Western world in the 1950s, translations of some of Dōgen's writings started to appear in Western languages. Over thirty books of Dōgen translations and studies have been published in English, which makes Dōgen by far the most extensively studied East Asian Buddhist in the Western world. How his influence will extend is yet to be seen.

The Contemporary Meaning of Dōgen

Over seven hundred years after his time, Dōgen's writings are still fresh and captivating for both Buddhists and non-Buddhists. The paradoxes, absurd images, and often impenetrable language in his essays are not merely exotic or intriguing. They point to a part of human consciousness that is often unnoticed. Dōgen's writing reveals a reality that is only experienced through a life-long investigation of nonduality. The freedom—including freedom from thinking itself and language itself—that we see in Dōgen's writing is stunning. It is ironic that his mind was so free while he was following a highly defined practice of meditation and while he was establishing meticulous guidelines for his monastery. It makes us wonder if his form of practice and teaching was part of the foundation of his freedom.

His meditation instructions remain among the most useful for Zen practitioners. Many of the forms he brought from China are still used in Japan, and are taking root in Western Zen groups. Although modern modes of cooking, cleaning, and earning a livelihood are vastly different from those in his time, Dōgen's teaching on attention to details and care about others is still valid.

Those of us who are familiar with contemporary Buddhist scholarship may have a different perspective from Dōgen on the historical development of Buddhism. Based on scientific findings since the nineteenth century, we now know that Mahāyāna sūtras were compiled in India centuries after the time of Shākyamuni Buddha and that many of the teachings may not represent the actual words of the Buddha himself. Also, the story that Mahākāshyapa smiled when he saw the Buddha hold up a flower, and that he received the treasury of the true dharma eye, may have been constructed in China, as there is no mention of it in Indian texts. The succession of Indian ancestors named in the Zen lineage is also seen

by scholars as a Chinese creation. Thus Dōgen's emphasis on the
authenticity of the Zen lineage does not convince the scientific
mind of modern times.

We now appreciate the teachings and practices of many religious traditions, as we have opportunities to witness and learn from
them first hand. From this perspective, Dōgen's criticisms of other
schools of Buddhism as mistaken or inferior may appear narrow-
minded. Nevertheless, his pure dedication to the path he followed,
passionately conveying to his students his understanding about it, is
moving. What makes practice authentic is not necessarily historical
evidence or comparative arguments, but genuine and sincere intention to practice.

Rich in scientific knowledge and highly advanced technology,
humans still face the transience of life, fear of death, and individual
and social suffering. We are back to the same question people have
been asking from the beginning of human society: how can we become free from suffering? Dōgen's invitation to us to experience
nonduality in meditation can be a way to inner freedom—freedom
from driving desires, self-centeredness, and the fear of isolation.
His teaching on the ultimate value of each moment is increasingly
relevant today, as we become more and more aware of the interconnectedness of all things throughout space and time.

Kazuaki Tanahashi

Notes

In the following notes, *SG* = *Shōbōgenzō, The Treasury of the True Dharma
Eye*, of Eihei Dōgen. *MD* = *Moon in a Dewdrop*, San Francisco: North
Point Press, 1985. "The editor" refers to Kazuaki Tanahashi.

1. Ōkubo, Dōshū, ed. *Dōgen Zenji Zenshū* (Entire Work of Zen Master
   Dōgen), 3 vols. Tokyo: Chikuma Shobō, 1970.
2. *Eihei-ji Sanso Gyōgō-ki* (Biographies of the First Three Ancestors of
   the Eihei Monastery), author unknown, already in existence in the
   Oei Era (1394–1428). *Shoso* Dōgen Zenji Oshō Gyōroku (Biography
   of the First Ancestor, Zen Master, Priest Dōgen), author unknown,

published in 1673. *Eihei Kaisan Gyōjō Kenzei-ki* (Kenzei's Biography of the Founder Dōgen of Eihei) by Kenzei (1417–1574).

3. Ejō, *SG Zuimon-ki* (Record of Things I Heard).
4. Ejō, ibid.
5. Dōgen, *SG Bendōwa* (On the Endeavor of the Way), *MD*.
6. *Dōgen*, ibid.
7. Dōgen, *Hōkyō-ki*, (Journal of My Study in China). See p. 3.
8. Ejō, ibid.
9. Dōgen, ibid.
10. Dōgen, Tenzo Kyokun (Instructions for the Tenzo), *MD*.
11. Dōgen, *SG* Kesa Kudoku (Power of the Robe). See p. 77.
12. Dōgen, *SG* Shisho (Document of Heritage), *MD*.
13. Dōgen, *Journal of My Study in China*. See p. 3.
14. Dōgen, ibid.
15. Dōgen, *SG Menju* (Face-to-face Transmission), *MD*.
16. Dōgen, *Journal of My Study in China*. See p. 3.
17. Dōgen, *Eihei Kōroku* (Extensive Record of Eihei, Fascicle Two).
18. Dōgen, *Shari Sōdenki* (Record of Bringing Master Myōzen's Relics). See p. 30.
19. Dōgen, *Fukan Zazen-gi* (Recommending Zazen to All People).
20. Dōgen, On the Endeavor of the Way.
21. Dōgen, ibid.
22. Dōgen, *SG Genjo Kōan* (Actualizing the Fundamental Point).
23. Dōgen, *Shinji SG* (The Chinese-Language Treasure of the True Dharma Eye). See Cases for Study, p. 40, for excerpt.
24. Dōgen, *Kannondōri-in Sōdō Konryū Kanjin-so* (Donation Request for a Monks' Hall at Kannondori Monastery). See p. 47.
25. Ejō, ibid.
26. Dōgen, Instructions for the Tenzo.
27. Dōgen, *SG Sansui-kyō* (Mountains and Waters Sutra).
28. Dōgen, *SG Uji* (The Time-Being). See p. xx.
29. Dōgen, *SG Kesa Kudoku* (The Power of the Robe). See p. 77.
30. Dōgen, *SG Keisei Sanshoku* (Valley Sound, Mountain Color). See p. 59.
31. Dōgen, *SG Shisho* (Document of Heritage), *MD*.
32. Dōgen, *SG Busshō* (Buddha Nature).
33. Dōgen, *SG Jinzū* (Miracles). See p. 104.
34. Dōgen, *SG Bukkōjōji* (Going beyond Buddha), *MD*.

35. Dōgen, *SG Gyōji* (Continuous Practice). See p. 114.
36. Dōgen, *SG Shinjin Gakudō* (Body and Mind Study of the Way), *MD*.
37. Dōgen, *SG Muchū Setsumu* (Within a Dream Expressing the Dream). See p. 165.
38. Dōgen, *SG Zenki* (Undivided Activity). See p. 173.
39. Dōgen, *Bendōhō* (Method of the Practice of the Way).
40. Dōgen, *Extensive Record of Eihei, Fascicle Two*. See p. xx.
41. Dōgen, *Eihei-ji Chiji Shingi* (Guidelines for Officers of the Eihei Monastery). See p. 210.
42. Dōgen, *SG Shukke* (Home-leaving).
43. Dōgen, waka poems for Lady Hōjō. See p. 256 for selected poems.
44. Dōgen, *Extensive Record of Eihei, Fascicle Three*.
45. Dōgen, *SG Semmen* (Face Washing).
46. Dōgen, Actualizing the Fundamental Point. See p. 35.
47. Dōgen, *SG Hachi Dainingaku* (Eight Awakenings of Great Beings). See p. 271.
48. Dōgen, Eihei Shitchū Kikigaki (Final Instructions at the Abbot's Room of the Eihei Monastery).
49. Dōgen, ibid.
50. Translated by Brian Unger and the Editor.
51. Dōgen, *Home-leaving*.
52. Dōgen, Continuous Practice, *Fascicle One*. See p. 114.
53. Dōgen, Undivided Activity. See p. 173.
54. Dōgen, *SG Mitsugo* (Intimate Language). See p. 179.
55. Dōgen, Actualizing the Fundamental Point. See p. 35.
56. Dōgen, Continuous Practice, Fascicle Two. See p. 137.
57. Dōgen, *SG Shinjin Inga* (Identifying with Cause and Effect). See p. 264.
58. Dōgen, *Journal of My Study in China*. See p. 3.
59. Dōgen, Identifying with Cause and Effect. See p. 264.
60. Ryōkan, "Reading the Record of Eihei Dōgen." An excerpt, translated by Taigen Daniel Leighton and the editor.

Texts and Translation Credits

ALL THE TEXTS IN THIS BOOK are translated from materials published in Dōshū Ōkubo's *Dōgen Zenji Zenshū* or *The Entire Work of Zen Master Dōgen*. We have also referred to *Dōgen Zenji Zenshū* or *The Entire Work of Zen Master Dōgen* by Tokugen Sakai, et al. The "Editor" refers to Kazuaki Tanahashi.

Journal of My Study in China (p. 3)

Known in Japan as *Hōkyō-ki*, or *Record of the Baoqing Era*, this is Dōgen's record of study with his teacher Rujing at Mt. Tiantong between the first and third year of the Baoqing Era (1225–1227). As Dōgen's successor Ejō wrote in the colophon, Dōgen did not show this text even to Ejō in his lifetime. Ejō found the draft soon after Dōgen's death and made a fair copy in 1253. It was written in Chinese and first published in 1750. Translated by Norman Fischer and the Editor.

Poems (p. 28)

These poems are written in Chinese and found in *Eihei Kōroku*, or *The Extensive Record of Eihei*, compiled by Dōgen's students after his death. They are among the six poems Dōgen wrote in exchange with the poet Wenben in 1226 during his stay at Mt. Tiantong. Translated by Jane Hirshfield and the Editor.

On a Portrait of Myself (p. 29)

This poem is calligraphed by Dōgen on a portrait of himself, owned by the Hommyō Temple, Kumamoto Prefecture. It is signed "Monk Dōgen of the Kennin Monastery, the third year of the Karoku Era (1227)." The poem is also found in *The Extensive Record of Eihei*. Translated by Tensho David Schneider and the Editor.

Record of Bringing Master Myōzen's Relics (p. 30)

Known in Japan as "Shari Sōden-ki," this text was written in Japanese in 1227 soon after Dōgen returned to Japan, according to the colophon. The photograph of a copy by one of his dharma descendants is owned by the Institute of Archive, Tokyo University. Translated by Gil Fronsdal and the Editor.

Recommending Zazen to All People (p. 32)

Known as "Fukan Zazen-gi" in Japan, this is one of the most revered texts in the Sōtō School, as it summarizes Dōgen's intention of establishing Zen practice in Japan. He wrote it in Chinese in 1227, as the colophon states. His own calligraphed text, dated 1233, still exists. We present the version edited by Dōgen even later, which is included in *The Extensive Record of Eihei*. Translated by Edward Brown and the Editor.

Actualizing the Fundamental Point (p. 35)

Titled "Genjō Kōan" in Japanese, this is probably the best known and most studied text of Dōgen. The word "kōan" usually means an exemplary Zen story given by a teacher to a student for investigation. But Dōgen used the word here to mean truth that is experienced. As the colophon states, Dōgen wrote this text and gave it to Kōshū Yō, a lay student, in 1233. This became the first fascicle of the seventy-five-fascicle version of *Shōbōgenzō*, or *The Treasury of the True Dharma Eye*, which was compiled later, probably by Dōgen himself. Dōgen revised this fascicle in 1252. ("Fascicle" is a chapter or a part of a book, originally bound in an independent bundle.) Translated by Robert Aitken and the Editor. Revised at San Francisco Zen Center, and later at Berkeley Zen Center.

Cases for Study (p. 40)

We are presenting the first ten of the three hundred enlightenment stories that Dōgen selected from Chinese Zen literature. Dōgen kept the text in Chinese and called it *Shōbōgenzō*, or *The Treasury of the True Dharma Eye*. But in order to distinguish this text from his collection of essays of the same title, it is called "Shinji" or "Mana" Shōbōgenzō (Shōbōgenzō written in Chinese), or Shōbōgenzō Sambyaku-soku (Shōbōgenzō Three Hundred Cases). Its preface is dated the first year of the Katei Era (1235). Translated by John Daido Loori and the Editor.

Donation Request for a Monks' Hall at the Kannondōri Monastery. (p. 47)

Dōgen wrote this fund-raising letter in Chinese, as a common form for writing a formal letter. It is dated the first year of the Katei Era (1235). The oldest known version is found in *Eihei Kaisan Gyōjō Kenzei-ki*, or *Kenzei's Biography of the Founder Dōgen of Eihei*, published in 1754. This text is known in Japanese as *Kannondōri-in Sōdō Konryū Kanjin-so*. Translated by Michael Wenger and the Editor.

Formal Talk upon Establishing the Kōshō (p. 49)

A formal talk in the Zen tradition is called *jōdō* in Japanese, which means ascending (the teaching seat) in the hall. The hall may be the dharma hall in a full-scale monastery, but in Dōgen's case at this time it was the monks' hall. This particular piece is Dōgen's first recorded jōdō, dated the fifteenth day, the tenth month, the second year of the Katei Era (1236). The attendant monk Senne recorded in Chinese a series of formal talks Dōgen gave in the Kōshō Hōrin Monastery, and these became the first fascicle of *The Extensive Record of Eihei*. Translated by Alan Senauke and the Editor.

Informal Talks (p. 50)

Dōgen calls an informal talk *yawa*, which literally means an "evening talk." These are excerpts from *Shōbōgenzō Zuimonki*, or *The Treasury of the True Dharma Eye: Record of Things Heard*, written in Japanese. Ejō collected the main materials for this book during the Katei Era (1235–1238), but some of his students completed the book after his death, based on his notes and words. Translated by Michael Wenger and the Editor, in part with Tensho David Schneider.

Valley Sounds, Mountain Colors (p. 59)

The original title of this piece is "Keisei Sanshoku." It is written in Japanese as part of *The Treasury of the True Dharma Eye*. Its colophon is dated the fifth day of the practice period in 1240. It is very likely that for Dōgen the practice period meant the summer practice period, which ran from the fifteenth day of the fourth month to the fifteenth day of the seventh month.

As with many other fascicles of *The Treasury of the True Dharma Eye*, this piece was presented to the assembly in the form of *jishu*, which is a dharma talk. It is likely that Dōgen's jishu consisted mainly of reading his draft to the group of practicing students. Translated by Katherine Thanas and the Editor.

The Time-Being (p. 69)

One of the philosophical pieces by Dōgen, it is called "Uji" and written in Japanese as part of *The Treasury of the True Dharma Eye*. As the colophon says, it was written on the first day, the tenth month of 1240. Translated by Dan Welch and the Editor.

The Power of the Robe (p. 77)

Its original title is "Kesa Kudoku." Dōgen wrote this fascicle of *The Treasury of the True Dharma Eye* in Japanese in 1240. As the colophon indicates, he presented this to the assembly of the Kōshō Hōrin Monastery on the day he completed "The Time-Being." Translated by Blanche Hartman and the Editor.

Encouraging Words (p. 102)

As formal talks, these two pieces were written in Chinese. They were recorded by Senne in 1241 and were later included in *The Extensive Record of Eihei*. Translated by Alan Senauke and the Editor.

Miracles (p. 104)

A fascicle of *The Treasury of the True Dharma Eye*, it was written in Japanese in 1241 under the title "Jinzū." Translated by Katherine Thanas and the Editor.

Continuous Practice, Fascicles One (p. 114) and Two (p. 137)

Written in Japanese, these texts are called "Gyōji." Exceptionally long as a chapter of *The Treasury of the True Dharma Eye*, Dōgen divided this collection of biographies of Indian and Chinese teachers into two fascicles. In Fascicle One, stories of three Indian ancestors are arranged in chronological order, followed by stories of Chinese teachers that seem to be arranged roughly by themes. In Fascicle Two, stories of Chinese teachers from Bodhidharma to Rujing are arranged, not necessarily following chronological order.

Dōgen wrote a colophon to Fascicle Two on the fifth day, the fourth month, the third year of Ninji (1242) at the Kōshō Hōrin Monastery. Ejō made a fair copy of Fascicle One and completed the checking of Fascicle Two on the eighteenth day, the first month of the following year. Translated by Mel Weitsman and the Editor, in part with Tensho David Schneider.

Within a Dream Expressing the Dream (p. 165)

A fascicle of *The Treasury of the True Dharma Eye*, this piece titled "Muchū Setsumu" was written in Japanese in 1242. "Expressing" in the title may also be translated as "explaining," "expounding," or "disclosing." Translated by Taigen Daniel Leighton and the Editor.

Undivided Activity (p. 173)

"Zenki," a fascicle of *The Treasury of the True Dharma Eye*, was written in Japanese in 1242. Translated by Edward Brown and the Editor.

Intimate Language (p. 179)

"Mitsugo," a fascicle of *The Treasury of the True Dharma Eye*, was written in Japanese in 1243, soon after Dōgen had moved to Echizen Province. "Mitsugo" can be translated "sacred words." Translated by Michael Wenger and the Editor.

Insentient Beings Speak Dharma (p. 185)

"Mujō Seppō," a fascicle of *The Treasury of the True Dharma Eye*, was written in Japanese in 1243. Translated by Alan Senauke and the Editor.

Turning the Dharma Wheel (p. 196)

Written in Japanese under the title "Tembōrin," this is a fascicle of *The Treasury of the True Dharma Eye*. It was written in Echizen Province in 1244, several days after construction of the Daibutsu Monastery had started. Translated by Taigen Daniel Leighton and the Editor.

In Honor of Master Rujing (p. 199)

According to the note for this Chinese-style poem, Dōgen wrote it on the seventeenth day, the seventh month of 1244, for the sixteenth memorial day of his teacher Rujing's death. As the official opening of the Daibutsu Monastery was scheduled for the following day, the community could not have a full service. So Dōgen presented this poem, possibly with some talk to the assembly. The text has been transmitted in the Keifuku Temple, Tottori Prefecture. Translated by Jane Hirshfield and the Editor.

On Carving the Buddha Image for the Daibutsu Monastery (p. 200)
This short record was written in Japanese and published in *Kenzei's Biography of the Founder Dōgen of Eihei*. The Daibutsu Monastery was constructed in 1244 and was renamed the Eihei Monastery in 1246. As the buildings of the Eihei Monastery burned down in 1473, the main statue of the monastery that Dōgen carved no longer exists. Translated by Gil Fronsdal and the Editor.

Space (p. 205)
Under the title "Kokū," this piece was written in Japanese in 1245 as part of *The Treasury of the True Dharma Eye*. Translated by Alan Senauke and the Editor.

Formal Talk on the First Day of the Practice Period (p. 205)
This jōdō, or formal talk, was given at the Daibutsu Monastery at the beginning of the summer practice period in the fourth month, the third year of the Kangen Era (1245). The text, written in Chinese, is found in Fascicle 2 of *The Extensive Record of Eihei*. Translated by Alan Senauke and the Editor.

Given to Hironaga Hatano (p. 206)
This Chinese-style poem is found in *Teiho Kenzei-ke Zue*, or *The Revised and Illustrated Version of Kenzei's Biography of Dōgen*, published in 1806. Translated by Jane Hirshfield and the Editor.

Formal Talk, upon Naming the Eihei Monastery (p. 209)
This talk was given on the occasion of naming the Eihei Monastery in 1246. It was written in Chinese and was later included in Fascicle 2 of *The Extensive Record of Eihei*. Translated by Alan Senauke and the Editor.

Guidelines for Officers of the Eihei Monastery (p. 210)
The original title for this text is "Nihon-koku Echizen (Echizen Province, Japan) Eihei-ji Chiji Shingi." The text is in Chinese, as are the texts of most of his *shingi*, or monastic guidelines. Dōgen wrote this in 1246. It was included in *Eihei Shingi*, or *Monastic Guidelines of Eihei*, after Dōgen's death and was first published in 1667. Translated by Mel Weitsman and the Editor.

Auspicious Beginning of Spring (p. 254)
This short piece, written in Chinese in 1247, was first published in *Teiho Kenzei-ki*, or *The Revised and Illustrated Version of Kenzei's Biography of Dōgen*. This text is known in Japan as "Risshun Daikichi-mon." Translated by Gil Fronsdal and the Editor.

Original Face (p. 256)
This waka poem was given to the wife of the Zen Person of the Saimyō Temple, a Buddhist title for Regent Tokiyori Hōjō, who ruled Japan as head of the warrior government in Kamakura. Dōgen presented it along with eleven other poems to Lady Hōjō in 1247 during his stay in Kamakura. Waka is an ancient Japanese

poetic form consisting of thirty-one syllables. Later it was published as part of *Sanshō Doei-shū*, or *Anthology of Enlightenment Poems by the Ancestor of Sanshō* in 1747. "Sanshō," meaning umbrella-like pine, is another name for the Eihei Monastery. Translated by Brian Unger and the Editor.

Transmission Outside Scripture (p. 257)

Along with the previous poem, this is among the waka poems given to Lady Hōjō. Translated by Jane Hirshfield and the Editor.

Formal Talk upon Returning from Kamakura (p. 258)

This talk, written in Chinese and dated 1248, is found in Fascicle 3 of *The Extensive Record of Eihei*. Translated by Alan Senauke and the Editor.

Omens of the Sixteen Arhats (p. 260)

This text was written in the third year of the Hōji Era (1249) in Chinese. A copy has survived at the Kinryū Temple, Ibaragi Prefecture. Translated by Gil Fronsdal and the Editor.

On a Portrait of Myself (p. 261)

Dōgen wrote this Chinese-style poem on a portrait of himself, on the harvest moon of the fifteenth day, the eighth month of the first year of the Kenchō Era (1249). The painting, called "Dōgen Viewing the Moon," owned by the Hōkyō Temple, Fukui Prefecture, is the most famous among his portraits. The poem is also included in *The Extensive Record of Eihei*. Translated by Tensho David Schneider and the Editor.

Three Auspicious Signs at the Eihei Monastery (p. 262)

A copy of this short writing in Japanese is now owned by the Tōkyō National Museum. Dōgen says these three events took place within eight years of the time he started living in the Daibutsu Monastery in 1244. (In East Asia a portion of the year is counted as a full year.) So it is assumed that this text was written in 1251. Translated by Gil Fronsdal and the Editor.

Identifying with Cause and Effect (p. 264)

Titled "Shinjin Inga," this undated piece was written in Japanese as a fascicle of *The Treasury of the True Dharma Eye*. Ejō's colophon says that he made a fair copy of the first draft of this text in the seventh year of the Kenchō Era (1255), one and a half years after Dōgen's death. Ejō indicates that Dōgen did not have an opportunity to make a final edited version of this text. It is presumed, therefore, that Dōgen wrote this text in the last part of his life. The maturity of his thinking on the theme seems to support this conjecture. Translated by Katherine Thanas and the Editor.

Eight Awakenings of Great Beings (p. 271)

Titled "Hachi Dainingaku" in Japanese, this essay was the last piece Dōgen wrote for *The Treasury of the True Dharma Eye*. According to Ejō's colophon, Dōgen wrote this essay while sick, in the first month of the fifth year of the Kenchō Era (1253), the year of his death. Translated by Tenshin Reb Anderson and the Editor.

Final Instructions (p. 276)

This is an excerpt of Gikai's writing in Chinese, known in Japan as *Eihei Shitchū Kikigaki*, or *Record of Things Heard in the Abbot's Room at the Eihei Monastery*. It is also known as *Goyuigon Kiroku*, or *Record of the Master's Will*. The text includes Dōgen's instructions to Gikai in 1253 and words by Ejō, who was Gikai's next teacher, in 1254–1255. After Dōgen and Ejō, Gikai became the third abbot of the Eihei Monastery in 1267. A version copied in 1326 is owned by the Eihei Monastery, Fukui Prefecture. Translated by Gil Fronsdal and the Editor.

Poem (p. 279)

Dōgen wrote this Chinese-style poem upon leaving the Eihei Monastery for Kyōto on the fifth day, eighth month of 1253. It was published in *Kenzei's Biography of the Founder Dōgen of Eihei*. Translated by Jane Hirshfield and the Editor.

Death Poem (p. 280)

This death poem by Dōgen was written in Chinese style. Included in *Kenzei's Biography of the Founder Dōgen of Eihei*. Translated by Philip Whalen and the Editor.

Emergence of the
True Dharma Eye

1223–1235

Journal of My Study in China

I WROTE TO MASTER RUJING shortly before I met him: "When I was young I aroused the aspiration* for enlightenment and visited various monasteries in my country. I had some understanding of the principle of cause and effect; however I was not able to clarify the real source of buddha, dharma, and sangha. I was only seeing the outer forms, the marks and names. Later I entered the chamber of Eisai, Zen Master Senkō, and for the first time heard the teaching of the Linji School. Now I have accompanied Monk Myōzen to the flourishing kingdom of Song China. After a voyage of many miles, during which I entrusted my phantom body to the billowing waves, I have finally arrived and have entered your dharma assembly. This is the fortunate result of my wholesome roots from the past.

"Great Compassionate Teacher, even though I am only a humble person from a remote country, I am asking permission to be a room-entering student, able to come to ask questions freely and informally. Impermanent and swift, birth-and-death is the issue of utmost urgency. Time does not wait for us. Once a moment is gone it will never come back again, and we're bound to be full of regret.

"Great compassionate reverend abbot,* grant me permission to ask you about the way, about the dharma. Please, I bow to you one hundred times with my forehead humbly touching the floor."

Rujing wrote back, "Yes, you can come informally to ask questions any time, day or night, from now on. Do not worry about formality; we can be like father and son." And he signed it, "Old man at Mt. Taibo."

ON THE SECOND DAY of the seventh month of the first year of the Baoqing Era [1225] I entered the abbot's room and asked, "Nowadays in many places they talk about transmission outside the teaching. They call this 'the essence of Bodhidharma's coming from India.' How do you understand it?"

Rujing said, "The great road of buddha* ancestors is not concerned with inside or outside. The reason they call it transmission outside the teaching is this: although Kashyapa Matanga and others had transmitted the teaching to China previously, in coming here from India Bodhidharma brought the teaching to life and showed the craft of the way. This is why they call it transmission outside the teaching. But there aren't two buddha-dharmas. Before Bodhidharma arrived in China there were practices but no master to enliven them. After Bodhidharma came to China it was as if an aimless people acquired a strong king who brought the land, people, and property of the kingdom into order."

I asked, "Nowadays elders of different monasteries say that only direct experience without discrimination—hearing the unhearable and seeing the unseeable—is the way of buddha ancestors. So they hold up a fist or a whisk, shout, or beat people with sticks. This kind of teaching doesn't do anything to awaken students.

"Furthermore, these teachers don't allow students to inquire about the essentials of the Buddha's* guidance and they discourage practices that aim to bear fruit in a future birth. Are these teachers really teaching the way of buddha ancestors?"

Rujing said, "To deny that there are future births is nihilism; buddha ancestors do not hold to the nihilistic views of those who are outside the way. If there is no rebirth there is no present birth. We know this present birth exists. How could it be that the next birth doesn't also exist?

"We have been followers of the Buddha for a long time. How can we hold views that are outside the way of the Buddha? To teach students the power of the present moment as the only moment is a skillful teaching of buddha ancestors. But this doesn't mean that there is no future result from practice.

"If you believe there is no future result of practice, then you won't study with teachers and buddhas won't emerge in the world. Just listen to what I'm saying here and realize it for yourself.

"If we do not have trust in future results and so do not practice the way of enlightenment, we would be like the people from the world of Uttarakuru. In that world no one can ever receive the Buddha's guidance and no one is ever awakened."

I asked, "Teachers in the past and present talk about inherent knowledge; they liken it to a fish drinking water and immediately knowing whether it's warm or cold. Awakening is this kind of knowledge, they say, and this is itself enlightenment. I don't understand this. If inherent knowledge is correct awakening, then all sentient beings will automatically become completely enlightened *tathāgatas*,* because all sentient beings already do have this kind of knowledge. Some people say this is how it is, that all sentient beings really are beginningless original tathāgatas. Others say that sentient beings are not necessarily tathāgatas. They say that only those sentient beings who become aware of their inherent wisdom are tathāgatas, and those who are not aware of it are not. Are any of these theories correct buddha-dharma or not?"

Rujing said, "Those who say that sentient beings are already buddhas are really professing a belief in spontaneous enlightenment. This view is not at all in accord with the way. To equate 'I' with buddha is to mistake unattainment for attainment and unenlightenment for enlightenment."

I ASKED, "When we students practice the way, how should we cultivate the mind in the midst of ordinary activity, while walking, sitting, standing, and lying down?"

Rujing said, "When Bodhidharma came from India, the body and mind of buddha-dharma truly entered China. Here are some things to pay attention to when you first undertake dharma study: don't spend a long time sick in bed; don't travel far away; don't read or chant too much; don't argue too much; don't overwork; don't eat leeks and onions; don't eat meat; don't drink too much milk or honey; don't drink alcohol; don't eat impure food; don't listen to singing or music; don't watch dancing women; don't look at mutilated bodies; don't look at pornography or talk about sex; don't be intimate with kings or ministers; don't eat raw or unripe foods; don't wear filthy clothes; don't visit slaughterhouses; don't drink aged tea or take medicines for mental disease like those they sell at Mt. Tiantai; don't eat fungi; don't pay any attention to matters of fame and fortune; don't eat too much cream; don't be associated with eunuchs or hermaphrodites; don't eat too many dried plums or chestnuts; don't eat too many longans, lichi nuts, or olives; don't have too much sugar or candy; don't wear quilted clothes but wear only plain cotton clothes; don't eat dry food for soldiers; don't pay attention to shouting and loud noises, or watch herds of pigs and sheep; don't stare at big fish, the ocean, bad pictures, hunchbacks, or puppets; instead look at mountains and streams.

"Illuminate the mind with ancient teachings and read sutras that contain complete meanings. Monks who practice zazen should always have clean feet. When the body and mind are confused, chant the beginning of the text called 'the bodhisattva precepts'."

Then I asked, "What text is that?"

Rujing said, "It's what the Japanese monk Ryūzen has been chanting. Don't associate with small-minded people."

I asked, "Who are small-minded people?"

Rujing said, "Those who are full of greed."

RUJING SAID, "Don't keep tigers, elephants, pigs, dogs, cats, or badgers. Nowadays elders in many monasteries keep cats; this is really unacceptable; only stupid people do this. The sixteen nasty habits are prohibited by buddha ancestors. Do not get accustomed to them."

I ASKED RUJING, "Lay people read *The Lankāvatāra Sūtra* and *The Complete Enlightenment Sūtra* and say that these are the ancestral teachings transmitted from India. When I opened up these sūtras and observed their structure and style, I felt they were not as skillful as other Mahāyāna* sūtras. This seemed strange to me. More than this, the teachings of these sūtras seemed to me to be far less than what we find in Mahāyāna sūtras. They seemed quite similar to the teachings of the six outsider teachers [who lived during the Buddha's time]. How do we determine whether or not these texts are authentic?"

Rujing said, "The authenticity of *The Lankāvatāra Sūtra* has been doubted by some people since ancient times. Some suspect that this sūtra was written by people of a later period, as the early ancestors were definitely not aware of it. But ignorant people in recent times read it and love it. *The Complete Enlightenment Sūtra* is also like this. Its style is similar to *The Lankāvatāra Sūtra*."

I ASKED, "Can the negative results that come from delusion, external conditions, and karma* really be the path of buddha ancestors [as Nāgārjuna's teachings say]?"

Rujing said, "You should always trust teachings by ancestors like Nāgārjuna; their views are never mistaken. As far as the negative effect of karma goes, one should practice wholeheartedly, and it will certainly be turned around."

I asked, "So should we always be aware of cause and effect?"

Rujing answered, "You should never ignore cause and effect. Yongjia said, 'Superficial understanding of emptiness* ignores cause and effect and invites calamity.' Those who ignore cause and effect cut off good roots in buddha-dharma. How can you regard them as descendants of buddha ancestors?"

I ASKED, "Why is it that nowadays elders everywhere keep long hair and long nails? They call themselves monks but look like lay people. Maybe we should call them lay people. Actually, they're nothing but bald-headed idiots! In the past, during the Ages of True Dharma and Imitation Dharma, disciples of buddha ancestors in India and China were never like this. What do you make of it?"

Rujing said, "They are indeed ignoramuses, corpses in the pure ocean of buddha-dharma."

Rujing continued, "Although you're still young, there is already a look of deep accomplishment in your face. It will be good for you to live in a deep mountain or quiet valley so that you can slowly gestate in the womb of the buddha ancestors. Then you will certainly arrive at the place of enlightenment of the ancient sages."

Then I stood up and made a prostration at his feet. Rujing chanted a verse:

Both the bower and the bowed-to
are empty and serene by nature
and the way flows freely between them.
How wondrous!

Then he spoke to me extensively about the practices of buddha ancestors in India and China. I was so moved that I cried until the lapel of my robe became soaked with tears.

I ENTERED THE ABBOT'S ROOM in the Great Light Storehouse Hall and Rujing said, "When you practice with the assembly, you should tie all the belts for your robes and undergarments quite firmly. Whenever you wear your belts like this, you will be able to make strong effort without too much exertion."

RUJING SAID, "One of the most essential practices for the training in the monks' hall is the practice of slow walking. There are many elders here and there nowadays who do not know about this practice. In fact, only a few people know how to do it. To do the slow walking practice you coordinate the steps with the breathing. You walk without looking at the feet, without bending over or looking up. You go so slowly it looks like you're not moving at all. Do not sway when you walk."

Then he walked back and forth several times in the Great Light Storehouse Hall to show me how to do it and said to me, "Nowadays I am the only one who knows this slow walking practice. If you ask elders in different monasteries about it, I'm sure you'll find they don't know it."

*   *   *

I ASKED, "The nature of all things is either good, bad, or neutral. Which of these is the buddha-dharma?"

Rujing said, "The buddha-dharma goes beyond these three."

I asked, "The wide road of the buddhas and ancestors* cannot be confined to a small space. How can we limit it to something as small as 'the Zen School'?"

Rujing replied, "To call the wide road of the buddhas and ancestors 'the Zen School' is thoughtless talk. 'The Zen School' is a false name used by bald-headed idiots, and all sages from ancient times are aware of this. Haven't you read *Record of Monasteries* by Shaman?"

I said, "I haven't."

Rujing went on: "It would be good for you to study it. What this book says is true. Briefly, the great dharma of the World-honored One* was transmitted to Mahākāshyapa alone and was passed on heir to heir for twenty-eight generations, and then for five generations in China to Huineng, the Sixth Ancestor. Today I, Rujing, hold the center of buddha-dharma. In a billion *sahā** worlds there can be no one comparable.

"Yet it is true that those who lecture on sūtras or treatises and carry on the various schools' teachings are also family members of buddha ancestors. Among them some are more important than others, depending on how close they are in the family."

I asked, "Then those who have become buddha ancestors' family members must still arouse the aspiration for enlightenment and visit true masters. But why would they throw away years of study in another school to join an assembly of buddha ancestors like yours here and practice day and night?"

Rujing said, "In India and China people often had to go beyond what they learned in the course of their advancement. It's this way when someone stops being a councilor and advances to prime minister. Though he's no longer a councilor, he can still teach his successors how to perform as a councilor. It's the same way in studying the way of buddha ancestors. Although someone becomes a prime minister because of his good work as a councilor, once he becomes a prime minister he no longer acts like a councilor but acts like a prime minister. Yet while he was a councilor he acted like a councilor, not like a prime minister. No matter what the role, all the activity is devoted to governing the nation and comforting the people. The mind of true dedication is one, not two."

I asked further, "None of the statements of elders in different places has been able to illuminate the way of buddha ancestors for me. But now I clearly see it. Buddha ancestors are indeed heirs of the World-honored One, the dharma king of this eon. Buddha ancestors preside over everything in the billion worlds, over all conditions in the dharma realm. There cannot be two kingdoms."

Rujing said, "What you say is right. As far back as India there have never been two legacies of the dharma storehouse. In China from the First Ancestor to the Sixth Ancestor there was no dual transmission of the robe. Therefore the single root of the buddha-dharma of the billion worlds is the way of buddha ancestors."

RUJING SAID, "Studying Zen is dropping off body and mind. Without depending on the burning of incense, bowing, chanting Buddha's names, repentance, or sūtra reading, devote yourself to just sitting."

I asked, "What is dropping off body and mind?"

Rujing said, "Dropping off body and mind is zazen. When you just sit, you are free from the five sense desires* and the five hindrances."*

I asked, "Is this freedom from the five sense desires and the five hindrances the same as what the sūtra schools are talking about? Does it mean we are to be practitioners of both the Mahāyāna and Hīnayāna?"*

Rujing said, "Descendants of ancestors should not exclude the teachings of either vehicle. If students ignore the Tathāgata's sacred teachings, how can they become the descendants of buddha ancestors?"

I ASKED, "Recent critics say that the three poisons* are themselves buddha-dharma and the five sense desires are nothing but the ancestral way. They say that trying to become free of them is dualistic discrimination, no different from the Hīnayāna way. What do you think about this?"

Rujing said, "If we don't try to free ourselves from the three poisons and the five sense desires, we would be practicing like people outside the way in the lands of King Bimbisāra and his son, King Ajātashatru. If buddha ancestors' descendants become free from even one moment of hindrance or desire, it will be a great benefit. To do this is to encounter buddha ancestors."

I ASKED, "Priest Changsha and Secretary Haoyue discussed the original emptiness of karma. It would seem that if karma is empty, the other two negative effects—those resulting from external conditions and those resulting from delusion—will also be empty. It seems wrong to discuss the emptiness of karma without discussing the other two.

"However when Haoyue asked, 'What is the original emptiness?' Changsha said, 'Karma.' And when Haoyue said, 'What is karma?' Changsha said, 'Original emptiness.' Is what Changsha said here correct or not? If the buddha-dharma is as Changsha stated, how could buddhas emerge in the world and Bodhidharma come from India?"

Rujing said, "What Changsha said is not at all correct. He did not clarify the karma in the three times from now."*

I ASKED, "Teachers in the past and present all say we should study the sūtras that contain complete meaning and not the sūtras that contain incomplete meaning. What are the sūtras that contain complete meaning?"

Rujing said, "Sūtras that contain complete meaning include descriptions of the events in the past lives of the Tathāgata. Sūtras that explain only events in this world and have a limited perspective, not a universal perspective, and sūtras that discuss temporal things but do not discuss timeless things are not sūtras of complete meaning. The sūtras that discuss the rise and fall of eons and the rise and fall of nations from limited and universal perspectives, as well as sūtras that deal with timeless realms, the world of relatives, businesses, and workers without leaving anything out are called the sūtras of complete meaning."

I asked, "Isn't it also true that just half a phrase can explain the essential meaning? Can't we also call this kind of brief sūtra a sūtra with complete meaning? How can we say that only sūtras that extensively expound the essential meaning should be called sūtras of complete meaning? Furthermore, there are some sūtras that teach eloquently and extensively but fail to clarify the essential meaning; these should not be regarded as sūtras with complete meaning."

Rujing said, "No, what you say is wrong. Whatever was spoken by the Tathāgata always exhausts the essential meaning regardless of the length of the teaching. An extensive sūtra always extensively exhausts the essential meaning. A brief sūtra always briefly exhausts the essential meaning.

"There is no way any of the sūtras are incomplete. Furthermore, sacred silence and sacred expounding are both buddha activities. The light of consciousness is the buddha activity; having a meal is the buddha activity; being born in heaven, coming down from heaven, becoming a monk, practicing asceticism, encountering demons, attaining the way, practicing begging, and entering nirvāna are all buddha activities. Sentient beings who see and hear this all attain benefit.

"Therefore you should be clear that all of these things are sūtras with complete meaning. To expound dharma through buddha activities is called expounding a sūtra of complete meaning. These sūtras are the dharma of buddha ancestors."

I said, "I respectfully accept your instruction as the buddhadharma and the ancestral path. Now I see that statements I've heard by elders of monasteries here and there in China, as well as statements by dilettantes of dharma in Japan, have no ground to stand on.

"Up to now my understanding of complete meaning was incomplete. Today for the first time I understand clearly with your guidance that sūtras of complete meaning go beyond sūtras of complete meaning. This understanding is rarely met with even in millions and billions of eons."

I ASKED AT MIDNIGHT, "In your dharma talk you said, 'The bower and the bowed-to are empty by nature. The mind-to-mind communication is wondrous and inconceivable; its heart is profound, and it cannot be known. There is no way to reach it superficially. Doubt cannot touch it.' Teachers in the scriptural school also talk about mind-to-mind communication. Is it the same as what is taught in the ancestral path?"

Rujing replied, "You should know very well the ultimate importance of mind-to-mind communication. Without it buddhas would not have appeared, and Bodhidharma would not have come to China. It is a mistake to regard the scriptural teachings as outside of the ancestral path. Regarding the scriptural buddha-dharma as incorrect is like using a round robe and a square bowl. You can't do that, can you? Please don't try to use a round robe and a square bowl. You should know that there is always mind-to-mind communication."

I SAID, "The other day I visited elder Daguang of Mt. Ayuwang and asked some questions. He said the buddha ancestors' way and the scriptural school are like water and fire, that they are as far apart as heaven and earth. He said that to agree with the scriptural school is to be far removed from the teachings of the ancestors. Can this statement by Daguang be true?"

Rujing answered, "It is not only Daguang who makes such mistaken statements. Elders of monasteries here and there are also like this. If they don't understand the teaching of the scriptural schools, how can they enter the ancestors' inner room? They are elders, but they speak nonsense."

I SAID, "The Buddha's teachings were originally compiled in two streams: the Mahāyāna scriptures were compiled by Manjushrī, the Bodhisattva of Perfect Wisdom, and the Hīnayāna scriptures were compiled by Ānanda, the Buddha's disciple.

"This being so, it is hard to see why Mahākāshyapa, another disciple of the Hīnayāna, became the First Ancestor entrusted with the dharma treasury. Why not the Bodhisattva Manjushrī? Manjushrī's perfect wisdom is after all the source of all buddhas including Shākyamuni Buddha, so it would seem that he should be regarded as the First Ancestor entrusted with the dharma treasury. Can it be that the Tathāgata's treasury of the true dharma eye, the wondrous heart of nirvāna, is actually the dharma of the Hīnayāna? What do you think of this?"

Rujing replied, "You are right in saying that Manjushrī's perfect wisdom is the source of all buddhas. So he is the teacher of all the buddhas, not their heir. Had he been a disciple of the Buddha, he would certainly have received the entrustment of dharma. Another point to consider is this: The tradition that Manjushrī compiled the Mahāyāna sūtras is only one of the traditions and is not commonly accepted. Even if he did compile them, it would appear that he did not know the Hīnayāna teachings, for his name doesn't appear there.

"Most accept that Ānanda compiled both the Mahāyāna and the Hīnayāna teachings because he was a person with exceptional listening and remembering abilities. This is why Ānanda assembled the discourses that the Tathāgata gave throughout his lifetime. As for Mahākāshyapa, he was a senior monk while the Buddha was alive and was recognized as the most senior and most skillful of teachers. This is why the dharma treasury was entrusted to him.

"If the dharma treasury had been entrusted to Manjushrī, who was not a disciple of the Buddha and did not study the Hīnayāna teachings, there would have been doubts about the wholeness of the dharma. You should trust the wholeness of the dharma of all buddhas. Do not doubt it."

RUJING SAID as we met informally one evening, "Dōgen, do you know about putting on socks while you are seated in the teaching chair?"

I made a small bow and said, "Will you show me?"

He said, "When you are seated in the teaching chair to give a talk in the monks' hall during zazen, you should wear ceremonial socks. As you put them on you cover your feet with your right sleeve. This is to avoid being rude to Manjushrī Bodhisattva, the Sacred Monk, whose image is on the altar facing you."

RUJING SAID, "During the time you are in training, practicing zazen intensively, do not eat wild rice. It may give you a fever. Also, do not do zazen in a drafty place."

RUJING SAID, "When you get up from zazen to walk, you should practice the method of slow walking meditation. Do not go more than half a step with each breath."

RUJING SAID, "Zen practitioners of ancient times all wore the simple robe,* but sometimes they wore the combined robe.* Now everyone wears the combined robe all the time; this is a degenerate custom. If you want to follow the ancient style, you should wear a simple robe, even when you visit the palace. Also, at the time of dharma transmission* or when receiving the dharma robe or the bodhisattva precepts, you should wear a simple robe.

"Monks who practice Zen nowadays say that the simple robe is the uniform of the Precepts School monasteries. They are wrong. They do not know the ancient custom."

RUJING SAID, "Since I became abbot of this monastery, I have never worn a decorated robe. Nowadays there are elders in name only who follow the crowds and wear decorated robes; to me this makes them appear that they have no true realization. I never wear robes like that. The World-honored One himself wore only robes made of coarse cloth throughout his lifetime; he never wore beautiful robes.

"On the other hand, it is also incorrect to make a point of wearing robes of inferior material and workmanship. If you make a point of wearing such a robe you'll be like Ajita Keshakambala [who wore robes made of his own hair] and others outside the way.

"Therefore descendants of buddha ancestors should simply

wear whatever plain robes come to hand. It's no good to be extreme one way or the other. Extremism doesn't work. It's like trying to carry a long board by holding it at one end. You can't hold it; it won't balance.

"Those who are concerned that their robes appear impressive are small-minded people. Don't forget that a robe made of excrement-cleaning cloth is an ancient model."

I offered incense to Rujing and asked, "But the World-honored One transmitted a brocade robe to Mahākāshyapa. Can you tell me about this?"

He said, "What a wonderful question! Most people don't ask this question because they don't know enough to ask it. This is where teachers struggle. When I was studying with late teacher Xuedou and asked this question he was very pleased. When the World-honored One first saw Mahākāshyapa coming to take refuge he immediately entrusted the buddha-dharma and brocade robe to him and made him the First Ancestor. Mahākāshyapa received this brocade robe and the dharma, yet he continued to follow ascetic practice day and night for the rest of his life without stint. He never lay down to sleep, and he always treated the *kashāya** with respect and full ceremony. Every day he did zazen, concentrating on the image of the Buddha or the Buddha's *stūpa.** Mahākāshyapa is an ancient buddha, ancient bodhisattva; whenever they were together the World-honored One always shared his seat with him.

"Of the thirty-two marks of the Buddha, Venerable Mahākāshyapa had thirty marks; he was lacking only a white tuft between his eyebrows and the knobby protuberance at the top of the head. He was very impressive, sitting side by side with the Buddha; it is said that humans and devas enjoyed looking at them together. He had miraculous understanding and a wonderful ability to communicate the entire buddha-dharma, and he received the full entrustment of the Buddha without any lack. Since Mahākāshyapa had these special qualities, the Buddha entrusted him with the brocade robe and the dharma the first time they met."

*   *   *

I WROTE A LETTER to Rujing, "Dear Abbot Master, in China there are four types of monasteries: Zen monasteries, monasteries of the Doctrinal School, monasteries of the Precepts School, and monasteries without lineage.

"As I understand it, the source experience of the Zen monasteries is that of the true descendants of buddha ancestors who transmit the dharma person to person and practice facing the wall as Bodhidharma did at Mt. Song. This experience is the treasury of the true dharma eye, the wondrous heart of nirvāna. It is indeed the heart of the Tathāgata, the center of buddha-dharma; all others are peripheral. This is incomparable and unarguable.

"In the monasteries of the Doctrinal School, the Tiantai way is practiced. This lineage was established by Zhiyi, Great Master Zhizhe, who was the heir of Nanyue, Meditation Master Huisi. Zhiyi received and refined the practice of the three stoppings* and three insights* of the one mind; he also attained the lotus flower *samādhi** and the revolving *dhāranī.** According to the Tiantai, studying with a teacher and scriptural study are equally important.

"When I was a Tiantai student extensively studying scriptures and commentaries, I found Meditation Master Zhiyi to be most outstanding in his understanding of the sūtras, precepts, and commentaries. His understanding is unprecedented and unmatchable. His teacher, the Great Priest Huisi of Nanyue, had received the dharma from Huiwen of the northern kingdom of Qi. Huisi aroused his mind and touched the fundamental root of meditation.

"Huiwen, his teacher, began by looking around blindly in the sūtras, eventually running into Nāgārjuna's *Treatise on Mādhyamika*. It was from this treatise that Huiwen established the practice of the three insights of one mind. Ever since his time the monasteries of the Doctrinal School have all been based on these teachings of the Tiantai School. But Huiwen's practice is based merely on the words of the *Treatise on Mādhyamika* without understanding the words of Nāgārjuna and without receiving an approval from Nāgārjuna. Furthermore, the rules of these monasteries are not thorough, and their buildings are not complete.

"In the present day, monasteries of the Doctrinal School have

added to their old practice the practice of the sixteen visualizations*
that comes from *The Sūtra of Infinite Life*, and the authenticity of
this sūtra is not established. Scholars of the past and today are
doubtful about it. Tiantai's original practice of three insights of one
mind cannot be the same as the sixteen visualizations from India.
The latter is merely expedient teaching, while the former is true
teaching, and so they are as different as heaven and earth, and they
contradict each other like water and fire. I suspect that students in
Great Song China have not clearly understood the teachings of the
Tiantai and have mistakenly added the sixteen visualizations. It is
also clear that the Doctrinal School monasteries have not transmitted the customs and traditions of monasteries from the Buddha's
time. They seem to have monastic styles begun not by the Buddha
but by Kāshyapa Mātanga and Zhu Falan.

"The monasteries of the Precepts School were originally
founded by Nanshan Daoxuan, who, without going to India, studied scriptures brought here to the East. Even if he had heard the
teaching of devas in addition to studying scriptures, it is still not as
good as directly receiving the teachings of the wise sages. Because
these monasteries were founded without direct teaching contact,
their building layout and design are doubted by scholars and practitioners.

"In China there are many large and famous Zen monasteries.
Some of them house over one thousand practitioners and consist of
over one hundred buildings with various towers and shrines, and
walkways running in many directions. They look like palaces. The
customs and traditions of these monasteries are completely in accord with what buddha ancestors taught face to face, and everything
is designed and built according to that direct teaching.

"But the magnificence of the buildings is not the most important thing. More important are such practice forms as morning tea
meeting and evening instruction; these forms are directly given by
Bodhidharma and cannot be compared with practices created by
those who work things out only through the interpretation of texts.
Only the Zen ways should be considered correct.

"I suspect that these practices of the ancient buddhas were

maintained even before the World-honored One emerged in this world. Didn't the World-honored One say once to Ānanda, 'You should follow the customs and traditions of the Seven Original Buddhas'? So it seems that the dharma of the Seven Original Buddhas is the dharma of Shākyamuni Buddha, and that Shākyamuni's dharma is also the dharma of the Seven Original Buddhas.

"From Shākyamuni Buddha through twenty-eight transmissions, this dharma reached Bodhidharma who came to China and correctly transmitted it to save deluded minds. After five transmissions this same dharma reached Huineng, and through him his two excellent students Qingyuan and Nanyue. Their descendants in turn became excellent teachers in their own right and spread this teaching of Shākyamuni.

"This is why we should consider the monasteries where these monks and their descendants abide as the true places of the buddha-dharma. These monasteries cannot be compared with monasteries of the Doctrinal School or the Precepts School any more than a country without a king can be compared to a country that has a rightful king.

"Please guide me on these points. Burning incense and making a hundred bows, I am your disciple, Dōgen."

Rujing said in reply, "Your letter is quite right and well presented. In ancient times monasteries did not carry names like the Doctrinal School, the Precepts School, or the Zen School. The use of such names is simply a bad habit of this declining age. Kings' officials who really do not know buddha-dharma mistakenly classify monks as monks of the Doctrinal School, the Precepts School, or the Zen School. Imperial tablets use these designations and their usage has spread so that now we hear of five types of monks: Precepts School monks, who are descendants of Nanshan; Doctrinal School monks, who are descendants from the Tiantai; monks of the Yoga School, who are descendants of Amoghavajra; monks of monasteries without lineages, who are not clear about who their ancestors are; and the Zen monks, who are all descended from Bodhidharma. It is truly pitiful that we have such a confusion of names and groups in this remote country, China, in this declining age.

"It is true that there were five schools* in India but these were only various styles of one buddha-dharma. In China the division into five schools is not like this. If there were a wise king in this country, such confusion would not exist. In the end, what is clear is that the design, customs, and traditions of the Zen monasteries are all direct teachings of the ancestors through direct transmission by the true heirs of the Buddha. The authentic way of the Seven Original Buddhas is only found in the Zen monasteries, although the term 'Zen' is really a mistaken name.

"Our customs and traditions are the ones transmitted by buddha ancestors, and our monasteries are central to the stream of the dharma. Precepts School and Doctrinal School monasteries are only tributaries. Buddha ancestors are the dharma kings; and when the king is installed, he is the king of the world and all people are subject to him."

RUJING SAID, "Descendants of buddha ancestors should first be free from the five hindrances* and then become free from the sixth hindrance. The sixth hindrance is the lack of understanding.

"When you are free from the hindrance of the lack of understanding you immediately become free of the five hindrances. But if you are not free from the hindrance of the lack of understanding, even though you are free from the five hindrances, you do not arrive at the practice-realization of buddha ancestors."

I bowed with gratitude, respectfully folding my hands across my chest, and said, "I have never heard of this teaching before. A lot of senior monks and brother monks don't seem to know or talk about it. It must be that I have good roots from the past that have enabled me today to hear for the first time this compassionate teaching. Master, please tell me further: What is the secret of being free from all these five hindrances and six hindrances*?"

Rujing smiled and replied, "Haven't you been practicing all along? What you have already been doing is exactly the way to be free from the six hindrances. Buddhas and ancestors do not wait for people to pass through various stages. They directly and personally transmit the way to be free from the six hindrances so that we are no longer controlled by the five sense desires.

"The practice of just sitting and dropping off body and mind *is* the way to become free from the five hindrances and the five sense desires. There's no other way and there's no point in talking about any other way."

I ASKED, "You have not worn the ceremonial dharma robe since you became abbot of this monastery. Why is this?"

Rujing said, "In fact I have not worn such a robe as an abbot. I forbear this for the sake of humility. The Buddha and his disciples should wear robes made of discarded cloth and use bowls made of humble materials."

I said, "Elders in different monasteries often do wear ceremonial dharma robes; this may show a lack of humility and perhaps it is a sign of petty greed. But how do you feel about Old Buddha Hongzhi? He wore a ceremonial dharma robe but no one would deny that he was a very humble person."

Rujing said, "Yes, Old Buddha Hongzhi wore a ceremonial dharma robe, but in his case it was out of respect, and it was an act of sincerity in the practice of the way. In your country, Japan, wearing a ceremonial dharma robe is not a problem. But here in China there's a tendency for elders to be greedy and ostentatious in the robes they wear. I do not wear a ceremonial dharma robe here because I do not want to participate in this way of doing things."

RUJING ONCE SAID, "The zazen of *arhats** and *pratyeka-buddhas** is free from attachment, but it lacks all-embracing compassion. This is very different from the zazen of buddha ancestors, where all-embracing compassion and the vow to awaken all sentient beings is the highest priority.

"People outside the way in India also practiced zazen, but this zazen still has the three problems of attachment, wrong views, and pride, and so it is permanently and utterly different from the zazen of buddha ancestors. *Shrāvakas** also practice zazen, but their compassion is limited. They do not penetrate the reality of all things

with wisdom; instead they merely improve themselves and thus remove themselves from the creative seed of the buddhas. So their
zazen, too, is permanently and utterly different from that of buddha
ancestors.

"The very essence of buddha ancestors' zazen is the vow to
accumulate all buddha qualities from the moment of arousing the
aspiration for enlightenment into the endless future. Buddha ancestors never forget or abandon sentient beings, but have compassion
for all creatures, even insects, and make a constant effort to rescue
them all, and they turn over whatever merit is produced by all this
to sentient beings. Because of this vow, buddha ancestors always
practice zazen in the desire realm, in our everyday world of Jambudvīpa, which has great opportunities for influencing cause and
effect. Buddha ancestors practice this way life after life, world after
world, and attain great flexibility of mind and heart."

I bowed and said, "How do we attain this flexibility of mind and
heart?"

Rujing said, "To actualize buddha ancestors' dropping off body
and mind is the essence of this flexibility. That is why dropping off
body and mind is called the mind seal* of buddha ancestors."

I bowed.

RUJING SAID, "In the dharma hall* there are lion images placed
to the east and west of the steps that lead up to the dharma seat.
Both of them face the steps, but are slightly angled to face south,
toward the audience. These lions, from tail to mane, should be pure
white. In recent times workers have produced lions that are white,
but with blue manes. This variation isn't based on tradition; in fact,
the lions should be all white, from mane to tail.

"Above the dharma seat there should be an eight-cornered lotus
canopy, which shelters the seat, just as the lotus flower covers the
earth. There should be a mirror in each of its eight facets, and a
streamer with a bell affixed to it hanging down from each corner.
There should be five layers of lotus petals, with a bell hung from
each petal. The canopy should be exactly like the one above the
dharma seat of this monastery."

*   *   *

I ASKED, "I heard your verse on the windbell. The first line says, 'The entire body is a mouth hanging in emptiness.' And the third line says, 'Joining the whole universe in chiming out prajñā.'[1] What is this emptiness? Is it just the lack of form? People who doubt the way say this. And nowadays even students of the way do not understand buddha-dharma; they regard the spaciousness of the blue sky as emptiness. This is regrettable."

Rujing said, "Emptiness is no other than prajñā. It's not the lack of form. Emptiness is neither having nor not having hindrances; therefore it is not emptiness in the sense of simple lack. It is not one-sided reality. Elders in different places have not yet clarified even form; how can they clarify this emptiness? I'm afraid that here in Great Song China the decline of buddha-dharma is beyond description."

I said, "Your verse on the windbell is supreme. Even if they had numberless eons, other elders would never be able to compose a verse like this. Brother monks should venerate it. Although I have come from a remote land and am not well versed in dharma, I have read collections of Zen masters' teachings, like *Transmission of the Lamp, Wide Lamp, Successive Lamp*, and *Universal Lamp*, as well as the recorded sayings of various masters, and I have not yet seen anything like your windbell verse. It is my good fortune to have seen it. I wet my robe with tears of joy and bow day and night in appreciation of its straightforwardness and its beautiful rhythm."

Rujing was about to ride off in a sedan chair; he smiled and said, "Your words are deep and your spirit is outstanding. I composed this verse when I was at Qingliang Monastery. At the time many people praised it, but none of them spoke as you have done. I acknowledge that you have a sharp dharma eye. When you compose a verse, you should do it in the same manner."

RUJING SAID to me at night, "If sentient beings, transmigrating through birth and death, arouse the aspiration for enlightenment

---

1. "Windbell" by Rujing: The real body is a mouth hanging in emptiness. / Whether the wind blows from the east, west, south, or north, / it joins the whole universe in chiming out prajñā. / Ting-ting, ting-ting, ting-ting.

and seek buddhahood, they are immediately children of buddha ancestors. Yet it's also true that all other sentient beings are children
of buddha ancestors as well. Understand this family lineage, but
don't speculate about its origins."

RUJING INSTRUCTED ME: "When you do zazen, place your
tongue on the roof of the mouth and allow it to press behind the
front teeth. If after forty or fifty years of zazen practice you are
accustomed to sitting without drooping or becoming drowsy, it is
all right to close your eyes during zazen. Those who are not so
accustomed to zazen should sit with the eyes open. If you sit long
and are tired, it is all right to shift the position of your legs. This
has been directly transmitted by the Buddha for fifty generations."

I ASKED, "Those in Japan and China who doubt say that the zazen
widely practiced in Zen monasteries is the dharma of the Hīnayāna.
How do we respond to this?"

Rujing said, "Such critics in China and Japan have not yet clarified buddha-dharma. Dōgen, you should know that the true dharma
of the Tathāgata goes beyond the external appearance of so-called
Great or Small Vehicles. The compassion of the ancient buddhas
falls as naturally as weeds cut by the mower and produces many
skillful means which we call Mahāyāna and Hīnayāna.

"You should know that Mahāyāna is seven pieces of vegetable
rice cake; Hīnayāna is three pieces of sesame rice cake. Furthermore, buddha ancestors have never deceived children by pretending
to have treasures in their closed fists. They open their hands and
give golden leaves or pieces of gold according to the situation. They
give predictions of enlightenment when called for, and skillful guidance when called for. None of their activities is ineffective, and
nothing they have given is not useful."

RUJING SAID, "I see that you do zazen in your place in the monks'
hall without sleep day and night. This is wonderful. You'll soon
experience the exquisite fragrance that is beyond compare in this
world. This is an auspicious sign. Visions of drops of oil falling on

the ground in front of you are also an auspicious sign, as are powerful and unusual bodily sensations. When you experience these things you should immediately increase your intensity of practice as if you were putting out a fire on your head."

RUJING SAID, "The World-honored One said that hearing and thinking about the way is like being outside the gate, but zazen is like coming home and sitting calmly inside. Therefore the merit of doing zazen even for one moment is immeasurable.

"I have been practicing the way for over thirty years without ever turning back, and although I am sixty-five years old I am more determined than ever. You too should practice with this intensity, as if you had received the prediction of enlightenment from the golden mouth of the Buddha himself."

RUJING SAID, "During zazen do not lean on the wall, screen, or the back of a chair. If you do, it will cause you to become ill. You should sit with a straight back, following the guidelines for zazen, never violating them."

Rujing said, "If you get up from zazen and do walking meditation, do not walk in a circle, but go in a straight line. If after twenty or thirty steps you want to turn around, always turn to the right. Always begin your steps with the right foot, then the left foot."

RUJING SAID, "The ruins of the place where the Tathāgata got up from zazen and did walking meditation still exist in Udyāna Kingdom in India. Also, Layman Vimalakīrti's house still exists today, and the foundation stones of Jeta Grove Monastery have not been buried. When people go to examine these sacred places, the results of their measurements always differ: some measure long, others measure short, some find the stones close together, and others find them farther apart. Their findings don't correspond to each other. This is the vitality of buddha ancestors.

"You should also know that the bowl and robe, as well as the fist and nostrils of the ancestors, which have been transmitted to us in China, cannot be definitively measured."

I stood up and bowed with my head down to the floor, shedding tears of joy.

RUJING SAID, "In zazen it is possible to develop samādhi by placing the mind in various locations. However, I would say, during zazen set your mind on the palm of your left hand. This is the way correctly transmitted by buddha ancestors."

RUJING SAID, "Although Kao at Yaoshan, being just a novice, did not receive monk's precepts, you should not imagine that he did not receive buddha ancestors' correctly transmitted precepts. He wore the buddha robe and used the buddha bowl; he was a true bodhisattva.

"When monks are seated in assembly, their seniority should follow the order of receiving the bodhisattva precepts, not that of receiving the novice or monk's precepts. This tradition of bodhisattva precept transmission is the correct one. Dōgen, I am very pleased with your deep aspiration for seeking dharma. Truly you are the fully entrusted vessel for the transmission of the Caodong School."

I ASKED, "The experience of the ancient and present buddha ancestors is an excellent guidepost for our own practice. In the beginning, when we first arouse our mind to understand dharma, it appears that there is a buddha way, but later when we become established in our understanding, it appears that there is no buddha way. On the other hand, when we begin to practice, it appears that we have not yet attained enlightenment. And when we really enter the dharma, it appears that there is a spirit of enlightenment that goes even beyond the ancients. My question is: where is real enlightenment? At the beginning or later on?"

Rujing replied, "Bodhisattvas and shrāvakas asked this same question of the World-honored One when he was alive. In India and China there has been correctly transmitted teaching about this.

"On the one hand it is taught that the dharma does not increase or decrease. If so, how can there be such a thing as attaining enlightenment? This teaching implies that only buddhas have enlightenment; bodhisattvas can never attain it, and this raises a serious question and a serious doubt for practitioners.

"It is also taught that enlightenment is the same in the beginner's mind and the experienced practitioner's mind. But how can this be possible? If this is so, then immediately upon first arousing the bodhisattva aspiration for enlightenment, you would already be a buddha. On the other hand, if there is no enlightened beginner's mind, how can we make steps toward the enlightened fulfillment of dharma? So the enlightened fulfillment of dharma must be the fruition of the beginner's enlightened experience. And the beginner's enlightened experience must be the seed of the fulfillment.

"Let me explain this more clearly with an analogy. It is like a candle with its illuminating flame. When the candle is lit there is a flame. As the candle burns there is still the same flame. So there's no difference between the beginning time and the later time of the candle burning. The candle burns straight down and it never burns backward. The flame is neither new nor old. It is neither the possession of the candle nor does it exist apart from the candle. The flame is like the light of the beginner's mind. The candle, when it is flameless, is like the lack of vision of one who has not begun the way.

"The wisdom flame of the beginner's mind is complete at the outset. The all-inclusive samādhi of buddha ancestors is the completion of that same wisdom over time, burning down the confusion of ignorance till the candle is no more. Can you see how this practice has no beginning and no end, how now and later are not really different? This is the essential teaching correctly transmitted by buddha ancestors."

On the tenth day, twelfth month, fifth year of the Kenchō Era [1253], this was copied in the abbot's room, in the Eihei Monastery in Echizen. This text was found among the late teacher's posthumous documents. It was in the form of a draft, and may not be complete. I shed many tears in my regret that the work was never completed. Ejō

 *1226, Zhejiang, China*

Poems

Break open a single particle and all the sūtras grow clear:
the great merit-wheel of the dharma turns as a whole.
The womb of a donkey gives birth to the noble horse.
Each time you look, you'll see it new.

The name "Three Teachings"* was empty right from the
    start—
miss even one word and all go wrong.
Looking inward or outward, see there is no fixed self.
Break the front door, if you want to enter your home.

On a Portrait of Myself

Cold lake, for thousands of yards, soaks up sky color.
Evening quiet: a fish of brocade scales reaches bottom, then
    goes
first this way, then that way; arrow notch splits.
Endless water surface, moonlight brilliant.

Record of Bringing Master Myōzen's Relics

IN QUIET REFLECTION it is understood that at the moment that knowing arises, the entire teaching reveals its form. And where awakening is complete no trace of movement remains.

The late teacher was from Iyo Province. His family name was Soga and his dharma name was Myōzen. At the age of eight, he left his parents and went up to study at Mt. Hiei. He became a monk at sixteen and journeyed in the ocean of studies. He clarified the deep meaning of the exoteric and esoteric teachings. He widely exhausted the depths of samādhi and prajñā.

However, realizing that such studies are merely counting letters, he practiced with Zen Master Eisai, the former bishop and founder of the Kennin Monastery. He learned the teachings outside the scriptures and clarified the path underneath words. It was like Mahākāshyapa at Vulture Peak or like Nanyue going to meet Huineng, the Sixth Ancestor. He merged with the correct lineage and he alone received Eisai's personal transmission of dharma.

On the twenty-first day of the second month of the second year of the Teiō Era [1223] he left the Kennin Monastery and went far away to Great Song China. On the thirteenth day of the fifth month he arrived at Jingde Monastery on Mt. Tiantong in Qingyuan Prefecture. Because it was where his root teacher Eisai had visited, it was there that he put his traveling staff to rest. He spent years deepening his practice. While his practice matured and his merit accumulated, his reputation flowed throughout the region. He came to be respected in all the nine regions of China.

He became ill on the eighteenth day of the fifth month of the first year of the Baoqing Era [1225]. On the twenty-seventh day of the same month at the hour of the dragon [about 8:00 AM], he straightened up his robes, sat upright and entered nirvāna.

Monks, gathering like clouds, came to make prostrations; lay people, coming like the mist, offered respect. The cremation ceremony took place during the dragon hour on the twenty-ninth day of the same month, and the fire transformed itself into five colors. When those present saw this they said that relics would certainly appear. And as expected, in the ashes there were three fragments of white crystalline relics. When the monastery was informed about this, the entire community gathered to honor them with a ceremony. Later people kept on searching and they found over 360 crystalline fragments.

In the Great Song there was no one who heard about this who was not reverential. Those near and far, those intimately acquainted and those not, all honored Myōzen. In the monastery an inscribed stone was erected to maintain his memory. It is over six hundred years since the buddha-dharma was first transmitted to Japan. However, until now we had not heard of relics remaining among the ashes of a Japanese monk.

Sister Chi of Kyōto was among those ordained by the late teacher. She is a devoted student of Myōzen, loving him deeply. Moved by her sincere request for his remains, I am giving her a portion. I hope that we not only cherish our fortune of meeting Myōzen in this lifetime, but will continue to be committed to his intention of guiding all beings.

I have written this brief chronology for future generations.

Disciple Dōgen

The fifth day of the tenth month,
the third year of the Karoku Era

Recommending Zazen to All People

THE REAL WAY CIRCULATES everywhere; how could it re-
quire practice or enlightenment? The essential teaching is fully
available; how could effort be necessary? Furthermore the entire
mirror is free of dust; why take steps to polish it? Nothing is separate from this very place; why journey away?

And yet, if you miss the mark even by a strand of hair, you are
as distant as heaven from earth. If the slightest discrimination occurs, you will be lost in confusion. You could be proud of your
understanding and have abundant realization, or acquire outstanding wisdom and attain the way by clarifying the mind. Still, if you
are wandering about in your head, you may miss the vital path of
letting your body leap.

You should observe the example of Buddha Shākyamuni of the
Jeta Grove, who practiced sitting up straight for six years even
though he was gifted with intrinsic wisdom. Still celebrated is Master Bodhidharma of the Shaolin Temple, who sat facing the wall for
nine years although he had already received the mind seal. Ancient
sages were like this; who nowadays does not need to practice as they
did?

Hence, you should stop searching for phrases and chasing after
words. Take the backward step and turn the light inward. Your
body-mind of itself will drop off and your original face will appear.
If you want to attain just this, immediately practice just this.

For zazen, a quiet room is appropriate. Drink and eat in moderation. Let go of all involvements and let myriad things rest. Do not think good or bad. Do not judge right or wrong. Stop conscious endeavor and analytic introspection. Do not try to become a buddha. How could being a buddha be limited to sitting or not sitting?

In an appropriate place for sitting, set out a thick mat and put a round cushion on top of it. Sit either in the full- or half-lotus posture. For the full-lotus posture, first place the right foot on the left thigh, then the left foot on the right thigh. For the half-lotus posture, place the left foot on the right thigh. Loosen the robes and belts and arrange them in an orderly way. Then place the right hand palm up on the left foot, and the left hand on the right hand, lightly touching the ends of the thumbs together.

Sit straight up without leaning to the right or left and without bending forward or backward. The ears should be in line with the shoulders and the nose in line with the navel. Rest the tongue against the roof of the mouth, with lips and teeth closed. Keep the eyes open and breathe gently through the nose.

Having adjusted your body in this manner, take a breath and exhale fully, then sway your body to left and right. Now sit steadfastly and think not-thinking. How do you think not-thinking? Beyond thinking. This is the essential art of zazen.

The zazen I speak of is not learning meditation. It is simply the dharma gate of enjoyment and ease. It is the practice-realization of complete enlightenment. Realize the fundamental point free from the binding of nets and baskets. Once you experience it, you are like a dragon swimming in the water or a tiger reposing in the mountains. Know that the true dharma emerges of itself, clearing away hindrances and distractions.

When you stand up from sitting, move your body slowly and rise calmly, without haste. We understand from past precedents that going beyond ordinary and sacred, where sitting and standing are effortless and boundless, depends solely on the power of zazen.

Furthermore, bringing forth the turning point by using a finger, a pole, a needle, or a mallet, or leading people to enlightenment with a whisk, a fist, a stick, or a shout cannot be understood by discriminatory thinking. How can it be understood by the use of supernatural powers? Zazen is an awesome presence outside form and color. How is it not the path preceding concept?

Thus, do not be concerned with who is wise and who is stupid. Do not discriminate the sharp from the dull. To practice whole-heartedly is the true endeavor of the way. Practice-realization is not defiled with specialness; it is a matter for every day.

Now, in this world and in other worlds, in India and China, buddha ancestors equally carry the buddha seal* and teach the practice of sitting immersed in steadfastness. Although circumstances may vary in a thousand ways, whole-heartedly practice Zen, giving yourself fully to the way. Why give up the sitting platform of your own house and wander uselessly in the dust of a remote land? Once a wrong step is taken, you depart from the way.

Having received a human life, do not waste the passing moments. Already upholding the buddha way, why would you indulge in the sparks from a flint? After all, form is like a dewdrop on the grass. Human life is like a flash of lightning, transient and illusory, gone in a moment.

Honored practitioners of Zen, please do not grope for the elephant or try to grasp the true dragon. Strive to hit the mark by directly pointing. Revere the mind that goes beyond study and surpasses all doings. Experience the enlightenment of the buddhas, correctly inheriting the samādhi of the ancestors. Practice thusness* continuously, and you will be thus. The treasury will open of itself for you to use as you wish.

Actualizing the Fundamental Point

As all things are buddha-dharma, there are delusion, realization, practice, birth and death, buddhas and sentient beings. As myriad things are without an abiding self, there is no delusion, no realization, no buddha, no sentient being, no birth and death. The buddha way, in essence, is leaping clear of abundance and lack; thus there are birth and death, delusion and realization, sentient beings and buddhas. Yet in attachment blossoms fall, and in aversion weeds spread.

To carry the self forward and illuminate myriad things is delusion. That myriad things come forth and illuminate the self is awakening.

Those who have great realization of delusion are buddhas; those who are greatly deluded about realization are sentient beings. Further, there are those who continue realizing beyond realization, who are in delusion throughout delusion. When buddhas are truly buddhas, they do not necessarily notice that they are buddhas. However, they are actualized buddhas, who go on actualizing buddha.

When you see forms or hear sounds, fully engaging body-and-mind, you intuit dharma intimately. Unlike things and their reflections in the mirror, and unlike the moon and its reflection in the water, when one side is illumined, the other side is dark.

To STUDY the buddha way is to study the self. To study the self is to forget the self. To forget the self is to be actualized by myriad things. When actualized by myriad things, your body and mind as well as the bodies and minds of others drop away. No trace of enlightenment remains, and this no-trace continues endlessly.

WHEN YOU FIRST SEEK dharma, you imagine you are far away from its environs. At the moment when dharma is correctly transmitted, you are immediately your original self.

When you ride in a boat and watch the shore, you might assume that the shore is moving. But when you keep your eyes closely on the boat, you can see that the boat moves. Similarly, if you examine myriad things with a confused body and mind you might suppose that your mind and nature are permanent. When you practice intimately and return to where you are, it will be clear that nothing at all has unchanging self.

FIREWOOD BECOMES ASH, and it does not become firewood again. Yet, do not suppose that the ash is after and the firewood before. You should understand that firewood abides in the phenomenal expression of firewood, which fully includes before and after and is independent of before and after. Ash abides in the phenomenal expression of ash, which fully includes before and after. Just as firewood does not become firewood again after it is ash, you do not return to birth after death.

This being so, it is an established way in buddha-dharma to deny that birth turns into death. Accordingly, birth is understood as no-birth. It is an unshakable teaching in the Buddha's discourse that death does not turn into birth. Accordingly, death is understood as no-death.

Birth is an expression complete this moment. Death is an expression complete this moment. They are like winter and spring. You do not call winter the beginning of spring, nor summer the end of spring.

*   *   *

ENLIGHTENMENT IS LIKE the moon reflected on the water. The moon does not get wet, nor is the water broken. Although its light is wide and great, the moon is reflected even in a puddle an inch wide. The whole moon and the entire sky are reflected in dewdrops on the grass, or even in one drop of water.

Enlightenment does not divide you, just as the moon does not break the water. You cannot hinder enlightenment, just as a drop of water does not hinder the moon in the sky. The depth of the drop is the height of the moon. Each reflection, however long or short its duration, manifests the vastness of the dewdrop, and realizes the limitlessness of the moonlight in the sky.

WHEN DHARMA DOES NOT fill your whole body and mind, you may assume it is already sufficient. When dharma fills your body and mind, you understand that something is missing. For example, when you sail out in a boat to the middle of an ocean where no land is in sight, and view the four directions, the ocean looks circular, and does not look any other way. But the ocean is neither round nor square; its features are infinite in variety. It is like a palace. It is like a jewel. It only looks circular as far as you can see at that time. All things are like this.

Though there are many features in the dusty world* and the world beyond conditions, you see and understand only what your eye of practice can reach. In order to learn the nature of the myriad things, you must know that although they may look round or square, the other features of oceans and mountains are infinite in variety; whole worlds are there. It is so not only around you, but also directly beneath your feet, or in a drop of water.

A FISH SWIMS in the ocean, and no matter how far it swims there is no end to the water. A bird flies in the sky, and no matter how far it flies there is no end to the air. However, the fish and the bird have never left their elements. When their activity is large their field is large. When their need is small their field is small. Thus, each of them totally covers its full range, and each of them totally experiences its realm. If the bird leaves the air it will die at once. If the fish leaves the water it will die at once.

Know that water is life and air is life. The bird is life and the fish is life. Life must be the bird and life must be the fish. You can go further. There is practice-enlightenment which encompasses limited and unlimited life.

Now if a bird or a fish tries to reach the end of its element before moving in it, this bird or this fish will not find its way or its place. When you find your place where you are, practice occurs, actualizing the fundamental point. When you find your way at this moment, practice occurs, actualizing the fundamental point; for the place, the way, is neither large nor small, neither yours nor others. The place, the way, has not carried over from the past, and it is not merely arising now. Accordingly, in the practice-enlightenment of the buddha way, to attain one thing is to penetrate one thing; to meet one practice is to sustain one practice.

Here is the place; here the way unfolds. The boundary of realization is not distinct, for realization comes forth simultaneously with the mastery of buddha-dharma. Do not suppose that what you attain becomes your knowledge and is grasped by your intellect. Although actualized immediately, the inconceivable may not be apparent. Its appearance is beyond your knowledge.

Mayu, Zen Master Baoche, was fanning himself. A monk approached and said, "Master, the nature of wind is permanent and there is no place it does not reach. Why then do you fan yourself?"

"Although you understand that the nature of the wind is permanent," Mayu replied, "you do not understand the meaning of its reaching everywhere."

"What is the meaning of its reaching everywhere?" asked the monk again. Mayu just kept fanning himself. The monk bowed deeply.

The actualization of the buddha-dharma, the vital path of its correct transmission, is like this. If you say that you do not need to fan yourself because the nature of wind is permanent and you can

have wind without fanning, you will understand neither permanence nor the nature of wind. The nature of wind is permanent.
Because of that, the wind of the buddha's house brings forth the
gold of the earth and makes fragrant the cream of the long river.

*Written in midautumn, the first year of the Tempuku Era
[1233], and given to my lay student Kōshū Yō of Kyūshū Island.
Revised in the fourth year of the Kenchō Era [1252].*

Cases for Study

QINGYUAN, ZEN MASTER HONG of the Jingju Monastery in Ji Region, once asked Shitou, "Where are you from?"

Shitou said, "I am from Caoxi."

Qingyuan held up a whisk and said, "Do they have this in Caoxi?"

Shitou said, "Not in Caoxi, or in India."

Qingyuan said, "Have you been to India?"

Shitou said, "If I had been there, it would have been there."

Qingyuan said, "You are saying this without having been there."

Shitou said, "Master, please say something, instead of letting me say it all."

Qingyuan said, "It's not that I mind saying something but that I fear it would be misunderstood later."

HUANGBO, Zen Master Duanji of Hong Region, asked his teacher Baizhang, "How do we explain the teaching that has been handed down?" Baizhang kept sitting without words in his seat.

Huangbo said, "If so, what will people in the future receive?"

Baizhang said, "I thought you were a true person." He then returned to the abbot's room.

ZHAOZHOU, Great Master Zhenji, asked his teacher Nanquan, "Where has the one who knows gone?"

Nanquan said, "Gone to a donor's house near the mountain and has become a buffalo."* Zhaozhou thanked him for his teaching. Nanquan said, "Late last night the moon reached the window."

ONCE LECTURER LIANG of Mt. Xi, Hong Region, studied with Mazu, who said, "Which sutra do you teach?"

Liang said, *"The Heart Sūtra."*

Mazu said, "How do you teach it?"

Liang said, "I teach it with the heart."

Mazu said, "The heart is like a main actor. The will is like a supporting actor. The objects of the six senses are like their accompanists. How do they understand your teaching of the sūtra?"

Liang said, "If the heart doesn't understand it, does emptiness understand it?"

Mazu said, "Yes, it does." Liang flipped his sleeves and started to walk away.

Mazu called, "Lecturer." Liang turned his head around.

Mazu said, "Just this, from birth till death."

At this moment Liang had realization. He hid himself at Mt. Xi and no one heard about him any longer.

LAYMAN PANGYUN of Xiang Region asked Shitou upon his first meeting with the teacher, "Who is the one that does not accompany all things?"

Shitou covered Pangyun's mouth with his hand. Pangyun had some understanding at this point. Later Pangyun asked Mazu the same question.

Mazu said, "Wait till you swallow up the Xi River, and I will say it for you." Pangyun was immediately awakened.

A MONK ASKED Langye, Zen Master Guangzhao of Chu Region, "Purity is originally present. How is it that mountains, rivers, and the great earth suddenly appear?"

Langye said, "Purity is originally present. How is it that mountains, rivers, and the great earth suddenly appear?"

* * *

PRIEST MIHU of Jingzhao had a monk ask Yangshan, "Can people nowadays realize enlightenment?"

Yangshan said, "It's not that there is no enlightenment, but how can we deal with falling into what is not essential?"

The monk returned and reported this to Mihu, who then approved Yangshan.

MAZU, Zen Master Daji of Hong Region in Jiangxi, was an attendant* to Nanyue and intimately received the mind seal from him, surpassing his peers.

Before that he lived in the Chuanfa Temple and did zazen all day long. Knowing that Mazu was a dharma vessel, Nanyue went to him and asked, "Great Monk, what do you intend to do by doing zazen?"

Mazu said, "I am intending to be a buddha."

Nanyue picked up a tile and started grinding it on a rock. Mazu said, "What are you doing?"

Nanyue said, "I am trying to make a mirror."

Mazu said, "How can you make a mirror by grinding a tile?"

Nanyue said, "How can you become a buddha by doing zazen?"

Mazu said, "What do you mean by that?"

Nanyue said, "It's like driving a cart. When it stops moving, do you whip the cart or the horse?" Mazu said nothing.

Nanyue said, "Do you want to practice sitting Zen or sitting buddha? If you understand sitting Zen, you will know that Zen is not about sitting or lying down. If you want to learn sitting buddha, know that buddha is merely a form of samādhi. Do not use discrimination in the nonabiding dharma. If you sit as buddha, you kill buddha. If you are attached to the sitting form, you are not mastering the essential principle."

Mazu heard this admonition and felt as if he were tasting a most delicious cream.

PRIEST HUANGBO once left his assembly at Mt. Huangbo and entered the Daan Monastery. There he joined the workers who cleaned the halls. Once Minister Peixiu visited the temple to offer incense and was greeted by the temple director.* Peixiu looked at a mural on the wall and said, "What kind of painting is that?"

The Director said, "It is a portrait of a high monk."

Peixiu said, "Obviously it is a portrait. But where is the high monk?" The Director could not answer.

Peixiu said, "Is there a Zen person around here?"

The Director said, "A monk has been working in this temple. He seems to be a Zen person."

Peixiu said, "Could you ask him to come so I can ask him questions?"

Huangbo was quickly brought to the minister, who was happy to see him and said, "I have a question, but all the masters of whom I have asked this question have refused to answer it. Reverend, would you please respond to it?"

Huangbo said, "Please present your question, my lord." Peixiu repeated the question he had asked the temple director.

Huangbo raised his voice and said, "My lord."

Peixiu said, "Yes."

Huangbo said, "Where are you?"

Peixiu understood it on the spot. It was just like getting a pearl from his own hair. So he said, "You are a true master." He asked Huangbo to open the buddha hall and let him enter.

ONCE A MONK asked Qingyuan, "How is it that Bodhidharma came from India?"

Qingyuan said, "He disappeared just like this."

The monk asked further, "What do you have to teach these days?"

Qingyuan said, "Come closer." The monk moved closer.

Qingyuan said, "Keep it in mind."

Raising Sages

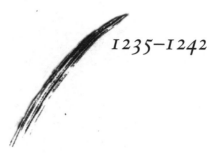

1235–1242

Donation Request for a Monks' Hall at the Kannondōri Monastery

WE RESPECTFULLY MAKE THIS ANNOUNCEMENT to all buddhas in the ten directions, to sages and monks in the heavenly and human worlds, to the eight types of guardians* in the dragon realm, and to generous men and women. We wish to construct a training hall with donations, however small they may be, from people's pure heart.

The Bodhisattva Precepts Sūtra says, "Children of the Buddha, you should guide sentient beings by constructing monasteries and building stūpas in the mountains, forests, gardens, and fields. You should establish training halls for holding winter and summer practice periods* for zazen and all other practices. You would be negligent if you failed to do so."

All temples and monasteries are practice places of buddhas. Buddhist monasteries in China are modeled after those in India. Japanese monasteries should follow these examples. Constructing a monastery is of great significance and its merit is profound; it has much to offer to people.

For some years now, ever since I returned to Japan from China, I have vowed to establish a monastery. But there has not been a place suitable to support monks' formal practice using bowls and robes. Now we have acquired an excellent place. It is located in the compound of the Gokuraku Temple near Fukakusa [in the southern vicinity of Kyōto]. We have named this place the Kannondōri [Avalokiteshvara's Guiding Power] Monastery. Although it is still covered with weeds and not yet functioning, we plan to build a training monastery here.

The primary components of a monastery are a buddha hall, a dharma hall, and a monks' hall. We have a buddha hall and we do not have a dharma hall. But we urgently need a monks' hall. We plan to build seven *ken* [about seventy feet] square with no interior walls. We will set up long platforms on which we will reside, practicing day and night without fail. A sacred figure of Manjushrī will be enshrined in the center of the hall, to be surrounded by the practicing monks.

The ancient practice of formally taking refuge in the three treasures together as a group in one hall is still alive today. Its merit is enormous and its effect is broad. We will thoroughly engage in each activity in order to cultivate fertile conditions to transform the ten directions.* In India and China we have excellent examples of monks who did this in the Ages of True Dharma and Imitation Dharma.

We will acknowledge the gifts by installing the donors' names inside the sacred image of Manjushrī. The enshrined names will form myriad syllables as seeds of wisdom illuminating everyone. Those who attain the way in this hall will be guiding masters of the people, and will not only reach the human realm, but beyond. They will transform beings in the heavenly realm and in the dragons' palace. Those in the realms of invisible and divine will also listen. Thus this dharma wheel* transmitted from Shākyamuni Buddha will reach everywhere.

Respectfully yours,
Abbot of the Kannondōri Monastery
THE TWELFTH MONTH,
THE FIRST YEAR OF THE KATEI ERA

Formal Talk upon Establishing the Kōshō Monastery

RECORDED BY SENNE, ATTENDANT MONK

ON THE FIFTEENTH DAY, the tenth month, the second year of the Katei Era, Master Dōgen assembled the monks, ascended the teaching seat, and expounded dharma for the first time here, at the Kōshō [Raising Sages] Zen Monastery: "The wind of our house depends on the grass and transmits the heartwood. The finest place for practice is a forest monastery. Hit the sitting platform once, strike the drum three times, express the Tathāgata's inconceivable voice. Those of you who are inside this Raising Sages Monastery, what do you say right at this moment?"

After a pause, Dōgen said, "Even in the golden region of Chinese Zen, south of the Xiang River, north of Tan Lake, countless ordinary people drown on dry land."

Informal Talks

RECORDED BY EJŌ, ATTENDANT MONK

MASTER DŌGEN SAID in an informal evening talk, "Don't scold or criticize monks with harsh words. Even when they make mistakes, don't put them down angrily. Whatever mistakes they make, if there are more than four monks assembled and practicing together, they should be respected as a treasure of the nation. Abbots, elders, and teachers should give them thorough instruction with a grandmotherly, compassionate heart. Those who need to be hit should be hit, and those who need to be scolded should be scolded, but don't insult or slander them.

"When my late teacher Rujing was abbot of Tiantong Monastery, he criticized some monks and hit them with his slipper during zazen to keep them awake. Those who were hit appreciated it and admired him.

"He said in a lecture, 'I am old now, overdue to be retired, passing my last years in a hut. But I'm here as abbot to help break your delusions, and to assist in your practice of the way. For this reason, I sometimes scold you, or hit you with a bamboo stick. But this is a dangerous thing to do. I only do this to guide you on behalf of the Buddha. My brothers, please pardon me with compassionate heart.'

"When he said this, all the monks wept. Guide people and extend the teaching with this heart. Even those who are in the position of abbot or elder should not scold and control the monks as if they were personal possessions. Furthermore, it is an error to discuss others' shortcomings and make accusations in their absence. Be extremely cautious of this. When you see others' faults, use skillful means not to arouse their anger. If you talk about their fault as if it were somebody else's, it will be easier for them to accept your point."

As an aside to a dharma talk, Dōgen said, "Even when you are clearly correct and others are mistaken, it is harmful to argue and defeat them. On the other hand, if you admit fault when you are right, you are a coward. It is best to step back, neither trying to correct others nor conceding to mistaken views. If you don't react competitively and let go of the conflict, others will also let go of it without harboring ill will. This is above all something you should keep in mind."

Dōgen said, "When Eisai, the late bishop, was abbot of Kennin Monastery, a man came and said, 'My family is very poor. We haven't eaten for several days. The three of us—my wife, my son, and myself—are starving to death. Please show your compassion and help us.' At that time there were no clothes, food, or money in the monastery. Eisai could find no way to help. But he remembered the copper sheet that was intended for the halo of the Medicine Buddha figure. He got this out, broke off a portion of it, crushed it together, and gave it to the poor man, saying, 'Please exchange this for food and satisfy your hunger.' The man departed overjoyed.

"The students were upset and said, 'That copper was for the radiance of the Medicine Buddha's image. Is it not a crime to give such sacred material to a lay person?'

"Eisai said, 'Yes, it is a crime. But think of the Buddha's intention. He gave up his own flesh and bones and offered them to sentient beings. We would honor the Buddha's intention even if we were to give the entire body of the Medicine Buddha to those who are starving now. We may fall into hell for this act. Still we should continue to save people from starvation.'

"Students nowadays should reflect on the great heart of our guiding master. Don't forget this."

ONE DAY A STUDENT ASKED, "Although I have been studying the way for years, I haven't been enlightened. The teachers of old have said, 'Don't depend on intelligence and learning.' So I believe that even if I am slow and have little wisdom, I should not become discouraged. Is there anything to learn from the teachers of old about this?"

Dōgen instructed, "You are right. Inherent intelligence or high capacity is not necessary. You should not depend on brilliance or smartness. Don't exclude those who are very slow or less talented. It is a mistake, however, to say that for the true study you should be like a blind, deaf, or dumb person. The true study of the way should be easy. But even among hundreds and thousands of students in the assembly of one teacher in Great Song China, those who genuinely attain the way and inherit dharma are only one or two. Therefore, we should keep the examples of the ancient masters in mind.

"I see that there are those who have the utmost aspiration and those who don't. Those who have the utmost aspiration and study accordingly will not fail to attain the way. You should remember that how much you study and how fast you progress are secondary matters. The joyfully seeking mind is primary.

"Those who vow to steal a precious treasure, to defeat a powerful enemy, or to know a beautiful lady, will follow their intention and keep it in mind on each occasion under all circumstances while walking, standing, sitting, and lying down. Nothing is left unachieved with such a commitment. If you seek the way with genuine intention, as you practice just sitting, as you work on kōans about ancient teachers, or face the teacher, then you can shoot a bird however high in the sky or catch a fish however deep in the water. But without arousing such a determined mind, how can you achieve the great matter of cutting off the transmigration of birth and death at the very moment the words 'buddha way' are uttered? Those who have such a determined mind will invariably be enlightened, whether or not they are less learned or are slow, whether or not they are dumb or unwholesome.

"Upon arousing this mind, you should reflect on the impermanence of the world. Impermanence is not something you merely visualize, or something you create and think about. Impermanence is the truth that is right in front of you. You need not study other people's words or textual evidence on this matter. To be born in the morning and to die in the evening, not to see someone today whom you saw yesterday—the impermanence of life is in your eyes and ears. You should not see or hear it only in terms of others but apply it to your own self.

"Even if you hope to live for seventy or eighty years, in the end you are destined to die. You should regard your pleasure and sorrow, relationship, and attachment in worldly affairs as your enemy. To do so is the way to a fuller life. You should keep in mind the buddha way alone and work for the bliss of nirvāna. Especially those of you who are elderly or who are middle-aged, how many years do you have left? How can you be lax in your practice of the way?

"Yet this is not urgent enough. You should examine both the mundane world and the buddha realm. Tomorrow, or even in the next moment, you might become gravely ill, lose your senses, and suffer from great pain. You might be suddenly killed by a demon, a robber, or an enemy. Truly nothing is for certain. Therefore in this transient world where the time of death is unpredictable, scheming to live forever or wasting your time plotting against others is quite stupid.

"The Buddhas spoke this truth to sentient beings. Ancestors expounded solely on this matter. I also speak of impermanence, the swift passage of time, and the urgency of birth and death. Do not ever forget this truth. Realize that you have just today, just this moment. You should concentrate your mind on the study of the way without wasting your time. If you do this, your practice becomes easy. To discuss the superiority or inferiority of your nature, the brilliance and slowness of learning, is not necessary."

* * *

DURING AN INFORMAL TALK Dōgen said, "To be poor is particularly important for those who study the way. When I look at the world, I see that those who have property create two types of problems: anger and shame. If you have property, other people want to take it. When you resist having it taken, anger arises. If you argue in court or fight over your problems, anger arises and shame comes. If you are poor and not greedy, you are free from such problems. Easy and blissful as can be, the truth is quite evident.

"Do not wait to see this teaching in sūtras. Teachers in ancient times and the wise in recent times caution against the acquisition of wealth. Buddha ancestors, as well as heavenly beings, are clear about this. To accumulate wealth, hold anger, and become foolish is truly regrettable. On the other hand, those who stay poor and care about the way are revered by the wise and sages and cause buddha ancestors and invisible beings to rejoice.

"It is easy to see that the practice of buddha-dharma is declining. Things have changed since I first entered the Kennin Monastery seven or eight years ago. Nowadays the dormitories have walled closets. Monks own various utensils, prefer beautiful robes, maintain personal property, love chatting, and are careless about greetings and bowing. From this, you can imagine what it must be like in other temples.

"You who practice buddha-dharma should not own anything other than robes and bowls. What do you need a closet for? You should not keep anything from others. Owning nothing makes your life easy. If you would rather kill than be killed, you have a lot of worries and are hurting yourself. If you are determined not to retaliate even if your life is threatened, you don't need to fear robbers or feel anxious. You will be relaxed and joyful every moment.

A MONK SAID, "I have an aged mother. I am her only child and the sole means of her support. As my love for her is deep, I am determined to help her. So I work for others to be able to buy food and clothing for her. If I abandoned the world and went into seclusion, it would be difficult for her to survive even for one day. That's why I am engaged in worldly affairs. It disturbs me that I cannot fully enter the buddha way. Should I give up everything for the buddha way? If so, why? Please explain it to me."

Dōgen said, "This is a difficult matter. Other people cannot decide it for you. You should think deeply. If you have a true intention to practice the buddha way, you may be able to come up with some skillful means to secure your mother's livelihood and also enter the buddha way. This would fill both needs. With a strong determination, it's possible to defeat a tough enemy, win the love of a beautiful person, or gain a rare treasure. So, your difficulty can be solved with the help of heavenly and earthly guardians.

"Huineng, the Sixth Ancestor, was originally a woodcutter in the Xin Region of China. He supported his mother by selling firewood. One day in the marketplace he heard a customer chanting *The Diamond Sūtra* and his mind was opened to the way. So he left his mother and studied with Daoxin, the Fifth Ancestor. It is said that he was then given thirty *liang* of silver which he used for buying food and clothing for his mother. I suppose this was a gift from heaven for his sincere determination. You should reflect deeply on this. This is an important point.

"If you stay with your mother till she dies and then enter the buddha way free from obligation, your intention will be fulfilled. But who knows? Age and death are not necessarily linked. Your mother may live long and you may depart first. In that case your intention will not be actualized. You will be sorry about not entering the buddha way and your aged mother will be responsible for preventing you from doing so. Both of you will be at fault and will achieve no good result.

"On the other hand, even if your mother dies of starvation, letting her only son enter the way will be greatly beneficial to her own attaining of the way. You may have been unable to discard family obligations and attachments throughout many lifetimes. Doing so now and meeting the buddha-dharma truly repays your parents' kindness, and matches the Buddha's heart. It is said that when one child becomes a monk the parents of seven generations attain the way. Don't lose the opportunity of attaining bliss for countless eons, through attachment to this present drifting life. You should carefully consider this."

ON THE LAST NIGHT of the second year of the Katei Era [1236], during an informal talk, Dōgen asked Ejō to take the teaching whisk, thus appointing him the first head monk* of the Kōshō Monastery. Dōgen instructed: "This is how the buddha-dharma of our school has been transmitted: Bodhidharma went to China from India. He stayed at the Shaolin Temple and sat in front of a wall, waiting for a time when a student would appear. At the end of one year, Huike came to study. Knowing that he was a fine vessel, Bodhidharma trained him and transmitted both the robe and dharma. Their descendants spread and the true dharma has come to us today.

"I am appointing you head monk for the first time and asking you to hold the teaching whisk. Do not be concerned that this assembly is small. Do not think that you are not advanced enough. Fenyang had only six or seven practitioners. Yaoshan had less than ten. However, they fully practiced the way of the buddha ancestors. This is why we say that their monasteries flourished.

"Look. There was one who was enlightened with the sound of a bamboo being struck and another who clarified his mind upon seeing peach blossoms. Is the bamboo bright or dull, deluded or enlightened? Are peach blossoms shallow or deep, wise or foolish? Although flowers blossom year after year, not everyone who sees them is enlightened. When a bamboo cracks, not everyone who hears it realizes the way.

"Enlightenment and clarity of the mind occur only in response to the sustained effort of study and practice. Endeavoring in the way ripens the conditions of your practice. It is not that the sound of the bamboo is sharp or the color of the blossoms is vivid. Although the sound of the bamboo is wondrous, it is heard at the moment when it's hit by a pebble. Although the color of blossoms is beautiful, they do not open by themselves but unfold in the light of springtime. Studying the way is like this. You attain the way when conditions come together. Although you have your own capacity, you practice the way with the combined strength of the community. So you should practice and search with one mind with others.

"A stone is turned to a jewel by polishing. A person becomes a sage by cultivation. What stone is originally shiny? Who is mature from the beginning? You ought to polish and cultivate yourself. Don't diminish yourself. Don't be lazy in your study of the way.

"A teacher of old said, 'Don't let time pass in vain.' Let me ask you. Does time stay with us if we value it? Does it not stay with us even if we value it? Let me tell you. Time does not pass in vain but you can let it pass in vain. The teacher of old meant that you should study the way without letting time pass in vain. Practice the way with this in mind.

"It's not easy for me to expound dharma all by myself, yet the buddha ancestors have practiced like this. Many people attained the way by studying with the Tathāgata, and there were some who were enlightened by studying with disciple Ānanda. You as the new head monk should not regard yourself as unworthy, but should raise Dongshan's three pounds of flax,* and teach the assembly."

Thus saying, Dōgen got down from his seat. The drum was hit and I, Ejō, held up the teaching whisk. This was how the first head monk was installed at the Kōshō Monastery. I was thirty-nine years old.

Dōgen said, "The essential thing for studying the way is zazen. This comes first. Many people in Song China attained the way through the power of zazen. Even those who cannot read or those who are dull without talent can fully engage in zazen and mature more than those who are longtime scholars. Therefore, students should engage in just sitting and not pursue other activities. The buddha ancestors' way is simply sitting. Do not go elsewhere."

I asked, "In addition to just sitting, if we study kōans and read the recorded sayings of old masters, there may emerge some insight. This might be as rare as one out of a hundred or a thousand instances. But zazen does not seem to do this. Do we still need to emphasize zazen?"

Dōgen said, "Even if you obtain some ideas by studying kōans and words, it may cause you to go further away from the buddha ancestors' path. Instead, dedicate your time to sitting upright, not seeking achievement, and not seeking enlightenment. This is the ancestral way.

"Although teachers of old used verbal studies along with just sitting, they were totally engaged in sitting. There were those whose enlightenment was revealed by verbal studies. But this was due to the strength of zazen. The true power lies in sitting."

Valley Sounds,
Mountain Colors

IN THE TRANSMISSION of unsurpassable enlightenment by numberless buddha ancestors, various practices have arisen. Study such examples as ancient practitioners crushing their bones and Huike chopping off his arm. Embody in yourself the dedication of a boy spreading his hair on muddy ground* for the Buddha to walk on.

Slipping out of your old skin, not held back by past views, you manifest immediately what has been dormant for boundless eons. As this very moment manifests, "I" don't know, "who" doesn't know, "you" have no expectations, and "the buddha eye" sees beyond seeing. This experience is beyond the realm of human thinking.

IN SONG CHINA there was a man who called himself Layman Dongpo. He was originally named Shi of the Su family, and his initiatory name was Zidan. A literary genius, he studied the way of dragons and elephants in the ocean of awakening. He descended deep chasms and soared freely through clouds.

One night when Dongpo visited Mt. Lu, he was enlightened upon hearing the sound of the valley stream. He composed the following verse, which he presented to Zen Master Changzong:

Valley sounds are the long broad tongue.
Mountain colors are no other than the unconditioned
    body.*
Eighty-four thousand verses* are heard throughout the
    night.
What can I say about this at a future time?

Seeing this verse, Changzong approved his understanding.

Changzong, also called Zen Master Zhaojue, was a dharma heir of Huanglong Huinan, who was a dharma heir of Zen Master Ciming Chuyuan. When Dongpo met with Zen Master Fuyin— Priest Liaoyuan—Fuyin transmitted the Buddhist precepts to him with a monk's robe, which Dongpo later wore when practicing. Dongpo presented Fuyin with a jeweled belt. People talked about this exchange as something uncommon.

The valley sounds of Dongpo would refresh practitioners of later generations. How sad for those who miss the dharma of the manifested buddha body! How are mountain colors seen and valley sounds heard otherwise? Are mountain colors and valley sounds one phrase or half a phrase? Are they eighty-four thousand verses of scripture? You may regret that mountains and waters conceal sounds and colors, but you may rejoice as well that the moment of enlightenment emerges through mountains and waters.

The tongue does not take a break. The colors are beyond coming and going. Are the sounds and colors intimate when they are apparent or are they intimate when they are obscured? Are they one whole expression or half an expression? During previous springs and autumns, Dongpo had not seen or heard the mountains and waters. But he saw and heard them for the first time that night. Bodhisattvas who study the way, you should open your minds to mountains flowing and to water not flowing.

Dongpo had this awakening soon after he had heard Zen Master Changzong talk about insentient beings speaking dharma. Although Dongpo did not leap when he heard Changzong's words, towering billows flew into the sky upon his hearing the sounds of the valley. Was it the valley sounds or the tide of awakening that jolted Dongpo? I suspect that the voices of insentient beings speaking dharma are resounding even now, still blended with the sounds of the night's stream. Who can fathom this water? Is it a bucketful or does it fill whole oceans? In the end was it Dongpo who was awakened or the mountains and waters that were awakened? Who today sees with clear eyes the long broad tongue and the unconditioned body?

Xiangyan Zhixian studied at the assembly of Guishan Lingyou, Zen Master Dayuan, who said, "You are bright and knowledgeable. Say something about yourself before your parents were born, but don't use words you have learned from sūtras and commentaries."

Xiangyan tried and tried but could not say anything. He poured through the many books he had collected over the years but could not come up with anything. Deeply ashamed, he burned his books and said, "A painting of a rice cake does not satisfy hunger. I will be just a gruel monk, not expecting to understand buddha-dharma in this lifetime." A gruel monk means one who supports the assembly by cooking rice, an equivalent of our kitchen assistant. He followed this vow for years.

One day Xiangyan said to Guishan, "My mind is undifferentiated; I cannot speak. Can you explain this to me, Master?"

Guishan said, "I wouldn't mind explaining it to you, but if I did, you would resent me."

Some time later, Xiangyan went to the memorial site of Nanyang, National Teacher Dazheng, at Mt. Wudang, and built himself a hut. For company, he planted some bamboo. One day while he was sweeping the path a pebble flew up and struck a bamboo. At the unexpected sound Xiangyan had thorough awakening. After bathing and cleansing himself he faced Mt. Gui, offered incense, prostrated himself, and said, "Master, if you had spoken for me at that time, this could not have happened. Your kindness is deeper than my parents'." Then he wrote a poem:

One stroke dissolves knowledge.
Struggle no longer needed.

I will follow the ancient path
not lapsing into quietude.
Noble conduct beyond sound and form—
no trace anywhere.
Those who have mastered the way
call this the unsurpassable activity.

He presented this poem to Guishan, who said, "This fellow has gone through."

ONE SPRING DAY Lingyun Zhiqin, who had been practicing for thirty years, walked into the mountains. While resting he saw peach blossoms in full bloom in a distant village and was suddenly awakened. He wrote this poem, which he presented to Guishan:

For thirty years I have looked for a swordmaster.
Many times leaves fell, new ones sprouted.
One glimpse of peach blossoms—
now no more doubts, just this.

Guishan said, "One who enters with ripened causes will never leave." He approved Lingyun in this way.

Who does not enter with ripened causes? Who enters and then leaves? This awakening is not limited to Lingyun. If mountain colors were not the unconditioned body, how could this awakening have occurred? This is how he inherited dharma from Guishan.

ONCE A MONK asked Changsha Jingcen, "How do you turn mountains, rivers, and the great earth into the self?"

Changsha said, "How do you turn the self into mountains, rivers, and the great earth?" Saying that the self returns to the self is not contradicted by saying that the self is mountains, rivers, and the great earth.

Langye Huijue, Great Master Guangzhao, was a dharma descendant of Nanyue. Once Zhixuan, a lecturer on scriptures, asked

Langye, "If originally unconditioned, how do mountains, rivers, and the great earth suddenly emerge?"

Langye responded, "If originally unconditioned, how do mountains, rivers, and the great earth suddenly emerge?"

Now we know. The mountains, rivers, and the great earth, which are originally unconditioned, should not be mistaken for mountains, rivers, and the great earth. The sūtra master had never heard this, so he did not understand mountains, rivers, and the great earth as just mountains, rivers, and the great earth.

YOU SHOULD KNOW that without mountain colors and valley sounds, Shākyamuni Buddha's taking up the flower and Huike's attaining the marrow would not have taken place. Because of the power of valley sounds and mountain colors, the great earth and sentient beings simultaneously attain the way, and there are countless buddhas who are enlightened upon seeing the morning star.* Such skin bags* are earlier sages whose aspiration for seeking dharma was profound. People today should be inspired by predecessors like these. Authentic study, free of concern for fame and gain, should be based on such aspiration.

In this remote nation in recent days those who genuinely seek buddha-dharma are rare—not that there are none. Many people leave their households, appearing to be free from worldly matters, but in fact use the buddha way to seek fame and gain. What a pity! How sad that they waste their time in unilluminated trades! When will they break off and attain the way? If they meet a true teacher, how can they recognize the true dragon?

My master, the late buddha Rujing, called such people "pitiful fellows." Because of unwholesome causes in previous lives, they do not seek dharma for the sake of dharma. In this life they are suspicious of the true dragon when they see it and are put off by genuine dharma when they meet it. As their body, mind, flesh, and bones are not ready to follow dharma, they are unable to receive it. Because the lineage of the ancestral school started a long time ago, the aspiration for enlightenment has become a distant dream. How pitiful that people do not know about or see treasure even though they were born on a mountain of treasure! Where can they find dharma treasure?

As soon as you arouse aspiration for enlightenment, even if you transmigrate in the six realms* and four forms of birth,* transmigration itself will be your practice of enlightenment. Although you may have wasted time so far, you should vow immediately, before this present life ends: "Together with all sentient beings, may I hear the true dharma from this birth on throughout future births."

When you hear the true dharma, do not doubt or distrust it. When you encounter the true dharma, relinquish ordinary affairs and uphold the buddha-dharma. Thus you realize the way together with the great earth and all sentient beings. This vow is the ground for genuine aspiration. Do not slacken in this determination.

JAPAN IS a remote land where people are extremely ignorant. Neither sages nor geniuses have been known to arise here, and genuine students of the way are rare. When we talk about way-seeking mind, those without it become resentful instead of reflecting on themselves.

When you arouse the aspiration for enlightenment, try to keep your practice private. Praising your own practice is out of the question. People nowadays rarely seek the truth. Deficient in practice and realization, they seek recognition for their effort and understanding. This is delusion on top of delusion. You should abandon such confused thinking.

Among those who study the way it is rare to find determination for true dharma. Such determination is the buddha light, the buddha mind, which has been transmitted from buddha to buddha.

From the time of the Tathāgata to this day there have been many who have been concerned with fame and gain in the study of the way. But if they meet a true master and turn toward true dharma, they will readily attain the way. You should know that there is a disease for fame and gain among practitioners of the way. Among beginners as well as longtime practitioners, some have the opportunity to receive the teaching while others don't. Some learn the ancient way, but there are also demons who slander the teaching. Do not be attached or upset in either case. When you remember how few realize the three poisons as the three poisons, you no longer have resentment.

DO NOT FORGET the aspiration that arises when you first seek the way. When you arouse the aspiration for enlightenment you do not seek dharma in order to be respected by others. You abandon fame and gain, and without veering off you aspire to attain the way. You do not look for respect or gifts from kings or ministers. Even though that may happen, it should not be your primary intention to become entangled with humans and devas. But foolish people, even those with way-seeking mind, quickly forget their original aspiration and hope for offerings from humans and devas. Receiving such offerings they rejoice that the merit of buddha-dharma has arrived. When kings and ministers come to take refuge in the buddha, foolish teachers may feel rewarded. This is a hazard of practice. Remember to have compassion for them but do not rejoice.

Do you recall that the Buddha said these golden words? "Even now at the time of the Tathāgata there are many who are antagonistic." Thus foolish people do not understand the wise; small-minded ones regard great sages as enemies. Also, the ancestors in India were sometimes overpowered by kings, those outside the way, or practitioners of the Two Lesser Vehicles.* It was not that the ancestors lacked deep understanding or that those others excelled.

When Bodhidharma came from India and stayed at Mt. Song, neither the Emperor of Liang nor the Emperor of Wei understood him. At that time there were two critics, Scripture Master Bodhiruchi and Precept Master Guangtong. They were afraid they would lose their fame and gain to a true teacher, so they tried to block him. It was as if they were trying to cover the sun. They were worse than Devadatta, who lived at the time of the Buddha. What a pity! The fame and gain they were attached to would have been discarded like excrement by Bodhidharma. Their behavior was the result of lack of understanding in buddha-dharma. They were like dogs barking at a well-intentioned person. Do not resent such dogs but vow to guide them with this blessing: "Arouse the thought of enlightenment, dogs." An old sage said, "There are animals who have human faces." On the other hand, there are demons who take refuge in the Buddha and make offerings to him.

An earlier buddha said, "Do not get close to kings, princes, ministers, administrators, Brahmans, and laypeople." Practitioners should remember this admonition so that, as their practice advances, the merit of their bodhisattva effort will accumulate.

There are stories of Indra, who came down to test the aspiration of a practitioner, or of the demon Pāpiman, who obstructed people's practice. Such things happen when practitioners cannot free themselves from desire for fame and gain. To those who have great compassion and whose vow to guide sentient beings is vast and mature, such things don't happen.

Through the merit of practice you may be given the gift of an entire nation, and this may appear to be a great achievement in the world. But do not be blinded; look deeply on such an occasion. Foolish people may rejoice, but they are like dogs licking a dry bone. Wise people and sages reject this just as worldly people are disgusted by excrement.

IN GENERAL, when you are a beginner you cannot fathom the buddha way. Your assumptions do not hit the mark. The fact that you cannot fathom the buddha way as a beginner does not mean that you lack ultimate understanding, but that you do not recognize the deepest point.

You should endeavor wholeheartedly to follow the path of earlier sages. You may have to climb mountains and cross oceans when you look for a teacher to inquire about the way. Look for a teacher and search for understanding with all-encompassing effort as if you were coming down from heaven or emerging from the ground. When you encounter your teacher, you invoke sentient beings as well as insentient beings. You hear with the body, you hear with the mind.

To hear with the ear is an everyday matter, but to hear with the eye is not. When you see buddha, you see self-buddha, other-buddha, a large buddha, a small buddha. Do not be frightened by a large buddha. Do not be put off by a small buddha. Just see large and small buddhas as valley sounds and mountain colors, as a broad long tongue, and as eighty-four thousand verses. This is liberation, this is complete seeing.

There is a common saying that expresses this: "Totally superb, totally solid." An earlier buddha said: "It covers heaven, it encompasses the earth." This is the purity of the spring pine, of autumn chrysanthemums. Just this.

When you reach this realm, you are a great master of humans and devas. If you teach others before arriving in this realm you will do great harm to them. Without knowing the spring pine or the autumn chrysanthemum, how can you nourish others, and how can you cut off their roots of confusion?

WHEN YOU ARE LAZY or doubtful, repent before the buddhas with sincere mind. If you do so the power of repentance will purify and save you. This power will nurture faith and effort free from hindrance. Once pure faith emerges, self and others are simultaneously turned. This benefit reaches both sentient and insentient beings.

Repentance is: "Although my past unwholesome actions have accumulated, causing hindrance in the study of the way, may buddhas and ancestors release me from these actions, and liberate me. May the merit of practicing dharma fill inexhaustible phenomenal worlds. May compassion be extended to me."

Before awakening, buddha ancestors were like us. Upon our awakening, we will become buddha ancestors. When we look at buddha ancestors we see only one buddha ancestor. When we look at their aspiration for enlightenment, we see one single aspiration. Fully working with compassion, we achieve facility and we drop off facility. Thus Longya said:

If you did not attain enlightenment in the past, do so now.
Liberate this body that is the culmination of many lifetimes.
Before enlightenment, ancient buddhas were like us.
When enlightened we will be like those of old.

This is the understanding of a realized buddha. We should reflect on it. With repentance you will certainly receive invisible help from buddha ancestors. With mind and body, you should repent to the buddhas. The power of repentance melts the root of unwholesomeness. This is the single color of true practice, true mind of faith, true body of faith.

When we have true practice, then valley sounds and colors, mountain colors and sounds all reveal the eighty-four thousand verses. When you are free from fame, profit, body, and mind, valleys and mountains are also free. Through the night the valley sounds and mountain colors do and do not actualize the eighty-four thousand verses. When your capacity to talk about valleys and mountains as valleys and mountains is not yet mature, who can see and hear you as valley sounds and mountain colors?

On the fifth day of the practice period, the second year of En'ō [1240], this was presented to the assembly of the Kannondōri Kōshō Hōrin Monastery.

1240, Fukakusa

The Time-Being

AN ANCIENT BUDDHA [Yaoshan] said:

> For the time being stand on top of the highest peak.
> For the time being proceed along the bottom of the deepest
>   ocean.
> For the time being three heads and eight arms [of a fighting
>   demon].
> For the time being an eight- or sixteen-foot body [of the
>   Buddha].
> For the time being a staff or whisk.
> For the time being a pillar or lantern.
> For the time being the children of [common families]
>   Zhang and Li.
> For the time being the earth and sky.

"For the time being" here means time itself is being, and all being is time. A golden sixteen-foot body is time; because it is time, there is the radiant illumination of time. Study it as the twelve hours of the present.[1] "Three heads and eight arms" is time; because it is time, it is not separate from the twelve hours of the present.

Even though you do not measure the hours of the day as long or short, far or near, you still call it twelve hours. Because the signs

---

1. A day is divided into twelve hours,* which correspond to the twelve zoological signs. The day begins with midnight, the hour of Rat.

of time's coming and going are obvious, people do not doubt it. Although they do not doubt it, they do not understand it. Or when sentient beings doubt what they do not understand, their doubt is not firmly fixed. Because of that, their past doubts do not necessarily coincide with the present doubt. Yet doubt itself is nothing but time.

THE WAY THE SELF arrays itself is the form of the entire world. See each thing in this entire world as a moment of time.

Things do not hinder one another, just as moments do not hinder one another. The way-seeking mind arises in this moment. A way-seeking moment arises in this mind. It is the same with practice and with attaining the way. Thus the self setting itself out in array sees itself. This is the understanding that the self is time.

KNOW THAT in this way there are myriad of forms and hundreds of grasses [all things] throughout the entire earth, and yet each grass and each form itself is the entire earth. The study of this is the beginning of practice. When you are at this place, there is just one grass, there is just one form; there is understanding of form and no-understanding of form; there is understanding of grass and no-understanding of grass. Since there is nothing but just this moment, the time-being is all the time there is. Grass-being and form-being are both time.

Each moment is all being, is the entire world. Reflect now whether any being or any world is left out of the present moment.

YET AN ORDINARY PERSON who does not understand buddha-dharma may interpret the words "the time-being" this way: "For a while I was three heads and eight arms. For a while I was an eight- or sixteen-foot body. This is like having crossed over rivers and climbed mountains. Even though the mountains and rivers still exist, I have already passed them and now reside in the jeweled palace and vermilion tower. Those mountains and rivers are as distant from me as heaven from earth."

It is not that simple. At the time the mountains were climbed and the rivers crossed, you were present. Time is not separate from you, and as you are present, time does not go away.

As time is not marked by coming and going, the moment you climbed the mountains is the time-being right now. If time keeps coming and going, you are the time-being right now. This is the meaning of the time-being. Does this time-being not swallow up the moment when you climbed the mountains and the moment when you resided in the jeweled palace and vermilion tower? Does it not spit them out?

Three heads and eight arms may be yesterday's time. The eight- or sixteen-foot body may be today's time. Yet yesterday and today are both in the moment when you directly enter the mountains and see myriad peaks. Yesterday's time and today's time do not go away.

Three heads and eight arms move forward as your time-being. It looks as if they are far away, but they are here and now. The eight- or sixteen-foot body moves forward as your time-being. It looks as if it is nearby, but it is exactly here. Thus, a pine tree is time, bamboo is time.

Do not think that time merely flies away. Do not see flying away as the only function of time. If time merely flies away, you would be separated from time. The reason you do not clearly understand the time-being is that you think of time only as passing. In essence, all things in the entire world are linked with one another as moments. Because all moments are the time-being, they are your time-being.

The time-being has the quality of flowing. So-called today flows into tomorrow, today flows into yesterday, yesterday flows into today. And today flows into today, tomorrow flows into tomorrow.

Because flowing is a quality of time, moments of past and present do not overlap or line up side by side. [Zen Master] Qingyuan is time, Huangbo is time, Mazu is time, Shitou is time. Self and other are already time. Practice-enlightenment is time. Being splattered with mud and getting wet with water [to awaken others] is also time.

ALTHOUGH THE VIEWS of an ordinary person and the causes and conditions of those views are what the ordinary person sees, they are not necessarily the ordinary person's truth. The truth merely manifests itself for the time-being as an ordinary person. Because you think your time or your being is not truth, you believe that the sixteen-foot golden body is not you.

However, your attempts to escape from being the sixteen-foot golden body are nothing but bits and pieces of the time-being. Those who have not yet confirmed this should look into it deeply. The hours of Horse and Sheep, which are arrayed in the world now, are actualized by ascendings and descendings of the time-being at each moment. The rat is time, the tiger is time, sentient beings are time, buddhas are time.

At the time you enlighten the entire world with three heads and eight arms, you enlighten the entire world with the sixteen-foot golden body. To fully actualize the entire world with the entire world is called thorough practice.

To fully actualize the golden body—to arouse the way-seeking mind, practice, attain enlightenment, and enter nirvāna—is nothing but being, nothing but time.

Just actualize all time as all being; there is nothing extra. A so-called extra being is thoroughly an extra being. Thus, the time-being half-actualized is half of the time-being completely actualized, and a moment that seems to be missed is also completely being. In the same way, even the moment before or after the moment that appears to be missed is also the time-being complete in itself. Vigorously abiding in each moment is the time-being. Do not mistakenly confuse it as nonbeing. Do not forcefully assert it as being.

You may suppose that time is only passing away, and not understand that time never arrives. Although understanding itself is time, understanding does not depend on its own arrival.

People only see time's coming and going, and do not thoroughly understand that the time-being abides in each moment. This being so, when can they penetrate the barrier? Even if people recognized the time-being in each moment, who could give expression to this recognition? Even if they could give expression to this recognition for a long time, who could stop looking for the realization of the original face? According to an ordinary person's view of the time-being, even enlightenment and nirvāna as the time-being would be merely aspects of coming and going.

THE TIME-BEING is entirely actualized without being caught up in nets or cages. Deva kings and heavenly beings appearing right and left are the time-being of your complete effort right now. The time-being of all beings throughout the world in water and on land is just the actualization of your complete effort right now. All beings of all kinds in the visible and invisible realms are the time-being actualized by your complete effort, flowing due to your complete effort.

Closely examine this flowing; without your complete effort right now, nothing would be actualized, nothing would flow.

Do not think flowing is like wind and rain moving from east to west. The entire world is not unchangeable, not immovable. It flows. Flowing is like spring. Spring with all its numerous aspects is called flowing. When spring flows there is nothing outside of spring. Study this in detail.

Spring invariably flows through spring. Although flowing itself is not spring, flowing occurs throughout spring. Thus, flowing is complete at just this moment of spring. Examine this thoroughly, coming and going.

In your study of flowing, if you imagine the objective to be outside yourself and that you flow and move through hundreds and thousands of worlds, for hundreds, thousands, and myriad of eons, you have not devotedly studied the buddha way.

YAOSHAN, Great Master Hongdao, instructed by Shitou, Great Master Wuji, once went to study with Mazu, Zen Master Daji.

Yaoshan asked, "I am familiar with the teaching of the Three

Vehicles and twelve divisions of scripture.* But what is the meaning
of Bodhidharma coming from India?"

Mazu replied:

> For the time being have him raise his eyebrows and blink.
> For the time being do not have him raise his eyebrows and
>   blink.
> For the time being to have him raise his eyebrows and blink
>   is right.
> For the time being to have him raise his eyebrows and blink
>   is not right.

Hearing these words, Yaoshan experienced great enlightenment
and said to Mazu, "When I was studying with Shitou, it was like a
mosquito trying to bite an iron bull."

What Mazu said is not the same as other people's words. The
"eyebrows" and "eyes" are mountains and oceans, because mountains and oceans are eyebrows and eyes. To "have him raise his
eyebrows" is to see the mountains. To "have him blink" is to understand the oceans. The "right" answer belongs to him, and he is
activated by your having him raise his eyebrows and blink. "Not
right" does not mean not having him raise his eyebrows and blink.
Not to have him raise eyebrows and blink does not mean not right.
These are all equally the time-being.

Mountains are time. Oceans are time. If they were not time,
there would be no mountains or oceans. Do not think that mountains and oceans here and now are not time. If time is annihilated,
mountains and oceans are annihilated. As time is not annihilated,
mountains and oceans are not annihilated.

This being so, the morning star appears, the Tathāgata appears,
the eye appears, and raising a flower appears. Each is time. If it were
not time, it could not be thus.

SHEXIAN, Zen Master Guixing, is the heir of Shoushan, a dharma
descendant of Linji. One day he taught the assembly:

For the time being mind arrives, but words do not.
For the time being words arrive, but mind does not.
For the time being both mind and words arrive.
For the time being neither mind nor words arrive.

Both mind and words are the time-being. Both arriving and not-arriving are the time-being. When the moment of arriving has not appeared, the moment of not-arriving is here. Mind is a donkey, words are a horse.[2] Having-already-arrived is words and not-having-left is mind. Arriving is not "coming," not-arriving is not "not yet."

The time-being is like this. Arriving is overwhelmed by arriving, but not by not-arriving. Not-arriving is overwhelmed by not-arriving, but not by arriving. Mind overwhelms mind and sees mind, words overwhelm words and see words. Overwhelming overwhelms overwhelming and sees overwhelming. Overwhelming is nothing but overwhelming. This is time.

As overwhelming is caused by you, there is no overwhelming that is separate from you. Thus you go out and meet someone. Someone meets someone. You meet yourself. Going out meets going out. If these are not the actualization of time, they cannot be thus.

Mind is the moment of actualizing the fundamental point; words are the moment of going beyond, unlocking the barrier. Arriving is the moment of casting off the body; not-arriving is the moment of being one with just this, while being free from just this. In this way you must endeavor to actualize the time-being.

THE OLD MASTERS have thus uttered these words, but is there nothing further to say?

Mind and words arriving part-way are the time-being.
Mind and words not arriving part-way are the time-being.

2. This refers to the following dialogue: A monk said, "What is the meaning of buddha-dharma?" Lingyun said, "While the donkey has not yet left, the horse has arrived."

In this manner, you should examine the time-being.

> To have him raise the eyebrows and blink is half the time-
> being.
> To have him raise the eyebrows and blink is the time-being
> missed.
> Not to have him raise the eyebrows and blink is half the
> time-being.
> Not to have him raise the eyebrows and blink is the time-
> being missed.

Thus, to study thoroughly, coming and going, and to study thoroughly, arriving and not-arriving, is the time-being of this moment.

On the first day of winter, the first year of the Ninji Era [1240], this was written at the Kōshō Hōrin Monastery.

1240, Fukakusa

The Power
of the Robe

BODHIDHARMA, THE HIGH ANCESTOR of Mt. Song, alone transmitted the correct teaching of the robe to China. He is the twenty-eighth-generation ancestor from Shākyamuni Buddha. In India twenty-eight generations of ancestors transmitted this teaching from heir to heir. The Twenty-eighth Ancestor entered China and became the First Ancestor there. After transmission of the teaching through five generations in China, Huineng became the thirty-third-generation ancestor. He is called the Sixth Chinese Ancestor.

Huineng, Zen Master Dijon, received a robe from Hongren at Mt. Huangmei and maintained it for the rest of his life. This robe is still enshrined at the Baolin Monastery on Mt. Caoxi, where he taught.

Over the generations, one emperor after another requested that the robe be brought to the palace. When it was, people made offerings and bowed to it. Thus the robe has been worshiped as a sacred object. Emperors Zong, Su, and Dai of the Tang dynasty occasionally commanded that the robe be brought to the palace. Each time it was brought and each time it was returned, an imperial messenger accompanied it.

Once when Emperor Dai sent this buddha robe back to Mt. Caoxi, he proclaimed: "We order Liu Chongjing, the Nation's Chief General, to transport the robe with great respect. We regard this robe as a national treasure. You should place it in the main temple with appropriate procedures. Make sure that the monks are notified of our command and protect the robe without failure."

There is more merit in seeing the buddha robe, hearing the teaching of it, and making offerings to it than in presiding over the billion worlds. To be the king of a nation where the robe exists is an outstanding birth among innumerable births and deaths; it is indeed the most supreme birth.

IN THE BILLION WORLDS where the Buddha's teaching reaches, is there any place there is no kashāya robe? Yet, Bodhidharma alone correctly transmitted the buddha kashāya face-to-face, heir to heir. Teachers who were not in this lineage were not given the buddha kashāya.

A transmission in the lineage of Bodhisattva Bhadrapāla, a descendant of the Twenty-seventh Ancestor, Prajnātāra, reached Dharma Teacher Sengzhao, but no buddha kashāya was transmitted to him. Daoxin, the Fourth Ancestor in China, guided Niutou, Zen Master Farong, but did not give him a buddha kashāya. Even for those who did not receive heir-to-heir transmission of kashāya, the power of the Tathāgata's dharma is not lacking and its benefit is broad for thousands of years. But those who received correct heir-to-heir transmission of kashāya are not the same as those who didn't. Therefore, when devas or humans receive a robe, they should receive a robe correctly transmitted by the buddha ancestors.

In India and China, even lay people received kashāya in the Ages of True Dharma and Imitation Dharma. Nowadays in the lands remote from India when the buddha-dharma is thin and declining, those who shave their heads and faces, calling themselves the Buddha's disciples, do not maintain the kashāya. They do not believe, know, or understand that the kashāya is to be maintained. What a pity! How can they know its form, color, and measurement? How can they know the proper way to wear it?

*　*　*

A KASHĀYA has been called the garment of emancipation. The hindrances of actions, defilements, and the effects of action are all liberated by it. If a dragon obtains a small piece of kashāya it can be cured of febrile diseases. If an ox touches a kashāya with one of its horns, its past wrongdoings disappear. When buddhas attain the way, they always wear a kashāya. Know that its power is unsurpassable and most venerable.

It is regrettable that we have been born in a remote land in the Age of Declining Dharma. However, we have the joy of meeting the teaching of the robe transmitted from buddha to buddha, heir to heir. In what lineage has Shākyamuni's teaching of the robe been transmitted as correctly as it has been in ours? Who would not revere and make offerings upon meeting the teaching of the robe? You should make such offerings just for one day, even if you need to give up immeasurable lives to do so. You should vow to meet, uphold, revere, and make offerings to the robe, birth after birth, generation after generation.

We are thousands of miles away from the land where the Buddha was born, beyond mountains and oceans. We are unable to go there, but due to the influence of our past good actions, we are no longer blocked by mountains and oceans nor excluded by our ignorance in this remote place. We have met the true teaching and are determined to practice it day and night. We maintain, uphold, and guard the kashāya continuously.

Thus the power of the kashāya is actualized through our practice, not merely with one or two buddhas but with as many buddhas as the sands of the Ganges. Even if it is your own practice, you should revere it, rejoice in it, and wholeheartedly express gratitude for the profound gift transmitted by the ancestral teachers. Even animals repay kindness; how should humans not recognize their kind help? If we do not understand kindness, we are more foolish than animals.

The power of the buddha robe, the buddha-dharma, cannot be known and understood except by ancestors who transmit the Buddha's true dharma. When you follow the path of buddhas, you should joyfully appreciate the buddha robe, the buddha-dharma.

You should continue this correct transmission even for hundreds and thousands of future generations. This is buddha-dharma newly actualized.

Correct transmission is not like mixing water with milk, but rather like the crown prince being installed as king. You can use milk mixed with water if there is not enough milk. But don't mix milk with oil, lacquer, or wine. If there is correct transmission, even an ordinary teacher of a mediocre lineage can be regarded as milk. How much more so with the correct transmission of buddhas and ancestors? It is like the installation of the crown prince. Even worldly kings say that they only wear the former king's robe. How could a buddha's child wear a robe other than the buddha robe?

After the tenth year of the Yongping Era [67 CE] of the Emperor Xiaoming of the Later Han Dynasty, monks and lay people often went back and forth between India and China. But none of them said that they had met an ancestor in India who had correct transmission from buddha ancestors. Thus there was no lineage of face-to-face transmission from the Tathāgata. These seekers only studied with masters of sūtras and treatises and brought back Sanskrit scriptures. They did not say they had met ancestors who had correctly inherited buddha-dharma. They did not say there were ancestors who had transmitted the buddha kashāya. Therefore, those people did not enter deeply into the chamber of buddha-dharma and clarify the meaning of the correct transmission of the buddha ancestors.

The Tathāgata Shākyamuni entrusted the treasury of the true dharma eye, the unsurpassable enlightenment, to Mahākāshyapa along with the kashāya which had been transmitted by his teacher, Kāshyapa Buddha. The robe was transmitted heir to heir for thirty-three generations, to Huineng. The shape, color, and measurements were intimately transmitted. After that, dharma descendants of Qingyuan and Nanyue, intimately transmitting the dharma, sewed and wore the ancestral dharma. The teaching of washing and maintaining the robe was not known except by those who studied in the chamber of a master who had transmitted this teaching face-to-face.

* * *

THERE ARE THREE TYPES OF kashāya: a five-panel robe, a seven-panel robe, and a great robe such as a nine-panel robe. One who is engaged in authentic practice receives only such robes as these, which are enough to offer to the body, and does not keep other types of robes. For work and traveling far or near, a five-panel robe is worn. For conducting formal activities or joining the assembly, a seven-panel robe is worn. For guiding humans and devas and arousing their respect and trust, you should wear a great robe such as a nine-panel robe. A five-panel robe is worn indoors and a seven-panel robe is worn while with other monks. A great robe is worn when entering the palace or in town.

Also, a five-panel robe is worn when it is mild and a seven-panel robe is added on top of it when it is cold. A great robe is further added when it is severely cold. Long ago in midwinter, when it was so cold that the bamboo was cracking, the Tathāgata wore a five-panel robe in the early evening. Later at night it got colder so he added a seven-panel robe. At the end of the night when it became even colder, he further added a great robe. The Buddha then thought, "In the future when the cold is severe, good monks can use these three robes to warm the body."

THESE ARE WAYS to wear the kashāya: The most common way is to leave the right shoulder uncovered. There is also a way to cover both shoulders, which is customary for tathāgatas and elders. When both shoulders are covered, the chest is either covered or revealed. Both shoulders are covered when a formal kashāya of more than sixty panels is worn.

When you put on a kashāya, you start by placing both ends on your left shoulder and upper arm, hanging the ends over your left elbow. If you put on a formal kashāya, you start by bringing the ends over the left shoulder and letting them hang down in back. There are many other ways to put on a kashāya. You should study deeply and make inquiries of your teacher.

For hundreds of years during the Liang, Chen, Sui, Tang, and Song dynasties, a number of scholars of Mahāyāna and Hīnayāna gave up lecturing on scripture, having learned that it was not the ultimate teaching. Intending to study the correctly transmitted dharma of buddha ancestors, they would invariably drop off their old robes and receive a correctly transmitted kashāya. This is departing from the limited and turning to the genuine.

The Tathāgata's dharma is rooted in India, where teachers in the past and present have gone beyond the limited views of ordinary people. As the realms of buddhas and the realms of sentient beings are neither limited nor unlimited, the teaching, practice, practitioner, and essence of Mahāyāna and Hīnayāna cannot be contained by ordinary people's views. However, in China practitioners often ignore teachings from India and regard recent interpretations of limited views as buddha-dharma, which is a mistake.

Those who arouse aspiration and wish to receive a kashāya should receive a correctly transmitted one. Do not receive a kashāya with a new design. What is called a correctly transmitted kashāya is what has been transmitted from Bodhidharma and Huineng, heir to heir, directly from the Tathāgata, without a generation's gap. This is the correctly transmitted kashāya worn by dharma heirs and dharma descendants. Newly designed kashāyas in China are not appropriate. The kashāyas worn by monks from India in the past and present are all like the buddha ancestors' correctly transmitted kashāyas. None of them wore kashāyas like those newly made by monks of the Precepts School in China. Those who are ignorant believe in the kashāyas of the Precepts School, but those who have clear understanding do not.

THE POWER of the kashāya transmitted by buddha ancestors is clear and easy to accept. The correct transmission has been handed down person to person. The true form has been shown to us directly. It still exists, as this dharma has been inherited up to the present. The ancestors who received a kashāya are all teachers and students who merged their minds and received dharma. Therefore you should make a kashāya in the manner correctly transmitted by buddha ancestors.

As this is the correct transmission, ordinary people and sages, humans and devas, as well as dragon kings, all know it. To be born to the abundance of this dharma and to wear a kashāya even once and to maintain it for a moment is no other than wearing an amulet that assures the attainment of unsurpassable enlightenment.

When one phrase or one verse permeates your body and mind, it becomes a seed for illumination for limitless kalpas, and this brings you to unsurpassable enlightenment. When one dharma or one wholesome action permeates your body and mind, it is also like this. Moment by moment a thought appears and disappears without abiding. Moment by moment a body appears and disappears without abiding. Yet the power of practice always matures. A kashāya is neither made nor not made, neither abiding nor not abiding. It is the ultimate realm of buddha and buddha. A practitioner who receives it invariably attains its power.

Those who have no wholesome past actions cannot see, wear, receive, and understand a kashāya even if they live for one, two, or innumerable lifetimes. When I look at practitioners in China and Japan, I see that there are those who are able to wear a kashāya and those who are not. Their ability to wear one does not depend on how noble or lowly they are, how wise or ignorant they are, but on their wholesome past actions. Therefore those who have received a kashāya should rejoice in their wholesome past actions, without doubting their accumulated merit. Those who have not received a kashāya should wish for one. Try to sow a seed for a kashāya immediately in this lifetime. Those who cannot receive one because of their hindrances should repent to buddha tathāgatas and the three treasures.

How strongly people in other countries wish to have the Tathāgata's correct transmission of the dharma of the robe in their countries, just as in China! How deep their regret is and how sorrowful they are that they do not have it! With what fortune we have encountered the correct transmission of the World-honored One's robe dharma. This is due to the great power of our having nurtured prajñā in the past.

Now in this unwholesome time—the Age of Declining Dharma—people have no regret that they do not have correct transmission, but they are jealous that others do. They are like a gang of demons. What they believe and where they abide are not genuine, but only bound by their past actions. They should take refuge in the correctly transmitted buddha-dharma as the true place of return in studying the buddha way.

You should know that a kashāya is what all buddhas respect and take refuge in. It is the buddha body, the buddha mind. It is called the clothing of emancipation, the robe of the field of happiness, the robe of no form, the unsurpassable robe, the robe of patience, the Tathāgata's robe, the robe of great love and great compassion, the robe as a victorious banner, and the robe of supreme, penetrating, perfect enlightenment. You should indeed receive it with utmost respect. This is why you should not alter it.

EITHER SILK or common cloth is used as the material for a robe, according to the situation. It is not necessarily true that common cloth is pure and silk is impure. On the other hand, it would be unreasonable and laughable to exclude common cloth and only choose silk. According to the usual practice of buddhas, a robe of discarded cloth is regarded as excellent.

There are ten types of discarded cloth, including burned cloth, cloth chewed by oxen, cloth chewed by rats, and cloth from corpses. People throughout India throw away such cloth on streets or fields, just as we do with excrement-cleaning cloth. So a robe of discarded cloth is actually called a robe of excrement-cleaning cloth. Practitioners pick up such cloths, wash and repair them for use. There can be pieces of silk and common cloth among them. You should give up discrimination between silk and common cloth and study the meaning of discarded cloth. Once when a monk washed such a robe of discarded cloth in Anavatapta Lake, the dragon king rained down flowers in admiration and respect.

There are teachers in the Lesser Vehicles who say that threads are incarnated bodies of the tree god.[1] Practitioners of the Great

1. An attempt to explain that the silk for kashāya was not produced by killing silkworms.

Vehicle should laugh about it. Which thread is not an incarnated body? Those who have ears to hear about incarnated bodies may not have the eyes to see them. You should know that among the cloths you pick up, there can be common cloth and silk. Because cloth is made differently in different regions, it is difficult to identify the materials. Eyes cannot see the difference. Do not discuss whether the material you pick up is silk or common cloth. Just call it discarded cloth.

Even if a human or a deva turns into discarded cloth, it is not sentient but just discarded cloth. Even if a pine or chrysanthemum turns into discarded cloth, it is not insentient but just discarded cloth. Discarded cloth is actualized only when you accept that discarded cloth is not silk or common cloth, not gold, silver, or a pearl. Discarded cloth is not yet dreamed of by those who have not yet dropped off discrimination between silk and common cloth.

Once a monk asked Old Buddha Huineng, "Is the robe you received at midnight at Mt. Huangmei common cloth or silk? In the end what is it?"

Huineng said, "Not common cloth, not silk."

You should know that a kashāya is neither silk nor common cloth. This is the profound teaching of the buddha way.

HONORABLE SHĀNAVĀSA is the third entrusted ancestor of the dharma storehouse. He was born wearing a lay person's robe. The robe turned into a kashāya when he became a monk. Nun Pundarīka was born with a kashāya, birth after birth, as a result of offering a carpet to the Buddha.

When we meet Shākyamuni Buddha and leave the household, the lay clothing we acquire at birth immediately turns into a kashāya, just as Shānavāsa's did. Thus a kashāya is neither silk nor common cloth. The power of buddha-dharma transforms body, mind, and all things in this way.

It is clear that our body, mind, and environs are immediately transformed when we leave the household and receive the precepts. But we often do not notice this because of our ignorance. This effect of buddha-dharma is not only applied to Shānavāsa and Nun

Pundarīka but to us all. We should not doubt this great benefit. You should endeavor to clarify this point. The kashāya that covers the body of the one who has received the precepts is not limited to common cloth or silk. The Buddha's transformation is beyond our comprehension. The pearl hidden inside the robe is beyond the understanding of those who count letters.

You should study the shape, color, and size of buddhas' kashāyas. See whether they have size or are sizeless, whether they have form or are formless. This is what the ancestors in India and China, and present, have studied and correctly transmitted. Those who see and hear this original inheritance that has come from ancestor to ancestor and yet do not accept it cannot be excused. This is due to their ignorance and distrust. It is throwing away the true and seeking for the false, giving up the essential and wishing for the trivial, making light of the Tathāgata.

Those who arouse the aspiration for enlightenment should without fail receive the authentic transmission of the ancestors. As dharma descendants we have not only encountered the rarely encountered buddha-dharma, but we have seen, studied, and received the correctly transmitted buddha kashāya. In this way we meet the Tathāgata, we hear the Buddha expound the dharma, we are illuminated by the Buddha, we enjoy the Buddha's enjoyment, we receive the one-to-one transmission of the Buddha's mind, and we attain the Buddha's marrow. Thus we are intimately covered by the kashāya of Shākyamuni Buddha. We personally accompany the Buddha and receive this kashāya from the Buddha.

THIS IS HOW to wash a kashāya: you put it unfolded into a clean wooden tub, cover it with thoroughly boiled water that has been purified by incense, and leave it for one hour [roughly two hours by the modern way of counting]. Another way is to boil water mixed with pure ash and cover the kashāya until the water cools. Nowadays it is common to use ash water. It is called *aku no yu* in Japan.

When the ash water cools, rinse the kashāya with clear hot water many times. Do not scrub it with your hands or stamp on it. After thus removing sweat and oil stains, mix fragrant powder of sandalwood or aloeswood with cold water and rinse the kashāya in it.

Then hang it on a clean rod to dry. When it is completely dry, fold it, and put it on the altar. Then burn incense, spread flower petals on the altar, circumambulate the kashāya clockwise a few times, and bow to it. After three, six, or nine full bows, kneel and put your palms together; then hold up the kashāya with both hands, chant the kashāya verse, and put it on properly.

THE WORLD-HONORED ONE, Shākyamuni Buddha, said to the great assembly: "Good assembly, long ago in my previous life when I was with Rātnakosha Buddha, I was called Mahākarunā Bodhisattva. Once in front of the Rātnakosha Buddha the bodhisattva made these vows:

> Rātnakosha Buddha, after I attain buddhahood, there may be those who, following my teaching, leave home and wear a kashāya and still break important precepts, hold wrong views, or ignore the three treasures. And there may be monks, nuns, laymen, or laywomen who commit serious wrongdoings but arouse respectful mind and honor the monk's robe, revering the buddha, dharma, and sangha. I vow that there will not be even one such person in the Three Vehicles,* who misses receiving a prediction of enlightenment or turns away from my teaching. Otherwise this would contradict the vows of all buddhas who have been present for limitless eons in the worlds of the ten directions, and thus I would not attain unsurpassable, perfect enlightenment.
>
> Rātnakosha Buddha, after I attain buddhahood if any devas, dragons, humans, or nonhumans revere, make offerings to, or admire one who wears the kashāya, I vow that such beings, holding even a small piece of kashāya, will practice in the three treasures without regressing.
>
> If there are sentient beings overcome by hunger or thirst, poverty-stricken, or in a most humble position, as well as hungry ghosts, who obtain a piece of a kashāya no bigger than a hand, I vow that such beings will be satisfied with food and drink and that their wishes will be immediately realized.

If there are sentient beings who are in conflict, harbor grudges, and fight one another, or if there are devas, dragons, *gandharvas,** *asuras,** *garudas,** *kinnaras,** *mahoragas,** *kumbhāndas,** *pishāchas,** humans, or nonhumans who fight one another, I vow that if such beings think of a kashāya, compassionate mind, gentle mind, generous mind, serene mind, wholesome mind will arouse them and they will attain purity.

If people who battle, quarrel, or are in legal conflict bring a patch of kashāya for self-protection and pay respect to it, they will always be victorious and will overcome difficulties, because others will not harm, confuse, or belittle them.

Rātnakosha Buddha, if my kashāya did not possess the above five sacred powers, I would be deceiving all buddhas who have been present for limitless eons in the worlds of the ten directions, and I would not achieve unsurpassable, perfect enlightenment for conducting buddha activities in the future; thus I would be without wholesome dharma and would be unable to overcome those who are outside the way.

"Good assembly, then Rātnakosha Buddha extended his golden right arm, stroked Mahākarunā Bodhisattva on the head and said in admiration, 'Splendid, splendid, courageous bodhisattva. Your vow is a rare treasure that expresses great wisdom. You will realize unsurpassable, perfect enlightenment and your kashāya robe will possess those five sacred powers and cause immeasurable benefit.'

"Good assembly, upon hearing Rātnakosha Buddha's admiration, Mahākarunā Bodhisattva rejoiced and became exuberant. Then Rātnakosha Buddha extended his golden right arm, with long and slender fingers and his palm as soft as a feathery celestial robe. Rātnakosha Buddha stroked the bodhisattva on the head and turned him into a youth of twenty.

"Good assembly, all the devas, dragons, gandharvas, humans, and nonhumans folded their hands together and dedicated flowers and music to Mahākarunā Bodhisattva. They admired and admired the bodhisattva and then sat still."

From the time when Shākyamuni Buddha was alive in this world up to the present, these five sacred powers of the kashāya have been described in sūtras and precept texts for bodhisattvas and shrāvakas. Indeed, the kashāya is a buddha robe of all buddhas of past, present, and future. Although the power of all kashāyas is unlimited, receiving a kashāya from the heritage of Shākyamuni Buddha is incomparable with receiving a kashāya from the heritage of other buddhas.

The reason for this is that Shākyamuni Buddha made these vows to initiate the power of the kashāya in his former life as Mahākarunā Bodhisattva, when he made five hundred vast vows to Rātnakosha Buddha. The power of the kashāya is unlimited and beyond thought. Thus, what transmits the skin, flesh, bones, and marrow of the World-honored One is the kashāya robe. Ancestors who have transmitted the treasury of the true dharma eye have always correctly transmitted a kashāya.

Sentient beings who maintain and pay respect to a kashāya have always attained the way within two or three lifetimes. Even wearing the kashāya as a joke or for profit can lead to attainment of the way.

Ancestor Nāgārjuna said, "Home-leavers in buddha-dharma, you can resolve your crimes and attain liberation even if you break precepts and commit crimes, as mentioned in *The Sūtra on the Former Birth of Nun Utpalavarnā*:

> At the time when the Buddha was in this world, Nun Utpalavarnā attained six miraculous powers* and became an arhat. She visited noble householders and talked about the life of home-leavers. She encouraged noble women to become nuns.
>
> They said, "We are young and beautiful. It would be hard to keep the precepts."
>
> Utpalavarnā said, "It's all right to break the precepts. Leave the household first."
>
> The women said, "If we break the precepts, we will fall into hell. How can we do that?"
>
> Utpalavarnā said, "Then go ahead and fall into hell."
>
> They laughed and said, "We would be punished in hell."
>
> Utpalavarnā said, "Reflecting on my former life, I was an entertainer, putting on various costumes and speaking memorized

lines. Once I put on a nun's clothes for a joke. As a result of this action, I was reborn as a nun at the time of Kāshyapa Buddha. Because of my high status and proper conduct, I grew arrogant and broke a precept. I fell into hell and experienced various punishments. In my next birth I met Shākyamuni Buddha, left the household, attained the six miraculous powers, and became an arhat. From this I know that if you leave the household and receive precepts, even if you break a precept, you can become an arhat because of the merit of the precepts you have received. But you cannot attain the way if you only create unwholesome deeds without receiving the precepts. I was once a criminal falling into hell and coming out of hell. If a mere criminal dies and enters hell, there is nothing to attain. So, you should know that even if you break a precept, you can attain the fruit of the way."

The cause of Nun Utpalavarnā becoming an arhat in this story is no other than putting on a kashāya for a joke. In her second birth, she became a nun at the time of Kāshyapa Buddha and in her third birth she became a great arhat at the time of Shākyamuni Buddha and accomplished the three types of knowledge* and six miraculous powers. The three types of knowledge are the celestial eye, insight into the future, and knowing how to remove misery. The six miraculous powers are the power of celestial activity, insight into others' minds, the celestial eye, the celestial ear, knowing the past, and removing misery.

Indeed, a mere criminal dies in vain and enters hell. The criminal comes out of hell and becomes a criminal. As Utpalavarnā had a causal connection with the precepts, even though she broke a precept, she was able to attain the way. As a result of putting on a kashāya for a joke, she could attain the way even in her third birth. How much more likely you are to attain the way if you arouse a pure heart of faith and put on a kashāya for the sake of unsurpassable enlightenment! Can the merit not be complete? Even further, the merit of maintaining a kashāya with utmost respect throughout a lifetime is vast and boundless.

Those who arouse the aspiration for enlightenment should immediately receive a kashāya. To encounter this fortunate life and not to plant buddha seeds is regrettable. Having received a human body in this world, Jambudvīpa, you have a chance to meet Shākya-muni Buddha's dharma, to share life with ancestors who are heirs of buddha-dharma and to receive a kashāya that has been directly transmitted from person to person. It would be a pity not to do this and to spend your life in vain.

In the transmission of kashāya, only transmission through the ancestors is correct heritage. Transmission through other teachers cannot compare with this. Even if you receive a kashāya from a teacher without transmission, the merit is profound. How much more merit there is in receiving a kashāya from a correct teacher of heir-to-heir, face-to-face transmission. Indeed, in this way you become a dharma child and a dharma grandchild of the Tathāgata. This is truly to inherit the Tathāgata's skin, flesh, bones, and marrow.

The kashāya is transmitted through buddhas of the ten directions in the past, present, and future without a break. Buddhas, bodhisattvas, shrāvakas, and pratyeka-buddhas of the ten directions in the past, present, and future maintain it.

FOR MAKING a kashāya, coarse cloth is basic. When coarse cloth is not available, more finely woven cloth may be used. In case there is neither coarse cloth nor finely woven cloth, plain silk may be used. When none of these are available, patterned or open-weave silk may be used. This is permitted by the Tathāgata. When no cloth is available, the Tathāgata permits making a leather kashāya.

Kashāya materials should be dyed blue, yellow, red, black, or purple. The color should be subdued and indistinct. The Tathāgata always wore a kashāya of skin color. This is the original kashāya color.

The kashāya transmitted by Bodhidharma was bluish black. It was made of *kārpāsaka* [core] cotton from India, and is still kept at Mt. Caoxi. This kashāya was transmitted for twenty-eight generations in India and five generations in China to Huineng of Mt. Caoxi. Now disciples of Huineng maintain the tradition of this buddha robe. Monks of other lineages have nothing close to it.

There are three types of kashāya material: excrement-cleaning cloth, animal hair or bird feathers, and patched cloths. I have already mentioned that a robe usually consists of excrement-cleaning cloth. A robe made of animal hair or bird feathers is called a down robe. A robe made of patched cloths is made of old, worn-out cloth. Cloth that is desirable by worldly standards is not used.

Senior Monk Upāli said to the World-honored One, "Great virtuous World-honored One, how many panels does a great robe have?"

The Buddha said, "There are nine kinds of robes. The number of panels may be nine, eleven, thirteen, fifteen, seventeen, nineteen, twenty-one, twenty-three, or twenty-five. The first three kinds of great robes consist of panels of one short and two long pieces of cloth. The second three kinds of great robes consist of panels of one short and three long pieces of cloth. The last three kinds of great robes consist of panels of one short and four long pieces of cloth. A robe with more panels is not standard."

Upāli said, "Great virtuous World-honored One, how many sizes of sanghātī robes [great robes] are there?"

The Buddha said, "There are three sizes: large, medium, and small. A large robe measures three hasta [length from elbow to middle fingertip] vertically and five hasta horizontally. A small robe measures two and one-half hasta vertically and four and one-half hasta horizontally. A medium robe measures between these two."

Upāli said, "Great virtuous World-honored One, how many panels does an uttarāsangha robe [over-robe] have?"

The Buddha said, "It has seven panels. Each panel consists of one short and two long pieces of cloth."

Upāli said, "Great virtuous World-honored One, what are the sizes of an uttarāsangha robe?"

The Buddha said, "There are three sizes. A large robe measures three hasta vertically and five hasta horizontally. A small robe measures half a hasta less each way. A medium robe measures between these two."

Upāli said, "Great virtuous World-honored One, how many panels does an *antarvāsa* robe [under-robe] have?"

The Buddha said, "It has five panels. Each panel consists of one short and one long piece of cloth."

Upāli said, "Great virtuous World-honored One, what are the sizes of an antarvāsa robe?"

The Buddha said, "There are three sizes: large, medium, and small. A large antarvāsa robe measures three hasta vertically and five hasta horizontally. A small and a medium antarvāsa robe measure the same as for the uttarāsangha robe." The Buddha also said, "There are two other types of antarvāsa robe. One measures two hasta vertically and five hasta horizontally. The other measures two hasta vertically and four hasta horizontally."

The sanghāti robe is the outermost robe. The uttarāsangha robe is the outer robe. The antarvāsa robe is the inner robe. The sanghātī robe is also called the great robe. It is a robe for visiting a palace or expounding dharma. The uttarāsangha robe is a seven-panel robe. It is a less formal robe for joining the assembly. The antarvāsa is a five-panel robe, which is an informal robe for work. You should always maintain these three types of robes. Also there is a sixty-panel sanghātī robe. You should be aware of this.

Some sources say that the height of human bodies varies corresponding to their maximum life span, which ranges between eighty thousand years and one hundred years. Other sources say that the height of human bodies does not vary. It is a correct teaching to say it does not vary. But the height of a buddha's body and that of a human body are different. Human bodies can be measured but the buddha's body cannot. Thus, when Shākyamuni Buddha wore the past Kāshyapa Buddha's robe, it was neither too long nor too wide. When the future Maitreya Buddha wears Shākyamuni Buddha's robe, it will be neither too short nor too narrow. You should be aware that a buddha's body is beyond long and short. Brahma, the king of gods who resides high in the form world,* could not see the top of the Buddha's head. Maudgalyāyana, a disciple of the Buddha, traveled all the way to the Heaven of Shining Banner and still heard the Buddha's voice. Thus the Buddha was seen and heard near and far. How marvelous it is! All the merits of the Tathāgata are like this. You should keep this in mind.

A KASHĀYA VARIES according to how it is sewn. It may be made of rectangular pieces sewn together, of narrow strips sewn in the same pattern onto one large piece, of one piece tucked and hemmed, or of one piece plain and flat. These are all authentic ways of sewing. You should choose the way of sewing to suit the cloth you have received. The Buddha said, "The kashāyas of the buddhas of past, present, and future are always stitched."

In acquiring materials, purity is of primary concern. What is called excrement-cleaning cloth is regarded as of utmost purity. Buddhas of past, present, and future all recognize its purity. Cloth that is donated by faithful lay people is pure. Cloth purchased in a marketplace with donated money is also pure. Although there are guidelines for the length of time to spend on sewing, we live in a remote land in a time of declining dharma; so the most important thing for you is to sew a kashāya when the faithful heart arises, and then receive it.

It is an essential characteristic of Mahāyāna that even a lay person, whether human or celestial, receives a kashāya. Kings Brahma and Shākyamuni both wore a kashāya. These are outstanding examples in the desire world and in the form world, and cannot be comprehended by ordinary human beings.

Lay bodhisattvas also wear kashāyas. In China, Emperor Wu of the Liang Dynasty and Emperor Yang of the Sui Dynasty both wore a kashāya. Emperors Dai and Su also wore a kashāya, studied with monks, and received the bodhisattva precepts. Other lay men and women of the past and present have also received a kashāya together with the Buddhist precepts.

In Japan, Prince Shōtoku wore a kashāya and expounded such sūtras as *The Lotus Sūtra* and *The Shrimālā Devī Sūtra*, when he perceived the marvel of celestial flowers raining down. Since then the buddha-dharma has spread widely in our country. Prince Shōtoku was not only Regent of the Nation, but also a guiding master of humans and devas. A messenger of the Buddha, he was both father and mother of sentient beings. Although the form, color, and measurements of a kashāya have not been transmitted accurately to us in Japan, still, because of Prince Shōtoku's influence, we are able to see and hear about kashāyas. If he had not introduced the Buddha's teaching, it would have been a great loss to us.

Later, Emperor Shōmu also received a kashāya and the bodhisattva precepts. In this way even those who are on a throne or those who are retainers can receive a kashāya and the bodhisattva precepts. There is no wholesome fortune for humans that excels this.

Some sources say that the kashāya worn by lay people is called a single stitch robe or a lay robe, and that double stitching is not used for that robe. Other sources say that when lay people go to the practice place they wear three types of dharma robes and use tooth cleaning twigs, rinsing water, eating utensils, and sitting mats to engage in pure practice just as monks do. These are words of ancient masters. However, in the direct transmission of buddha ancestors, the kashāya given to kings, ministers, lay practitioners, and warriors is invariably double stitched. Laborer Lu [Huineng] did receive the buddha kashāya when he was a layman, which is an excellent precedent.

THE KASHĀYA is a banner of the Buddha's disciple. When you have received a kashāya, wear it respectfully every day.

First put it on top of your head, place your palms together, and recite this verse:

Great is the robe of liberation,
the robe of no form, the field of happiness!
I wear the Tathāgata's teaching
to awaken countless beings.

Then put it on. Visualize your teacher, or visualize a stūpa in the kashāya. Also recite this verse when you put on the kashāya after washing it.

The Buddha said, "When you shave your head and wear a kashāya, you are protected by all buddhas. Having left the household, you are given offerings by celestial beings."

From this we clearly know that as soon as you shave your head and wear a kashāya, you are guarded by all buddhas. With this protection, you realize unsurpassable enlightenment. Thus you are given offerings by humans and devas.

The World-honored One said to Monk Jnānaprabha, "The dharma robe brings forth the ten victories: It covers your body, providing modesty, and the practice of wholesome conduct. It protects you from cold, heat, insects, beasts, and snakes and provides comfort in the practice of the way. It manifests the form of a mendicant home-leaver and arouses joy in those who see it, relieving them of ill intentions. It is a sacred banner of humans and devas. Revering it and bowing to it will cause you to be born in the heaven of purity. By wearing it you arouse the thought of a sacred banner, avert wrongdoing, and bring forth happiness. It has been dyed with subdued color to help you become free from the five desires, undefiled by greed and attachment. It is the Buddha's pure robe that cuts off delusion and creates a wholesome field of happiness. When you wear it your unwholesome actions will disappear and the path of the ten wholesome actions* will increase moment by moment. It is like an excellent rice field as it nurtures the bodhisattva mind. It is like armor that protects you from the poison arrows of delusion."

Thus Monk Jnānaprabha understood that, thanks to these ten victories, all buddhas in the past, present, and future, all pratyeka-buddhas, *shramanas,** and pure home-leavers wear the kashāya while they sit on the sacred platform of emancipation, holding the sword of wisdom to subdue the demon of delusion, and together they enter nirvāna.

Then the World-honored One said in a verse:

Listen carefully, Jnānaprabha.
The great happiness-field robe has ten victorious qualities:
While worldly clothes increase defilement,
the dharma robe of the Tathāgata does not.
The dharma robe provides modesty, completes repentance,

and creates the rice field of happiness.
It protects you from cold, heat, and poisonous creatures
and strengthens your way-seeking mind for attaining
    ultimate understanding.
Manifesting the form of a mendicant home-leaver,
it frees people from greed and desire, cuts off five wrong
    views,
and helps you to hold correct practice.
By revering and bowing to the sacred banner kashāya,
you will have the happiness of King Brahma.
When a Buddha child wears the kashāya a vision of a stūpa
    arises,
creating happiness, eliminating unwholesomeness,
and joining humans and devas.
The noble form of the kashāya arouses respect
in a true seeker who is free from worldly dust.
All buddhas praise it as an excellent field
most beneficial to sentient beings.
The inconceivable miraculous power of the kashāya
nurtures practice for enlightenment.
The sprout of practice grows in the spring field,
the splendid fruit of enlightenment is like a harvest in
    autumn.
The kashāya is true armor, impenetrable as diamond,
the deadly arrows of delusion cannot pierce it.
I have now recited the ten excellent merits of kashāya.
For eons, more comments could be made, but I'll say this:
A dragon who wears even a shred of kashāya
can't be devoured by a gold-winged garuda.
A person who holds a kashāya while crossing the ocean
will not fear dragons, fish, or harmful beings.
Lightning and thunder, heaven's wrath,
will not frighten a monk who wears a kashāya.
When a lay person carries a kashāya with respect,
no evil spirits draw near.
When one arouses the beginner's mind,

leaves home and worldly affairs to practice the way,
demon palaces in the ten directions will tremble
and such a person will immediately realize the dharma
    king's body.

These ten victorious qualities encompass the wide-ranging
merits of the buddha way. Understand clearly the merits expounded
in these prose and verse lines. Do not put them aside after reading,
but continue to study them phrase by phrase. These victorious
qualities come from the power of the kashāya, not from the power
of a practitioner's vigorous effort or long practice.

The Buddha said, "The miraculous power of the kashāya is beyond thought." It is not something ordinary people or wise sages
can comprehend. When the dharma king's body is immediately actualized, the kashāya is invariably worn. Those who do not wear a
kashāya have never actualized the dharma king's body.

THE ROBE of utmost purity is one made of excrement-cleaning
cloth. Its merits are clearly and extensively stated in sūtras and commentaries of the Great and Lesser Vehicles, which you should inquire into and study broadly. You should also study other sources
about materials for robes. Buddha ancestors who have always understood and transmitted the robe of excrement-cleaning cloth cannot be compared with those who have not.

The Madhyamāgama Sūtra says, "Venerable assembly: Suppose
there is someone whose practice is pure in body, but not pure in
speech and mind. If you see this person and feel disgust, the disgust
needs to be removed.

"Venerable assembly: Suppose there is someone whose practice
is not pure in body, but pure in speech and mind. If you see this
person and feel disgust, the disgust needs to be removed. How is
this removed?

"Venerable assembly: It is like a monk who practices outdoors
and finds stained cloth. When he sees cloth discarded in the toilet
which is stained with excrement, urine, mucus, or other impurities,

he picks it up with his left hand, opens it with his right hand, and tears it up and saves the parts that are not stained or damaged.

"Venerable assembly: Suppose there is someone whose practice is not pure in body, but pure in speech and mind. Do not think of this practice as impure in body, but just think of this practice as pure in speech and mind. If you see the impurity and feel disgust, the disgust needs to be removed."

This is the way for a monk who practices outdoors and collects discarded cloths. There are four types as well as ten types of discarded cloths. When you collect cloths, you should save pieces without holes. Also, the parts heavily stained with urine and excrement are not taken. Save the pieces that can be washed clean.

The ten types of discarded cloths are those that have been chewed by cows, gnawed by rats, burned, stained by menstrual blood, stained during childbirth, used as a shrine robe, found in a cemetery, used as an offering with a prayer, given by royalty, and used as a shroud.[2] These cloths are abandoned by people, and not ordinarily used any more. You pick them up and turn them into pure material for the kashāya.

This is what buddhas in the past, present, and future admire and use. Thus discarded cloths have been respected and guarded by humans, devas, and dragons. You should pick up such discarded cloths, the material of utmost purity, to create a kashāya. There is no robe like this in Japan now. Even if you look for one, you won't encounter it. How sorrowful! Even if you search, you won't find one in this small remote country.

To make a kashāya, you should use pure material given by donors, offered by humans or devas, or purchased with the earnings from pure livelihood. Discarded cloth, as well as cloth obtained by pure livelihood, is neither silk, cotton, gold, silver, jade, nor brocade; it is nothing other than discarded cloth. It is used not for making tattered or elegant clothes, but just for the sake of buddha-dharma. To wear this cloth is to transmit the skin, flesh, bones, and

2. Cloth given by royalty: viewed as polluted because it may have been stained by the former owner's desire for fame and pride.

marrow of buddhas of past, present, and future, to transmit the treasury of the true dharma eye. Do not ask humans and devas about the power of the robe. Just study it with buddha ancestors.

Postscript

Once when I was in Song China, practicing on a long sitting-platform, I observed the monks around me. At the beginning of zazen in the morning, they would hold up their kashāyas, set them on their heads, and chant a verse quietly with palms together:

> Great is the robe of liberation,
> the robe of no form, the field of happiness!
> I wear the Tathāgata's teaching
> to awaken countless beings.

This was the first time I had seen the putting on of the kashāya in this way and I rejoiced, tears wetting the lapel of my robe. Although I had read this verse of veneration for the kashāya in *The Āgama Sūtra*, I had not known the procedure. Now I saw it with my own eyes. In my joy I also felt sorry that there had been no master to teach this to me and no good friend to recommend it in Japan. How sad that so much time had been wasted! But I also rejoiced in my wholesome past actions. If I had stayed in my land, how could I have sat side by side with the monks who had received and were wearing the buddha robe? My sadness and joy brought endless tears.

Then I made a vow to myself: However unsuited I am, I will become an authentic holder of the buddha-dharma, receiving correct transmission of the true dharma, and with compassion show the buddha ancestors' correctly transmitted dharma robes to those in my land. I rejoice that the vow I made at that time has not been in vain, and that there have been many bodhisattvas, lay and ordained, who have received the kashāya in Japan. Those who maintain the kashāya should always venerate it day and night. This brings forth most excellent merit. To see or hear one line of the kashāya verse is not limited to seeing and hearing it as if we were trees and rocks, but pervades the nine realms of sentient beings.*

In the tenth month of the seventeenth year of the Jiading Era of Song China [1224], two Korean monks visited Qingyuan Prefecture. One was named Zhixuan, and the other Jingyun. They were men of letters who often discussed the meaning of sūtras, but just like lay people they did not have kashāyas or bowls. What a pity! They had shaven heads but not the manners of monks. This was perhaps because they had come from a small country in a remote land. When some monks from Japan visit other countries, they might be like Zhixuan and his company.

During the twelve years of his practice before attaining the way, Shākyamuni Buddha venerated the kashāya without putting it aside. As a remote descendant, you should keep this in mind. Turn your head away from worshiping heaven, gods, kings, and retainers for the sake of name and gain, and joyfully dedicate yourself to venerating the buddha robe.

This was presented to the assembly of the Kannondōri Kōshō Hōrin Monastery on the first day of winter, the first year of the Ninji Era [1240].

Encouraging Words

RECORDED BY EJŌ, ATTENDANT MONK

MONK EUN WAS APPOINTED work leader* on the last day of last year, the second year of the En'ō Era [1240]. Then on the twenty-fifth day, the fifth month of this year, we were in the middle of the rainy season and the thatched-roof hut was leaking. When I went to zazen, billowing waves spread from the eaves across the floor of the monks' hall and the adjacent hallway. The monks' assembly of pure ocean moved to the center of the monks' hall and was stranded there.

I asked Eun to fix this. He took off his dharma robe and, together with the carpenters, he went up hatless onto the roof to oversee the work. Although the rain was falling hard, it didn't bother him. I felt like writing a poem for him. In my lineage there is a precedent for this kind of appreciation. Since then six months, nearly two hundred days, have passed. I have not yet composed my poem, but I have not forgotten about it either. It was common for ancient buddhas not to pick up the brush to write poems in the hot season, but to do so in the cold season. We need to respect this custom.

We're heading toward the one-year mark since Eun took his position. The monastery fences have been constructed. This is a fortunate sign that our efforts ripen. I see him share his knowledge with the community, just like a boat coming down the river and

being unloaded. I also personally see him present his subtle understanding. His effort brings joy to all of us.

This monastery is far from the main road and people do not
visit casually. Those who have high aspirations and a monk's traveling bag find their way here. They leave the world and join this
patch of grass. With full commitment, sharp ears, and joyous heart
they strive for the ancestral field, sometimes taking the form of a
fighting demon; sometimes they use a thousand hands and eyes.
Who would say that receiving dharma and continuing the ancestors' path is not an artisan's craft?

Beyond the traditional words about participating in the assembly and working together, here is a verse for Eun:

Hit the mark in one hundred activities.
Craft ten out of ten.

Zen person Kenne left his village in the west, bidding farewell to
his parents, and has just joined us in the practice of the ancient
buddha ancestors. He should maintain and treasure his joy. People
from the east, south, and north cannot have equal fortune. And they
never will.

There are different ways for newly arrived monks to work in
this community. One is to be the leader of new monks. The other
is to be an ordinary new member. Now I am appointing Kenne to
the head of purity [in charge of the toilets]. It is the second year of
the Ninji Era. You should respectfully attend the buddha ancestors
of the ten directions, whether you are the leader or one of the newly
arrived monks.

Once you present yourself, you are brand new. What is presenting? To forget great enlightenment. What is brand new? To be
greatly enlightened all of a sudden. Tell me now! How so? Do you
get it? Drop a coin in the river, and look for it in the river. Free
your horse at the foot of the mountain, and search for it at the foot
of the mountain.

Miracles

THE MIRACLES I AM SPEAKING OF are the daily activities of buddhas, which they do not neglect to practice. There are six miracles [freedom from the six sense desires], one miracle, going beyond miracles, and unsurpassable miracles. Miracles are practiced three thousand times in the morning and eight hundred times in the evening. Miracles arise simultaneously with buddhas, but are not known by buddhas. Miracles disappear with buddhas, but do not overwhelm buddhas.

Miracles occur throughout practice and enlightenment, whenever buddhas seek and teach, and wherever they search in the Himālayas or become a tree or a rock. When the buddhas before Shākyamuni Buddha appeared as his disciples, bringing a robe and a stūpa to him, he said, "This is a miracle caused by the inconceivable power of all buddhas." Thus we know that this miracle can also happen to buddhas now and to buddhas in the future.

GUISHAN IS THE thirty-seventh ancestor, a direct descendant of Shākyamuni Buddha. He was a dharma heir of Baizhang. Today, buddha ancestors in the ten directions, even those who do not call themselves descendants of Guishan, are all in fact his remote descendants.

One day while Guishan was lying down, Yangshan Huiji came to see him. Guishan turned around to face the wall.

Yangshan said, "I am your student. Please don't be formal." Guishan started to get up. Yangshan rose to leave.

Guishan said, "Huiji." Yangshan returned. Guishan said, "Let me tell you about my dream." Yangshan leaned forward to listen.

Guishan said simply, "Would you interpret my dream for me? I want to see how you do it." In response Yangshan brought a basin of water and a towel. Guishan washed his face and sat up. Then Xiangyan came in. Guishan said, "Huiji and I have been communicating intimately. This is no small matter."

Xiangyan said, "I was next door and heard you."

Guishan said to him, "Why don't you try now?" Xiangyan made a bowl of tea and brought it to him. Guishan praised them, saying, "You two students surpass even Shāriputra and Maudgalyā-yana with your miraculous activity!"

IF YOU WANT to understand buddhas' miracles, you should study Guishan's words. As "this is no small matter," to practice miracles is to study the buddha way. Not practicing miracles is not studying the buddha way. This miraculous activity is transmitted heir to heir. Do not study miracles from those outside the way, from the Two Lesser Vehicles, or from interpreters of sūtras.

When we study Guishan's miracles, we see that they were un-surpassable; each action was extraordinary. Beginning with Guishan lying down, there are: turning around to face the wall, getting up, calling "Huiji," talking about the dream, washing his face, and sitting up. Yangshan leaned forward to listen, then brought a basin of water and a towel. Then Guishan described this as: "Huiji and I have been communicating intimately." You should study these miracles.

These ancestors who correctly transmitted buddha-dharma talked in this way. Do not merely interpret it as Guishan expressing his dream by washing his face. You should regard their interaction as a series of miracles.

Guishan said, "This is no small matter." His understanding of miracles is different from that of practitioners who follow the Small Vehicles, have limited understanding, or hold lesser views. It is not the same as that of bodhisattvas of the ten stages and three classes. People of limited views study small miracles and attain limited understanding. They do not experience the great miracles of buddha ancestors.

These are miracles of buddhas, and miracles going beyond buddha. Those who study such miracles are beyond the reach of demons or those outside the way. Teachers and interpreters of sūtras have never heard of this teaching, nor would they have accepted it even if they had heard. Rather than studying great miracles, teachers and interpreters of sūtras, those outside the way, and practitioners of the Two Lesser Vehicles study lesser miracles.

Buddhas abide in and transmit great miracles, buddha miracles. Had it not been for buddha miracles, Yangshan would not have brought water and a towel and Guishan would not have turned to the wall while lying down, or sat up after washing his face.

Encompassed by the power of great miracles, lesser miracles occur. Great miracles include lesser miracles but lesser miracles do not know great miracles. Lesser miracles are a tuft of hair breathing in the vast ocean, a mustard seed storing Mt. Sumeru, the top of the head spouting water, or feet spreading fire.[1] Miracles like these are lesser miracles. Those who practice them never dream of buddha miracles. The reason I call them lesser miracles is that they are limited by circumstances and depend upon special practices and realizations. They may occur in this lifetime but not in another lifetime. They may be available to some people but not to others. They may appear in this land but not elsewhere. They may appear at times other than the present moment but not at the present moment.

Great miracles are not like that. The teaching, practice, and enlightenment of buddhas are all actualized through miracles. They are actualized not only in the realm of buddhas but also in the realm of going beyond buddhas. The transformative power of miracle buddhas is indeed beyond thinking. This power appears before the

---

1. In *The Lotus Sūtra*, there is a story that King Subhavyūha's two sons showed him the power of dharma by dancing in the air, shooting water out of their heads, shooting fire out of their feet, and expanding and shrinking their bodies.

buddha bodies appear, and is not concerned with past, present, or future. The aspiration, practice, enlightenment, and nirvāna of all the buddhas would not have appeared without buddha miracles.

In the inexhaustible ocean of the phenomenal world the power of great miracles is unchanging. A tuft of hair not only breathes in the great ocean [as in lesser miracles] but it maintains, realizes, breathes out, and utilizes the great ocean. When this activity arises, it encompasses the entire phenomenal world. However, do not assume that other activities do not also encompass the entire phenomenal world.

A mustard seed containing Mt. Sumeru is also like this. A mustard seed breathes out Mt. Sumeru and actualizes the inexhaustible phenomenal world. When a tuft of hair or a mustard seed breathes out a great ocean, breathing out happens in one moment, and it happens in myriad eons. Breathing out myriad eons and breathing out one moment happen simultaneously. How are a tuft of hair and a mustard seed brought forth? They are brought forth by great miracles. This bringing forth is a great miracle. What enables a tuft of hair and a mustard seed to do such things? Miracles enable them to do so. Miracles bring forth miracles. Do not think that miracles sometimes do and sometimes do not happen. Buddhas always abide in miracles.

LAYMAN PANGYUN was an outstanding person in the ancestral seat. He not only trained with Mazu and Shitou, but met and studied with many enlightened teachers. One day he said, "Miracles are nothing other than fetching water and carrying firewood."

You should thoroughly investigate the meaning of these words. Fetching water means to draw and carry water. Sometimes you do it yourself and sometimes you have others do it. Those who practice this are all miracle buddhas. Although miracles are noticed once in a while, miracles are miracles. It is not that things are eliminated or perish when they are unnoticed. Things are just as they are even when unnoticed. Even when people do not know that fetching water is a miracle, the fact that fetching water is a miracle is undeniable.

Carrying firewood means doing the labor of hauling, as in the time of Huineng, the Sixth Ancestor. Even if you do not know that miracles happen three thousand times in the morning and eight hundred times in the evening, miracles do happen. Those who see and hear the inconceivable function of miracles by buddha tathāgatas do not fail to attain the way. Attaining the way of all buddhas is always completed by the power of miracles.

Causing water to spout out of the head is a practice of the Lesser Vehicles. It is merely a minor miracle. On the other hand, fetching water, which Layman Pang speaks of, is a great miracle. The custom of fetching water and carrying firewood has not declined, as people have not ignored it. It has come down from ancient times to today, and it has been transmitted from there to here. Thus miracles have not ceased even for a moment. Such are great miracles, which are "no small matter."

DONGSHAN LIANGJIE, Great Master Wuben, was once attendant to Yunyan, who said, "Liangjie, what are miracles?"

Dongshan politely brought his hands together at his chest and stood near him.

Yunyan asked again, "What are miracles?"

Dongshan bid farewell and walked away.

In this story words are heard and the meaning of miracles is understood. There is merging, like box and cover joining. You should know that it is a miracle to have a disciple like Dongshan who does not veer off, or to have a high ancestor like Yunyan who does not come forward. Do not think that the miracles they are speaking of are the same as those taught outside the way or in the Two Lesser Vehicles.

On the road of buddhas there are also great miracles that happen at the top or bottom of the body. The entire world of ten directions is the true body of a single monk. Thus, the Nine Mountains and the Eight Oceans around Mt. Sumeru, as well as the ocean of thusness and the ocean of wisdom, are no other than water spouting from the top, bottom, and center of the body. It is also water spouting from the top, bottom, and center of the formless body. The spouting out of fire is also like this.

Not only is there the spouting out of water, fire, and air, but also there is the spouting out of buddhas from the top and bottom of the body. There is the spouting of ancestors from the top and bottom of the body. There is the spouting of immeasurable eons from the top and bottom of the body. There is also the spouting out of the ocean of the phenomenal world and the swallowing of the ocean of the phenomenal world from the top of the body. To spit out the lands of the world seven or eight times and to swallow them two or three times is also like this. The four, five, or six great elements,* all elements, and immeasurable elements, are also great miracles that appear and disappear, are spit out and swallowed. The great earth and empty space are miracles that are swallowed and spit out.

Miracles have the power of being activated by a mustard seed and of responding to a tuft of hair. Miracles arise, abide, and return to the source beyond the reach of consciousness. The realm of buddha miracles is beyond long or short—how can this be measured by discriminatory thinking?

LONG AGO when a sorcerer who had the five miraculous powers was attending the Buddha, he asked, "You have six miraculous powers and I have five. What is the one I am missing?"

The Buddha called to him, "Sorcerer."

"Yes," he responded.

The Buddha said, "What miraculous power are you asking about?"

You should thoroughly study the meaning of this dialogue. How did the sorcerer know that the Buddha had six miraculous powers? The Buddha has immeasurable miraculous wisdom, which is not limited to six miraculous powers. Even if you see six miraculous powers you cannot master them. How can those who have lesser miraculous powers dream of the Buddha's six miraculous powers?

You should say, "When the sorcerer saw Old Man Shākyamuni,

did he actually see the Buddha? When he saw the Buddha, did he actually see Old Man Shākyamuni? If the sorcerer saw Old Man Shākyamuni and saw the Buddha, did he also see himself, the sorcerer of the five miraculous powers?"

You should study the words of the sorcerer's questions and study going beyond the words of this dialogue. Isn't this question about the Buddha's six miraculous powers like counting the treasure of a neighbor? What is the meaning of Old Man Shākyamuni's words, "What miraculous power are you asking about?" He did not say whether the sorcerer had this miraculous power or not. Even if Old Man Shākyamuni had spoken about it how would the sorcerer have understood the single miraculous power? Although the sorcerer had five miraculous powers, they are not the same as the five miraculous powers of the Buddha.

Although the sorcerer's powers may look like those of the Buddha, how can his powers compare with those of the Buddha? If the sorcerer attained even one of the Buddha's powers, he could reach the Buddha by this power. When we see the sorcerer he had powers similar to the Buddha's, and when we see the Buddha he had powers similar to the sorcerer's. But the sorcerer did not have the Buddha's miraculous powers. If one of the sorcerer's powers could not reach one of the Buddha's powers, none of his five powers could be equal to those of the Buddha. So what is the use of asking the Buddha, "What miraculous power am I missing?" Old man Shākyamuni thought the sorcerer should have asked about the powers the sorcerer already had. The sorcerer had not even mastered one of those powers. In this way the Buddha's miraculous powers and other people's miraculous powers look alike but in fact are completely different.

ABOUT THE BUDDHA'S six types of miracles, Linji, Great Master Huizhao, said, "According to an old teacher, the excellent marks of the Buddha Tathāgata's body are listed to accommodate the needs of people's minds. To counter the common tendency toward nihilistic views, such provisional names as the thirty-two marks or the eighty appearances of the Buddha are used as expedient means. But they are imaginary concepts. Such a body is itself not awakening. Having no form is the Buddha's true form.

"You say that the Buddha's six types of miracles are wondrous. Devas, sorcerers, fighting spirits, and demons also have miraculous powers. Are they buddhas? Fellows of the way, do not be mistaken. A spirit defeated by Indra took his eighty-four thousand retainers and hid inside a lotus stem. Do you call this a miracle?

"The miracles I have described of these devas, sorcerers, fighting spirits, and demons are the result of past actions or present skills. But the six types of miracles of a buddha are different. A buddha enters forms, sounds, smells, tastes, touchables, and objects of mind and is not confused by them. Thus a buddha masters the six sense objects, which are all marked with emptiness. A buddha is free of conditions. Even having a body of five *skandhas** accompanied by desires, a buddha does not depend on anything. A buddha practices miracles that are grounded on the earth.

"Fellows of the way, a true buddha has no form, and the true dharma has no marks. From your mind's illusions, marks and appearances are created. What you get is a wild fox's spirit, which is the view of those outside of the way, and not of a true buddha."

Thus, the six types of miracles of the buddhas cannot be reached by those of the Two Lesser Vehicles, or of devas or demons. The six types of miracles of the buddha way cannot be measured. They are only transmitted to disciples of the buddha way, person to person, but not to others. Those who have not inherited such miracles do not know them. Those who have not inherited such miracles are not persons of the buddha way.

BAIZHANG, Zen Master Dazhi, said, "The eyes, ears, nose, and tongue are not defiled by form or formlessness. This nondefiling is called receiving the four lines of a verse of vows and receiving the four fruits of the arhats.* Leaving no trace in the six sense organs is called the six types of miracles. Not to be hindered by either form or formlessness, and not to depend on intellectual understanding, are miracles. Not abiding in these miracles is called 'going beyond miracles.' A bodhisattva who goes beyond miracles does not leave

traces. This is a person going beyond buddha. It is a most inconceivable person, an uncreated self."

The miracles transmitted by buddha ancestors are as Baizhang
described. A miracle buddha is one who goes beyond buddha, a
most inconceivable person, the uncreated self, a bodhisattva of
going beyond miracles. Miracles do not depend upon intellectual
understanding, do not abide in themselves, and are not hindered by
form and formlessness. There are the six types of miracles in the
buddha way, which have been maintained by buddhas ceaselessly.
There has not been a single buddha who has not maintained them.
Those who do not maintain them are not buddhas. These six types
of miracles leave no trace in the six sense organs.

An old teacher [Yongjia] said, "The six types of miracles are
neither empty nor not empty. A circle of light is neither inside nor
outside."

"Neither inside nor outside" means leaving no trace. When you
practice, study, and realize no-trace, you are not disturbed by the
six sense organs. Those who are disturbed should receive thirty
blows.* The six types of miracles should be studied like this. How
can those who are not authentic heirs of the buddha house learn
about this? They mistakenly regard running around inside and outside as the practice of returning home.

"The four fruits of the arhat" mentioned by Baizhang are the
essentials of the buddha way. But no teachers of the scriptures have
correctly transmitted them. How can those who study letters or
wander in remote lands receive these fruits? Those who are satisfied
with minor achievements cannot master them. The four fruits are
transmitted only by buddha and buddha. The so-called four fruits
are to receive four lines of verse, and this means that eyes, ears,
nose, and tongue are undefiled in all things. Undefiled means unstained. Unstained means undivided mind—"I am always intimate
with this."*

The six types of miracles and the four fruits have been correctly
transmitted in this manner. Anything different from this is not
buddha-dharma. Thus, the buddha-dharma is invariably actualized
through miracles. When actualized, a drop of water swallows the

great ocean, and a speck of dust hurls out a high mountain. Who can doubt that these are miracles?

On the sixteenth day, the eleventh month, the second year of the Ninji Era [1241], this was presented to the assembly of the Kannondōri Kōshō Hōrin Monastery.

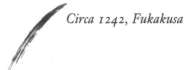
Circa 1242, Fukakusa

Continuous Practice, Fascicle One

On the great road of buddha ancestors there is always unsurpassable practice, continuous and sustained. It forms the circle of the way and is never cut off. Between aspiration, practice, enlightenment, and nirvāna there is not a moment's gap; continuous practice is the circle of the way. This being so, continuous practice is unstained, not forced by you or others. The power of this continuous practice confirms you as well as others. It means your practice affects the entire earth and the entire sky in the ten directions. Although not noticed by others or by yourself, it is so.

Accordingly, by the continuous practice of all buddhas and ancestors, your practice is actualized and your great road opens up. By your continuous practice, the continuous practice of all buddhas is actualized and the great road of all buddhas opens up. Your continuous practice creates the circle of the way. By this practice, buddha ancestors abide as buddha, nonabide as buddha, have buddha mind, and attain buddha without cutting off.

Because of this practice, there are the sun, the moon, and the stars. Because of this practice, there are the great earth and the open sky. Because of this practice, there are body, mind, and their environs. Because of this practice, there are the four great elements and the five skandhas. Continuous practice is not necessarily some-

thing people in the world love, but it should be the true place of
return for everyone. Because of the continuous practice of all buddhas of past, present, and future, all buddhas of past, present, and
future are actualized.

The effect of such sustained practice is sometimes not hidden.
Therefore you aspire to practice. The effect is sometimes not apparent. Therefore you may not see, hear, or know it. You should
understand that although it is not revealed, it is not hidden.

As it is not stained by what is hidden, apparent, existent, or not
existent, you may not notice the causal conditions that led you to
be engaged in the practice that actualizes you at this very moment
of unknowing. The reason you don't see it is that becoming conscious of it is not anything remarkable. You should investigate in
detail that it is so because the causal condition [the aspiration] is no
other than continuous practice, but continuous practice is not limited by the causal condition.

Continuous practice that actualizes itself is no other than your
continuous practice right now. The now of this practice is not originally possessed by the self. The now of this practice does not come
and go, enter and depart. The word "now" does not exist before
continuous practice. The moment when it is actualized is called
now. This being so, your continuous practice of this day is a seed
of all buddhas and the practice of all buddhas. All buddhas are actualized and sustained by your continuous practice.

By not sustaining your continuous practice, you would be
excluding buddhas, not nurturing buddhas, excluding continuous
practice, not being born and dying simultaneously with all buddhas,
and not studying and practicing with all buddhas. Blossoms opening
and leaves falling now is the actualization of continuous practice.
Polishing a mirror and breaking a mirror is not other than this
practice.

Even if you might try to ignore it in order to hide a crooked
intention and escape from it, this ignoring would also be continuous
practice. To go off here and there looking for continuous practice
appears similar to the aspiration for it. But it is like leaving behind
the treasure at the home of your true father and wandering poor in

another land. Wandering through wind and water at the risk of your life, you should not discard the treasure of your own father. While you were searching in this way, the dharma treasure would be missed. This being so, continuous practice should not slacken even for a moment.

COMPASSIONATE FATHER, Great Teacher Shākyamuni Buddha, was engaged in continuous practice in the deep mountains from the time he was nineteen years old. At age thirty, after practicing continuously, he attained the way simultaneously with all sentient beings and the great earth. Until he was in his eighties, his practice was sustained in mountains, forests, and monasteries. He did not return to the imperial palace nor did he claim any property. He wore the same robes and held the same bowls throughout his lifetime. From the time he began teaching he was not alone even for a day or for an hour. He did not selfishly receive offerings from humans and devas. He was patient with the criticism of people outside the way. The Buddha wore the pure robes and begged for food; his lifetime of teaching was nothing but continuous practice.

Mahākāshyapa is Shākyamuni Buddha's heir. Throughout his lifetime he was engaged without negligence in the twelve ascetic practices: Not to accept invitations from people. To practice begging daily. Not to receive money as an alternative for food. To stay on mountains and not in villages or towns. Not to ask for or accept clothing, but to take clothing from the dead in cemeteries, and to sew and dye the cloth for robes. To take shelter under a tree in the field. To have one meal a day, which is called *ekāsanika*. Not to lie down day or night, but to practice walking meditation and sleep sitting up. This is called *naishadika*. To hold three robes and nothing more, and not to lie down with a robe on. To live in cemeteries rather than in monasteries or houses; to sit zazen and seek for the way while gazing at skeletons. To seek out a solitary place, with no desire to lie down with or to be close to others. To eat fruit before the meal and not after. To sit in an open space and not desire to sleep under a tree or in a house. Not to eat meat or cream and not to rub the body with flax oil.

These are called the twelve ascetic practices. Venerable Mahā-kāshyapa did not turn back or deviate from them throughout his lifetime. Even after correctly receiving the Tathāgata's treasury of the true dharma eye, he did not retire from these practices.

Once the Buddha said, "You are old now. You should eat like the rest of the monks."

Mahākāshyapa said, "If I had not encountered the Tathāgata, I would have remained a self-enlightened buddha, living in mountains and forests. Fortunately I have met the Tathāgata. This is a beneficent gift of dharma. Thus, I cannot forego my ascetic practice and eat like the rest of the monks."

The Tathāgata admired his determination. At another time Mahākāshyapa looked exhausted because of his ascetic practices and the monks looked down on him. Then the Tathāgata graciously called Mahākāshyapa up to him and offered him half of his seat. Thus Mahākāshyapa sat on the Tathāgata's seat. You should know that Mahākāshyapa was the most senior monk in the assembly of the Buddha. It is impossible to list all the practices of his lifetime.

VENERABLE PĀRSHVA, the Tenth Ancestor, did not lay himself down on his side to sleep throughout his lifetime. Although he started his practice in his eighties, he soon received the great dharma, one to one. As he did not waste a moment, within three years he received the true eye of complete enlightenment.

Pārshva was in his mother's womb for sixty years and was born with long, gray hair. As he had a vow not to lay himself down on his side to sleep, he was called Venerable Undefiled Sides. In order to pick up a sūtra in the dark, he would radiate his inner light, an ability he had from birth.

When Pārshva was about to give up his household and wear a monk's robe at the age of eighty, a young boy in the town criticized him saying, "You are ignorant. What you are going to do doesn't make sense. Monks maintain two types of practice: learning samādhi and chanting. You are too old and frail to learn these things. You will only confuse the pure stream and eat monks' food in vain."

Hearing this criticism, he thanked the boy and reaffirmed his vow: "Until I master the Tripitaka, become free of desires in the three worlds, achieve the six miraculous powers, and attain the eight types of emancipation, I will not lie down on my side."

After that he did not skip even one day of contemplation while walking, sitting, and standing. During the day he studied the teachings and at night he practiced tranquil concentration. After three years he mastered the Tripitaka. He became free of desires in the three worlds and attained proficiency in the three types of knowledge.

Thus Pārshva was in his mother's womb for sixty years before his birth. Did he seek the way in the womb? Eighty years after his birth, he left his household to study the way. It was one hundred and forty years after he was conceived. Although outstanding, he was older and more frail than anyone else. In the womb he was old and at birth he was old. However, he did not mind people's criticisms and had unrelenting determination. That's why after only three years his endeavor to attain the way was fulfilled. Upon seeing the wise and being inspired by them, how could we be slack in our endeavor? We should not be hindered by old age and frailty.

Birth is hard to fathom. Is this birth or not birth? Is this old age or not? The views of water by four types of beings vary. We should just focus our aspiration and endeavor on the practice of the way. We should understand that the practice of the way is no other than seeing into birth and death. Yet our practice is not bound by birth and death.

It is extremely foolish of people nowadays to put aside endeavor of the way when they become fifty or sixty years old, even seventy or eighty. If we are concerned about how many months and years we have lived, this is merely a limited human view, which has nothing to do with the study of the way. Do not consider whether you are in your prime or old and frail. You should single-mindedly aspire to study and master the way, standing shoulder to shoulder with Pārshva. Do not look back or cling to a heap of dust in the graveyard. If you do not have single-minded aspiration and are not awakened, who would pity you? You should practice to gain sight just as you would be adding eyeballs to a skeleton lying in the wilderness.

* * *

HUINENG, the Sixth Ancestor in China, was a woodcutter from Xin Region who could hardly be called learned. He had lost his father when very young and had been brought up by his old mother. He worked as a woodcutter to support her. Upon hearing a phrase from a sūtra at the crossroads in town, he left his mother and set out in search of dharma. He was a great vessel, rare for any time, an outstanding practitioner of the way. Separating from his loving mother must have been more difficult than cutting off his own arm; setting aside his filial obligation was not lightly done.

Throwing himself into Hongren's assembly, he pounded rice day and night for eight months without sleep or rest. He received the authentic transmission of the robe and bowl at midnight. After being entrusted with the dharma he continued to pound rice for eight years, traveling with a grinding stone on his back. Even after he emerged in the world and expounded dharma to awaken people, he did not neglect this grinding stone. His continuous practice was rare in the world.

Mazu from Jiangxi did zazen for twenty years and received the intimate seal from Nanyue. Thus, Mazu did not say anything that might discourage anyone from practicing zazen when expounding dharma and saving people. Whenever new students arrived, he would allow them to intimately receive the mind seal. He was always the first one to engage in communal work and was not lax even when he was old. The current school of Linji is descended from Mazu.

Yunyan and Daowu both studied with Yaoshan. Together they made a vow to study single-mindedly without laying their sides on the platform for forty years. Yunyan transmitted dharma to Dongshan, Great Master Wuben. Dongshan said, "Twenty years ago I wanted to be just one piece, and I have been engaged in zazen ever since." Nowadays this statement is widely acclaimed.

Yunju, Great Master Hongjue, was always served food by a heavenly being when he was living in his Sanfeng Hut. During that time Yunju went to study with Dongshan, under whose teaching he settled the great matter of the way and returned to his hut. When the heavenly being brought food again, he looked for Yunju for three days but could not see him. Without depending on heavenly offerings, Yunju was fully dedicating himself to the great way. You should ponder his aspiration for practice.

Baizhang, Zen Master Dazhi, from the time when he was the attendant to Mazu until he died, did not let a single day pass without working for the assembly or for others. He graciously gave us the model of "A day of no work is a day of no eating." When Baizhang was old he labored just like those in their prime. The assembly was concerned for him but he did not stop working. At last some students hid the tools from him during the work period. He refused to eat that day, expressing his regret that he could not join the assembly's communal work. This is Baizhang's exemplification of "A day of no work is a day of no eating." The wind of the Linji School which is now widely spread in Song China, as well as the wind of the other schools, represents the continuous practice of Baizhang's profound teaching.

When Priest Jingqing was abbot of his monastery, he was so inconspicuous that the deities of the region never saw his face, nor did they even hear about him.

Sanping, Zen Master Yizhong, used to receive meals that were delivered by devas. After encountering his teacher Dadian, Sanping could no longer be found by the devas.

Changqing Daan was called the Later Guishan. He said, "I lived on Mt. Gui for twenty years. I ate Mt. Gui's rice and shit Mt. Gui's shit. I was not studying the words of Ancestor Guishan [Lingyou] but was just taming a water buffalo, wandering around all day long."

You should know that raising a single water buffalo is the sustained practice of living on Mt. Gui for twenty years. Ancestor Guishan had studied in the assembly of Baizhang. You should quietly think about and remember Changqing's activities of those twenty years. There are many who study Guishan's words, but the continuous practice of "not studying the words of Ancestor Guishan" is rare.

*   *   *

ZHAOZHOU, Priest Congshen, Great Master Zhenji of the Guanyin Monastery, first aroused the bodhi-seeking mind at the age of
sixty-one. He traveled around, carrying a water gourd and a staff
with metal rings on top. He told himself, "I will inquire about
dharma of anyone who excels me, even a seven-year-old child. I will
teach dharma to anyone who has less understanding, even a hun-
dred-year-old."

Thus he studied and understood Nanquan's way and his words.
It was an endeavor of twenty years. Finally when he was eighty
years old, he became abbot of the Guanyin Monastery, east of the
city of Zhaozhou [Zhau Province]. After that he guided humans
and devas for forty years.

Zhaozhou did not write a single letter of request to donors. The
monks' hall was small and without front or back platforms. Once a
leg of Zhaozhou's teaching chair broke. He replaced it with a
charred stick from the fireplace, tying it on with a rope, and taught
from it for many years. When an officer asked for permission to get
a new leg, he did not allow it. You should follow the spirit of this
old buddha.

Zhaozhou became abbot after receiving dharma transmission in
his eighties. This was correct transmission of the true dharma. People called him Old Buddha. Those who have not yet received true
transmission of the dharma are lightweights compared with Zhaozhou. Those of you who are younger than eighty may be more
active than Zhaozhou. But how can you younger lightweights be
equal to him even in his old age? Keeping this in mind, you should
strive in the path of continuous practice.

During the forty years Zhaozhou taught, he did not store
worldly property. There was not a grain of rice in the monastery.
So the monks would pick up chestnuts and acorns for food, and
they would adjust the meal time to fit the situation. Indeed this was
the spirit of the dragons and elephants of the past. You should long
for such practice.

Zhaozhou once said to the assembly, "If you do not leave the
monastery in your lifetime and do not speak for five or ten years,

no one can call you speechless. Even buddhas would not know what to make of you."

Zhaozhou expresses sustained practice in this way. You should know that "not to speak for five or ten years" may have the appearance of being speechless, but because of the merit of "not leaving the monastery," not speaking is not the same as being speechless. The buddha way is like this. One who is capable of speaking but doesn't speak is not like an ordinary person who has not heard the voice of the way. Thus, unsurpassable continuous practice is "not leaving the monastery." Not leaving the monastery is total speech that is dropping off. Most people do not know or speak of "going beyond speechless." No one keeps them from speaking of it, but nevertheless they don't speak of it. They do not discover or understand that to go beyond speechlessness is to express thusness. How regrettable!

You should quietly engage in the sustained practice of "not leaving the monastery." Do not be swayed east or west by the winds of east and west. The spring breeze and the autumn moon of five or ten years, unbeknownst to us, have the ring of emancipation beyond sound and form. This voice is not known to the self, not understood by the self. You should learn to treasure each moment of sustained practice. Do not assume that not to speak is useless. It is entering the monastery, leaving the monastery. The bird's path is the forest. The entire world is the forest, the monastery.

MT. DAMEI IS in Qingyuan Prefecture. Zen Master Fachang from Xiangyang founded the Husheng Monastery on this mountain. When Fachang was studying in the assembly of Mazu, he asked him, "What is buddha?"

Mazu said, "Mind is buddha." Upon hearing these words Fachang had realization.

Fachang climbed to the top of Mt. Damei and dwelt there in a hut. He ate pine cones and wore lotus leaves, as there were many lotus plants in a small pond on that mountain. He practiced zazen for over thirty years and was completely detached from human affairs. Without paying attention to which day it was, he only saw the green and yellow of the surrounding mountains. Those were rugged years.

During zazen he set an iron stūpa eight *cun* [about ten inches] in height on his head. It was like wearing a jeweled crown. As his intention was not to let the stūpa fall down, he would not sleep. This stūpa is still kept in the kitchen of the Husheng Monastery. He practiced in this way continuously, without slackening.

After many years a monk from the assembly of Yanquan went to the mountain looking for wood to make a staff. He lost his way and after a while found himself in front of Fachang's hut. Seeing Fachang he asked, "How long have you been on this mountain?"

Fachang said, "I have seen nothing but the green and yellow of the surrounding mountains."

The monk said, "How do I get off this mountain?"

Fachang said, "Follow the stream." Mystified by Fachang, the monk went back and told Yanquan about him.

Yanquan said, "When I was in Jiangxi, I saw a monk like that but I haven't heard of him since. This might be him." Yanquan sent the monk to Fachang and invited him to come to the monastery. Fachang would not leave the mountain but responded with a poem:

A decayed tree remains in the cold forest.
Meeting springs, there is no change of mind.
Woodcutters see me, but I ignore them.
How come the wood master seeks me out?

Fachang stayed on the mountain. Later, when he was about to move deeper into the mountain, he wrote this poem:

Wearing lotus leaves from this pond, I have an inexhaustible
    supply.
Eating pine nuts from several trees, I have still more left.
Having been spotted by people from the world
I am moving my hut further away.

So he moved his abode. Later his teacher Mazu sent a monk to Fachang to ask him, "Reverend, when you studied with Mazu, what did you understand that led you to live on this mountain?"

Fachang said, "Mazu said to me, 'Mind is buddha.' That's why I am living here."

The monk said, "Nowadays buddha-dharma is different."

Fachang said, "How is it different?"

The monk said, "Mazu says, 'Not mind, not buddha.' "

Fachang said, "That old man always confuses people. Let it be 'not mind, not buddha.' As for me, mind is no other than buddha."

The monk brought Fachang's response to Mazu.

Mazu said, "The plum is ripe."

This story is widely known among humans and devas. Tianlong is Fachang's excellent student. Tianlong's heir Juzhi is Fachang's dharma grandchild. Kaji of Korea transmitted Fachang's dharma and became the first ancestor of his country. All masters in Korea are dharma descendants of Fachang.

While Fachang was alive a tiger and an elephant attended him without contending with each other. After he died the tiger and elephant carried rocks and mud to help erect a tower for him. This tower still exists in the Husheng Monastery.

Fachang's sustained practice has been admired by teachers both past and present. Those who do not appreciate him lack wisdom. To suppose that buddha-dharma is present in the pursuit of fame and gain is a limited and foolish view.

ZEN MASTER Wuzu Fayan said, "When Yangqi Fanghui became abbot of Yangqi, the monastery buildings were old and dilapidated, barely able to provide shelter from wind and rain. It was deep winter and all the buildings were badly in need of repair. The monks' hall in particular was damaged to the point where snow and hail would pile up on the sitting platforms and there was hardly any place to settle down. It was very hard to do zazen there. The elders of the monastery were so concerned that they made a request to Yangqi to have the buildings repaired.

"Yangqi said, 'According to the Buddha's teaching, this is the time when the human life-span is decreasing, and the high lands and the deep valleys are always changing. How can we achieve complete satisfaction in all things? Sages in the past sat under trees and did walking meditation on bare ground. These are excellent examples, the profound teaching of practicing emptiness. You have left the household to study the way and are not yet accustomed to the daily activities with hands and legs. You are only forty or fifty years old. How can you have the leisure to enjoy a comfortable building?' Thus Yangqi did not approve their request. On the following day, he sat on the teaching seat and presented this poem to the assembly:

"When I began living here in this building with crumbling
    walls,
all the platforms were covered by jewels of snow.
Scrunching up my shoulders to my neck, I exhaled into
    darkness,
reflecting on the ancient one abiding under a tree.

"Even though the monks' hall was still in disrepair, monks in cloud robes and mist sleeves from the Four Seas and Five Lakes of China wanted to practice in Yangqi's assembly. We should be joyous that there were so many who were immersed in the way. You should dye your mind with his words and inscribe them in your ears."

Later Fayan gave instruction, saying, "Practice does not go beyond thinking. Thinking does not go beyond practice."

You should take this teaching seriously, thinking of it day and night and putting it into practice morning and evening. Do not be like those who are blown about by winds from east, west, south, and north.

IN JAPAN even the Imperial Palace is not a magnificent edifice, but is built of coarse plain wood. How can monks who study the way live in a luxurious building? Such a building can only be acquired by devious means; cases of acquisition through pure means are rare. I am not discussing something you may already possess. But do not try to acquire something luxurious. Grass huts or plain wooden hermitages were abodes loved by ancient sages. Those who study nowadays should long for and study this simplicity.

Although the Yellow Emperor, Emperor Xiao, and Emperor Shun were worldly monarchs, they lived in grass huts. They set excellent examples for the world. *Shizhi* says, "If you want to know the deeds of the Yellow Emperor, you should see his abode called the He Palace. If you want to see the deeds of Emperors Xiao and Shun, you should see their Courts of Affairs of State. The Yellow Emperor's abode was roofed with grass. That is why it was called the Thatched Palace. Xiao and Shun's courts were also roofed with grass. And it was called the Headquarters."

Keep in mind that these palaces were thatched with grass. If we compare ourselves to the Yellow Emperor, Emperor Xiao, or Emperor Shun, the gap is wider than that between heaven and earth. Those emperors made thatched-roof buildings their quarters. If lay people could live in grass huts, how should monks make tall buildings with breathtaking views their abode? It would be shameful. People of old lived under trees in the forest. Both lay people and home-leavers love such places.

The Yellow Emperor was a disciple of a Daoist named Guang-cheng, who lived in a grotto called Kongdong. Many kings and ministers of Great Song China still follow his example. Knowing that people in the dusty realms lived humbly, how can home-leavers be more worldly or more murky than they?

Among the buddha ancestors of the past, many received offerings from devas. However, after they attained the way, the devas' celestial eyes could not see them and demonic spirits could no longer communicate with them. You should be aware of this.

When devas and gods follow the practice of buddha ancestors, they have a way to approach them. But when buddha ancestors actualize going beyond, devas and gods have no way to find and come close to them. So Nanquan said, "As I lack the power of practice, a spirit is able to find me." You should know from this that to be seen by spirits means that your power of practice is lacking.

The guardian spirit of the monastery buildings at Mt. Tiantong said to Hongzhi, Abbot Zhengjue, "I know that you have been abbot of this monastery for over ten years. But whenever I go to see you in your sleeping quarters, I cannot quite reach you." This is indeed an example of someone who was engaged in the way. The monastery on Mt. Tiantong was originally a small practice place. When Hongzhi was abbot, he removed the Daoist temple, the nunnery, and the scriptural seminary and turned it into the current Jingde Monastery.

After Hongzhi died, Wang Boxiang, the imperial historian, was writing a biography of Hongzhi. Someone said, "You should record that Hongzhi plundered the Daoist temple, the nunnery, and the scriptural seminary and turned the compound into the current Jingde Monastery." Boxiang said, "It should not be recorded because it is not a meritorious thing for a monk to do." The people of his time agreed with Boxiang.

Know that such a deed by Hongzhi is what a worldly person might tend to value but it should not be seen as the achievement of a monk. Upon entering the buddha way, you go beyond the humans and devas of the three worlds, and are no longer measured by the standards of those in the three realms. Examine this closely. Study it thoroughly involving body, speech, mind, and your surroundings. The continuous practice of buddha ancestors has a great power to awaken both humans and devas, who, however, may not notice that they are helped by it.

IN THE CONTINUOUS PRACTICE of the way of buddha ancestors, you should not be concerned about whether you are a great or modest hermit, whether you are brilliant or dull. Just forsake name and gain forever and don't be bound by myriad conditions. Do not waste the passing time. Put out the fire on top of your head. Do not wait for great enlightenment, as great enlightenment is the tea and rice of daily activity. Do not wish for nonenlightenment, as nonenlightenment is a jewel concealed in your hair.

If you have a home, leave your home. If you have beloved ones, leave them. If you have fame, abandon it. If you have gain, escape from it. If you have fields, get rid of them. If you have relatives, separate from them. If you don't have name and gain, stay away from them. Why should you not remain free from them, while those who already have name and gain need to give them up? This is the single track of continuous practice.

To forsake name and gain in this lifetime and practice one thing thoroughly is the vast continuous practice of the Buddha's timeless life. This continuous practice is bound to be sustained by continuous practice. Love and respect your body, mind, and self that are engaged in this continuous practice.

Priest Daci, Zen Master Huanzhong, said, "Speaking ten feet does not compare with practicing one foot. Speaking one foot does not compare with practicing one inch."

It may appear that Daci was warning the people of his day not to ignore continuous practice and not to forget about mastering the buddha way. However, he was not saying that speaking ten feet is of no value, but rather that the practice of one foot has greater power. The comparison between speech and practice is not limited to one foot or ten feet. It is also like Mt. Sumeru and a poppy seed. Sumeru reveals its entire size. A poppy seed reveals its entire size. The great point of continuous practice is like this. These are not simply the words of Daci but the words of the Huanzhong [Boundless World].

Dongshan, Great Master Wuben, said, "Speak what cannot be practiced. Practice what cannot be spoken." These are words spoken by the high ancestor. It means that practice clarifies the way to speech and there is a way that speech approaches practice. This being so, you practice all day while speaking all day. You practice what cannot be practiced and you speak what cannot be spoken.

Yunju, Great Master Hongjue, investigating Dongshan's words seven or eight ways, said, "At the time of speaking, there is no road of practice. At the time of practicing, there is no path of speaking." His words show that there is neither practicing nor speaking. At the time of speaking, you do not leave the monastery for your lifetime. At the time of practicing, you wash the head and request Xuefeng to shave it.[1] You should not waste the time of speaking or the time of practicing.

BUDDHA ANCESTORS have said since ancient times, "Living for one hundred years without encountering a buddha does not compare with living for one day and arousing determination for the way."

These are not merely the words of one or two buddhas, they have been spoken and practiced by all buddhas. Within the cycles of birth and death for myriad *kalpas*,* one day of continuous practice is a bright jewel in the banded hair, the ancient mirror of all-inclusive birth and all-inclusive death. It is a day of rejoicing. The power of continuous practice is itself rejoicing.

When the power of your continuous practice is not sufficient and you have not received the bones and marrow of buddha ancestors, you are not valuing the body-mind of buddha ancestors, nor are you taking joy in the face of buddha ancestors. Although the face, bones, and marrow of buddha ancestors are beyond going and not going, beyond coming and not coming, they are always transmitted through one day's continuous practice. Therefore, each day is valuable. A hundred years lived in vain is a regrettable passage of time, a remorseful life as a living corpse. But even if you run around as a servant of sound and form for a hundred years, if you attain one day of continuous practice, you not only attain the practice of one hundred years, but you awaken others for a hundred years. The living body of this one day is a living body to revere, a form to revere. If you live for one day merged with the activity of the buddhas, this one day is considered as excellent as many kalpas of lifetimes.

1. This refers to the following story: A student of Xuefeng asked a hermit who lived nearby, growing his hair long, "What is the meaning of Bodhidharma coming from India?" The hermit said, "This valley is deep and my dipper is long." The monk bowed and reported this to Xuefeng. Xuefeng went to the hermitage with his attendant monk, bringing a razor. Xuefeng said to the hermit, "Say something, or I will shave your head." The hermit washed his head and presented himself to Xuefeng.

Even when you are uncertain, do not use this one day waste-
fully. It is a rare treasure to value. Do not compare it with an enormous jewel. Do not compare it with a dragon's bright pearl. Old
sages valued this one day more than their own living bodies. Reflect
on this quietly. A dragon's pearl may be found. An enormous jewel
may be acquired. But this one day out of a hundred years cannot be
retrieved once it is lost. What skillful means can retrieve a day that
is passed? No historical documents have recorded any such means.
Not to waste time is to contain the passage of days and months
within your skin bag, without leaking. Thus, sages and wise ones in
olden times valued each moment, day, and month more than their
own eyeballs or the nation's land. To waste the passage of time is to
be confused and stained in the floating world of name and gain.
Not to miss the passage of time is to be in the way for the way.

Once you have clarity, do not neglect a single day. Wholeheartedly practice for the sake of the way and speak for the sake of the
way. We know that buddha ancestors of old did not neglect each
day's endeavor. You should reflect on this every day. Sit near a
bright window and reflect on this, on mellow and flower-filled days.
Sit in a plain building and remember it on a solitary rainy evening.
Why do the moments of time steal your endeavor? They not only
steal one day but steal the merit of many kalpas. What kind of
enemy is the passage of time? How regrettable! Your loss of time
would be all because of your negligence of practice. If you were not
intimate with yourself, you would resent yourself.

It is not that buddha ancestors lacked family obligations and
attachments, but they abandoned them. It is not that buddha ancestors were not bound by relationships, but they let them go. Even if
you are bound by relationships, you cannot keep them. If you do
not throw away family obligations and attachments, the family obligations and attachments will throw you. If you want to cherish the
family obligations and attachments, then cherish them. To cherish
the family obligations and attachments means to be free from them.

NANYUE, Priest Huairang, Zen Master Dahui, went to study with
Huineng, the Sixth Ancestor, and was his attendant for fifteen years.

He received the way and the craft, just like receiving a vessel of water from another. Such an example from olden times should be longed for.

There must have been a lot of hardship during the wind and frost of those fifteen years. In spite of it Nanyue single-heartedly pursued his investigation. This is a mirror for later generations. Without charcoal in the cold stove, he slept alone in an empty hall. Without lamplight on summer evenings, he sat at a window by himself. Not having one piece of knowledge or a half of understanding, he reached the place of no effort, going beyond study. This is no other than continuous practice. As Nanyue had subtly abandoned greed for name and love for gain, he simply accumulated the power of continuous practice day by day. You should not forget the meaning of this. His statement to Huineng, "Speaking about it won't hit the mark," is his continuous practice of eight years.[2] Such continuous practice is rare throughout past and present, aspired to by those who are wise and by those who are not.

Xiangyan, Zen Master Zhixian, cultivated the way with Guishan. When Xiangyan tried to come up with one phrase of understanding, he could not utter it even after trying several times. In anguish, he burned his sūtras and books of commentary, and for many years he took up the practice of serving meals. Later he climbed up Mt. Wudang to visit the remains of National Teacher Nanyang and built a retreat hut there. One day when he was sweeping the path, a pebble flew up and struck a bamboo. At the crack he was suddenly enlightened.

Later he became abbot of Xiangyan Monastery and maintained the practice of one bowl and one robe. He lived his life discreetly in this monastery of extraordinary rocks and clear springs, and rarely left the mountain. Many spots where he practiced are still there.

2. Huineng said, "Where are you from?" Nanyue said, "From Mt. Song." Huineng said, "What is this that thus comes?" Nanyue said, "Speaking about it won't hit the mark." Huineng said, "Does it rest on practice and realization?" Nanyue said, "It is not that there is no practice and no realization; it is just that they cannot be defiled." Then Huineng said, "This nondefilement has been guarded by all buddhas. You are like this and I am like this."

* * *

LINJI, Great Master Huizhao, was an heir of Huangbo. He was in Huangbo's assembly for three years. After concentrated endeavor of the way, following the encouragement of his senior dharma brother, Venerable Chen, he asked Huangbo three times about the essential meaning of buddha-dharma. He received sixty blows of the stick, but still he did not slacken his determination. He was sent to see Dayu and had great realization. This was the result of his study with these two reverend masters, Chen and Huangbo.

Linji and Deshan are called heroes of the ancestral seats. But how can Deshan compare with Linji? Indeed, Linji was extraordinary. Those who were ordinary in his time excel those who are outstanding in our time. It is said that Linji strove wholeheartedly and that his continuous practice was extraordinary. No guess on how it was would hit the mark.

When Linji was at the assembly of Huangbo, he planted cedar and pine trees with Huangbo. Huangbo asked him, "Why are we planting so many trees deep in this mountain?"

Linji said, "First, for the landscape around the monastery. Second, as a landmark for later generations." Then he hit the ground twice with his hoe.

Huangbo held up his staff and said, "That's why I have just given you thirty blows." Linji heaved a deep sigh. Huangbo said, "When you get my teaching, it will flourish in the world."

In this way, you should know that when they planted cedar and pine trees after attaining the way, they were carrying hoes in their hands. "When you get my teaching, it will flourish in the world" is a result of this. You should transmit person to person and directly point to this ancient example of planting trees. Both Huangbo and Linji planted trees.

In the past Huangbo had had the continuous practice of joining the workers in the Daan Monastery and cleaning the halls. He swept the buddha hall and the dharma hall. He did not wait for the continuous practice of cleaning the mind and cleaning the lamp. It was at this time that he encountered Minister Peixiu.[3]

3. *Huangbo's Encounter with Peixiu*: See Cases for Study, p. 40.

*   *   *

EMPEROR XUAN was the second son of Emperor Xian. He was bright from the time he was young. He loved to sit in the lotus position and would do zazen in the palace.

Emperor Mu was Xuan's elder brother. When Mu was reigning, Xuan went to the throne room, sat on the throne early in the morning, and pretended to greet his retainers. The ministers saw this and, thinking he was out of his mind, reported it to the Emperor. Seeing this, Mu stroked Xuan's head and said, "Brother, you have inherited the excellent qualities of our family lineage." At that time Xuan was thirteen years old.

Mu passed away in the fourth year of the Changqing Era [825]. He had three sons: Jing, Wen, and Wu. Jing inherited the throne but passed away three years later. One year after Wen was installed, the ministers rebelled and replaced him with Wu. Xuan, not yet having been enthroned, lived in the country of his nephew. Wu called Xuan "my dull uncle."

Wu was on the throne during the Huichang Era [841–846], when he prohibited Buddhist teaching. One day he summoned Xuan and had him beaten into unconsciousness and covered with urine as punishment for having climbed up onto Mu's throne. Xuan was left in the imperial garden. When he regained consciousness, he left his homeland. Disguising himself, Xuan joined the assembly of Xiangyan, Zen Master Zhixian, had his head shaved, and became a novice. However, he did not receive the full precepts.

As a novice, Xuan traveled with his teacher, Xiangyan, to various places. When they arrived at Mt. Lu, Xiangyan wrote a verse on the waterfall there:

> The water gouges the cliff and pounds the rocks
> unceasingly.
> Even from a distance we know how high it is.

Xiangyan was trying to engage Xuan, to see how mature he was. Xuan added a verse to it:

How can the valley stream be blocked?
It will end up in the ocean as billows.

Seeing these lines, Xiangyan realized that Xuan was no ordinary person. Later Xuan went to the assembly of Yanguan, National Teacher Qian of Hang Region, and served as secretary of the monastery. At that time Huangbo was head monk. Thus Xuan was sharing the meditation platform with Huangbo.

When Huangbo went to the buddha hall and made prostrations to the Buddha, the secretary joined him and said, "Seek without being attached to the Buddha. Seek without being attached to the dharma. Seek without being attached to the sangha. Elder, why are you making prostrations?"

In response, Huangbo slapped the novice secretary and said, "Seek without being attached to the Buddha. Seek without being attached to the dharma. Seek without being attached to the sangha. Therefore we make prostrations like this." Then Huangbo slapped him again.

Xuan said, "That's pretty rough."

Huangbo said, "What is right here? How can you say it's rough?" and gave him another slap. Xuan was silent.

After Wu's reign ended, Xuan returned to the laity and ascended the throne. He stopped Wu's persecution of Buddhism and reinstituted the Buddhist teaching.

Before he was installed as emperor, he had left his father's kingdom and traveled widely, practicing the way wholeheartedly. It is said that while emperor, he practiced zazen day and night. Indeed, Xuan had been a pitiable wanderer after his father passed away and again after his brother passed away. He was punished and ordered beaten by his nephew. But his aspiration did not waver and he continued his practice. His genuine continuous practice was an excellent example, rare in history.

XUEFENG, Priest Yicun, Great Master Zhenjue, never slackened in zazen both day and night from the time when he aroused the bodhi-seeking mind. During the long course of entering various monasteries, he did not discriminate among them, but hung up his traveling staff and joined their practice. He did not relax his effort and completely perished in zazen. After that he founded an unadorned monastery on Mt. Xuefeng.

When Xuefeng first studied, he traveled to Dongshan nine times and to Touzi three times. His effort was so outstanding that when teachers encourage continuous practice, pure and solemn, they use "Xuefeng's lofty aspiration" as an example. Although Xuefeng's dullness is not different from others', his brilliance is beyond compare. This is due to his continuous practice. Those of you who follow the way nowadays should wash yourselves with the snow of Xuefeng [Snow Peak]. If you quietly reflect on the muscle power of Xuefeng to study at various monasteries, you will see that it is no other than the spiritual bone power he carried over from former lives.

Nowadays, when you join the assemblies of various masters who maintain the way, and you want to receive instruction, it is hard to find an opportunity. Not merely twenty or thirty skin bags, but one hundred or one thousand faces each desire to return to the true source. The day of the masters' guiding hand ends at sunset. The evening of pounding rice goes quickly. At the time when the masters expound dharma, you may lack eyes and ears; your seeing and hearing may be blocked. And when you are ready, your teacher's time may come to an end. While senior reverend masters clap their hands in laughter, those of you who are newly ordained and low in seniority may have difficulty even joining the assembly at the end of the mat.

There are those who do and those who do not enter the inner chambers. There are those who do and those who do not hear the essential words of the teachers. The passage of time is faster than an arrow. Life is more fragile than a dewdrop. Even when you have teachers, you may not be able to study with them. When you want to study with teachers, you may not have them. I have personally seen and heard of such cases.

Although great teachers all have the power to know people, it is rare to have a good relationship with a teacher and become intimate while cultivating the way. When Xuefeng visited Dongshan and Touzi, he must have had a hard time. We can all sympathize with the dharma aspiration of his continuous practice. Those who don't study or practice will be regretful.

Editing completed on the eighteenth day, the first month of the first year of the Ninji Era [1243].

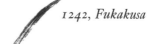

Continuous Practice, Fascicle Two

BODHIDHARMA CAME FROM INDIA to China at the request of his teacher, the venerable Prajnātāra. How severe the wind and snow throughout his three-year journey! How innumerable the waves of the ocean, under clouds and mist, as he sailed toward an unknown country! This journey is beyond the imagination of those attached to body and life.

This is continuous practice due solely to his great compassionate determination to transmit dharma and to save deluded beings. It is continuous practice because of his dedication to transmitting dharma, because of the all-inclusive world where dharma is to be transmitted, because the entire world of the ten directions is the true path, and because the entire world of the ten directions is the entire world of the ten directions. What place is not Bodhidharma's palace? What palace can hinder his practice of the way?

Thus Bodhidharma left India. As his vow was to save deluded beings, he had no doubt or fear. As what he embodied was the all-inclusive practice for saving deluded beings, he had no doubt or fear. Bidding farewell to the country of his father, the king, he sailed on a large ship through the South Sea and entered the Province of Guang. Although there were many people, including his attendant monks, on board, no record of the voyage has remained. No one knows what happened to his entourage.

On the twenty-first day, the ninth month, the eighth year of

Putong Era [527 CE] of the kingdom of Liang, the Governor of Guang Province, called Xiaoang, officially welcomed Bodhidharma. Carrying out his duty he reported Bodhidharma's arrival to Emperor Wu. On the first day of the tenth month Emperor Wu sent a messenger to Bodhidharma to invite him to the palace.

Bodhidharma went to the capital city of Jinling and met with Wu, who said, "Ever since I became Emperor, I have built temples, copied sūtras, and approved the ordination of more monks than I can count. What is the merit of having done all this?"

Bodhidharma said, "There is no merit."

The Emperor said, "Why is that so?"

Bodhidharma said, "These are minor achievements of humans and devas, which become the causes of desire. They are like shadows of forms and are not real."

The Emperor said, "What is real merit?"

Bodhidharma said, "When pure wisdom is complete, the essence is empty and serene. Such merit cannot be attained through worldly actions."

The Emperor said, "What is the foremost sacred truth?"

Bodhidharma said, "Vast emptiness, nothing sacred."

The Emperor said, "Who is it that faces me?"

Bodhidharma said, "I don't know."

The Emperor did not understand. Bodhidharma knew that there was no merging and the time was not ripe. Thus without a word he left on the nineteenth day of the tenth month and he traveled north of the River Yangzi.

He arrived in Luoyang in the Kingdom of Wei on the twenty-third day of the eleventh month of the same year. He stayed at the Shaolin Temple of Mt. Song, where he sat facing the wall in silence day after day. But Emperor [Xiaoming] of Wei was unaware of his presence and was not ashamed of being unaware of it. Bodhidharma was from the warrior class in southern India, a prince of a major kingdom, where sophisticated customs had been developed. In contrast, the customs of the minor kingdom of Wei must have looked uncivilized in the eyes of Bodhidharma, but it did not affect him. He did not abandon the country or people. Although he was attacked by the monk Bodhiruchi, he did not defend himself, nor did he hate him. He was not resentful of Precept Master Guangtong's ill intention, but simply ignored him.

Although Bodhidharma did many outstanding things, he was often regarded as an ordinary Tripitaka master or a scholar of sūtras and commentaries, because of the lack of understanding and small-mindedness of some monks in China. They saw no difference between the true teaching of Bodhidharma, who focused on the single dharma gate of the Zen School, and the teachings of scholarly commentators. Those who see in this way are beasts who defile the buddha-dharma.

Bodhidharma is the twenty-eighth authentic heir of Shākya-muni Buddha. He left the large kingdom of his father to save sentient beings of the eastern country. Who can be compared with him? If he had not come from India, how could sentient beings of the eastern lands see and hear the Buddha's true dharma? They would have been stuck with countless names and forms. Now some barbarians like us, who have hair and horns, are able to hear the true dharma. Today even farmers and village people can see and hear it due to the continuous practice of Bodhidharma, who voyaged to China.

China was much less civilized than India. Their customs were not as wholesome as those of India. An outstanding sage like Bodhidharma, who had received and maintained the treasury of dharma, would not have bothered to go had he not had great patience and vast compassion. There was no established place for practice and there were few people in China who would be able to appreciate a true teacher.

Bodhidharma stayed on Mt. Song for nine years. People called him a wall-gazing Brahman. Later historians listed him as a practitioner of learning meditation. But that is not the whole truth. The ancestor alone transmitted the treasury of the true dharma eye, buddha to buddha, heir to heir.

The Record within the Forest by Shimen says, "Bodhidharma at first visited the Kingdom of Liang and then the Kingdom of Wei. He then went to Mt. Song and rested his traveling staff at the Shao-

lin Temple, where he simply sat at ease facing the wall. It was not a
step-by-step practice of learning meditation. For a long time people
could not guess why he was doing it. So they regarded Bodhidharma as a practitioner of learning meditation.

"Now, meditation is only one of many activities of Zen. It does
not cover the entire practice of the sage. But those who recorded
the history of that time classified him among practitioners of learning meditation and lumped him together with those who engaged
in the static practice of a decayed tree and dead ash. The sage is not
limited to meditation, yet does not contradict meditation. It is like
the Yijing [I-ching] not being limited to yin and yang, yet not con-
tradicting yin and yang.

"When Emperor Wu of Liang met Bodhidharma, the Emperor
asked, 'What is the primary meaning of the sacred truth?' Bodhidharma said, 'Vast and empty, nothing sacred.' The Emperor asked
further, 'Who is facing me?' Bodhidharma said, 'I don't know.' Had
he not been so familiar with the local language, he would not have
communicated so well."

Thus it is clear that Bodhidharma moved from Liang to Wei.
He walked to Mt. Song and stayed at the Shaolin Temple. Although
he sat in stillness facing the wall, he was not engaged in so-called
learning meditation. Although he had not brought even one volume
of sūtra, he was a genuine master who transmitted true dharma.
However, historians did not understand and classified him in the
section about teachers of learning meditation. This was the utmost
stupidity, which is lamentable.

When he arrived on Mt. Song, a doglike monk barked at him.
What a pity! How foolish! With what mind could one ignore Bodhidharma's compassionate gift? How could one fail to repay his
kindness? In the worldly realm, there are those who do not forget
the kindness of others. People call them worthy beings. The great
kindness of Bodhidharma surpasses that of one's parents. His compassion is beyond filial love. The low birth of Japanese people is
amazing, if we think about it. Not having been born in the center
of the world, we haven't seen flourishing lands. We haven't known
sages nor seen the wise. There has been no one who has ascended

to heaven from our land, Japan. We are all equally immature. From the time our nation was founded, no one has guided lay people. We have never heard of anyone purifying the nation, as no one has known what is pure and what is murky. We are not familiar with yin and yang, or with heaven, earth, and humans. How, then, could we understand the undulation of the five types of matter?* This ignorance comes from not knowing the sound and form before our very eyes. It is the result of not knowing the sūtras, nor having true teachers to study them with.

Having no true teachers, we do not know how many scores of volumes, how many hundreds of verses, and how many thousands of words the sūtras have. We just read the remote aspects of the writing, instead of understanding the essential meaning of the thousands of verses and myriad words. We come to know the ancient sūtras and texts as a result of our longing for the authentic teaching. As we long for the ancient teaching, the sūtras of old come forth.

The founders of the Han and the Wei dynasties in China—emperors Gao and Dai—understood the verses of heaven and transmitted the expression of the terrestrial forms. When we clarify their words, we understand the fundamentals of heaven, earth, and humans. People who have not encountered the guidance of such virtuous leaders do not know what it is to truly serve the emperor or to truly serve their parents. They are unfortunate subjects of the emperor and unfortunate children of their parents. As subjects or children, they miss a precious jewel and waste the passage of time. Born into such a family, they have no authority to govern but cling to petty positions. Thus the nation is murky, rarely known for its purity. Since we have a lowly life in such a remote land as Japan where the Tathāgata's true dharma is not heard, what is the use of clinging to this bodily life? Why do we cling to this bodily life and to what do we devote ourselves?

Those who have a worthy and noble life should not cling to it for anything, even for the sake of dharma. This is also true for those with a lowly life. On the other hand, if those with a lowly life dedicate themselves to following the way for the sake of dharma, their life is more worthy than the life of the heavenly devas, a wheel-turning king,* the gods of heaven and earth, or sentient beings in the three realms.

Now, Bodhidharma, the First Ancestor in China, was the third son of the King of Xiangzhi in southern India.[1] As a prince from a royal family, of noble background, he was to be respected. But in the remote land of China, people did not know how to respect him. They had no incense, flowers, royal cushions, or palace for him. Japan is an even more distant steep cliff away, where no one knows how to honor a prince from a great nation. Even if we learn the manners, we may have difficulty in mastering them. The way to honor a lord is different from the way to honor royalty; one way is less formal than the other. But here we can't tell the difference, as we are unaware of the degrees of nobility even among ourselves. As we don't understand the difference, we don't know the degrees of our own nobility.

Bodhidharma was a dharma heir, twenty-eight generations from Shākyamuni Buddha. After he attained the way, his importance increased. A great sage, the most venerable one, he followed his teacher's request to transmit dharma for saving beings, and did not cling to his bodily life. In China they had not seen a buddha child, an authentic heir, nor had anyone received person-to-person transmission of the ancestral face. No one had met a buddha before Bodhidharma appeared. No buddhas other than his descendants emerged in China after that.

It is possible to meet the Buddha when the udumbara flower* is in bloom. People count the years looking forward to this. But the coming of the First Ancestor from India will never happen again. And yet those who call themselves descendants of the ancestors are like the one in the Kingdom of Chu who treasured an ordinary green stone thinking it was jade. Unable to tell jade from stone, they think that teachers of sūtras and treatises are equal to Bodhidharma. It is so because of their limited learning and shallow understanding. Those who do not recognize the correct seed of prajñā do not become descendants of the ancestral path. They wander around in the crooked paths of name and gain. How sad!

1. *Xiangzhi:* Its Indian name is unknown.

*   *   *

EVEN AFTER the Putong Era of the Kingdom of Liang, there were
monks who went to India. For what reason? It is quite stupid. Because of their unwholesome past actions, they wander around in a
foreign land. Step by step they go on the crooked paths of slandering dharma. Step by step they go further away from their parental
land. What do they gain by arriving in India? They merely bear
hardships in the mountains and waters.

Although they are supposed to seek for buddha-dharma, they
lack right aspiration for buddha-dharma, and so even in India they
do not meet a true teacher but only teachers of treatises and sūtras.
The reason for this is that although there are true teachers in India,
seekers who lack the right mind to search for true dharma cannot
find it. We have never heard of people who went to India and met
true teachers. If they had done so, they would have spoken about it.
But because they didn't, they did not speak about it.

Also in China, there have been many monks who have de-
pended upon sūtras and treatises without seeking for true dharma,
even after Bodhidharma came from India. Although they read sūtras and treatises, they are ignorant about the meaning of them.
This dark activity does not only come from today's action but also
from unwholesome actions of the past. In this lifetime they do not
learn the true teaching of the Tathāgata, are not illuminated by
the face-to-face transmission of the Tathāgata, do not actualize the
buddha mind of the Tathāgata, and do not listen to the wind of the
house of all buddhas. It is regrettable.

There were many people like that in the Sui, Tang, and Song
dynasties. But those who have once nurtured the seeds of prajñā,
even if they enter the gate unintentionally, are freed from counting
grains of sand, and they become descendants of Bodhidharma.
They are persons of excellent roots, the highest of the high, persons
of good seeds, while those who are ignorant merely lodge forever
in the huts of sūtras and treatises.

Therefore, we should look up at the profound teaching that
Bodhidharma brought from India without avoiding or abhorring

the steep path. For what other purpose should we save our stinky
skin bags?

Zen Master Xiangyan said:

Hundreds of plans, thousands of means,
your body is dust in the tomb.
Don't say white hair has no words.
It is a message from the yellow springs.*

Thus, even if you make hundreds of plans and create thousands
of means to save yourselves, you will in the end turn to dust in
the tomb. Furthermore, driven by a king of a small nation and his
retainers, you run around east and west, with thousands of hardships and myriad sufferings of body and mind. You give your life
over to royalty, even to the extent of following your king to the
grave. A future driven by worldly obligations is clouds and mists of
darkness. Many people since olden times have been occupied by
minor pursuits and have given up their lives. Those human lives
might have been saved, as they could have become vessels of the
way.

Now that you have met the true dharma, you should study it
even if you have to give up the lives of hundreds and thousands of
kalpas. Why would you give up your life for worthless petty people,
instead of devoting yourself to the broad and profound buddha-
dharma? Neither those who are wise nor those who are not should
hesitate in making this decision. Think quietly. When the true
dharma is not spread, you cannot meet it even if you want to give
up your life for it. You should wish right now for the self that meets
the true dharma. You should be ashamed of the self that would not
offer your life for the sake of the true dharma. If there is anything
to be ashamed of, this is it.

This being so, to appreciate the great gift of Bodhidharma is
the continuous practice of this day. Do not look back on your bodily
life. Do not cling to a love that puts you lower than birds and beasts.
Even if you cling to that love, you cannot maintain it forever. Do

not hold on to the house of the family that is like trash. Even if you retreat to that place, it cannot be your ultimate abode.

The wise buddha ancestors in olden times let go of the seven types of treasure and a thousand servants, leaving behind jeweled palaces and vermilion towers. They saw these luxuries as drool and manure. These actions by the ancient buddha ancestors exemplify their kindness.

According to an ancient Chinese legend, even a sick sparrow remembered the beneficence of someone who had cared for it and presented a jade ring that carried a prediction of an auspicious future. A captured tortoise did not forget the beneficence of someone who helped release it and exhibited its tortoise figure in all the seals the person commissioned. How sad that some with human faces lack the virtue of expressions of gratitude like these animals!

Your ability to see buddhas and hear dharma right now is the result of the compassionate continuous practice of each buddha ancestor. Without the one-to-one transmission of buddha ancestors, how could the dharma have reached us today? You should gratefully repay the beneficence of having received one phrase, one dharma. How much more beneficent is the unsurpassed great dharma, the treasury of the true dharma eye? How could you not repay it with gratitude? You should vow to surrender to this day your lifetimes, which could be as immeasurable as the sands of the Ganges.

Your corpse of a body that is dedicated to dharma should be revered with bows and offerings, generation after generation. Such a corpse is what devas and dragon kings respect, guard, and admire. There has been a Brahman custom for a long time in India to sell and buy skulls, because people there revere the merit of the skulls of those who have practiced dharma. If you don't dedicate your bodily life to the way right now, the power of practicing dharma will not arrive. To fully engage without sparing your bodily life is to mature your practice of dharma. Then your skull will be revered. But who would bow to your skull if you do not dedicate yourself to the way? Who would want to sell or buy such a skull found in a field? You will be regretful when your spirit looks back to this day, if you do not dedicate yourself to the way.

A demon beat the bones of his own corpse for his unwholesome past actions, and a deva bowed to his own skeleton for his wholesome past actions. Thinking upon the time when your body will turn to dust or mud, you should care about the future generations without self-concern. Then, those who see your remains will be moved to tears. Even if you turn to dust or mud, leaving a skull that people might want to avoid, you will be very fortunate if you engage in continuous practice of the true buddha-dharma.

Thus, do not fear the suffering from cold. The suffering from cold has never crushed the way. You should only be concerned about not practicing. Lack of practice leaves a person divided and hinders the way. Do not be put off by the suffering from heat. The suffering from heat has never crushed the way. You should only be concerned about not practicing. Lack of practice leaves a person divided and hinders the way.

The Buddha accepted an offering of barley for horses as food for himself. Sages of olden times lived on bracken in the mountains. These are excellent examples for both buddhas and laity. You should not be like a demon looking for blood or milk. A day of fully engaged activity is the continuous practice of all buddhas.

HUIKE, Great Master Zhengzong Pujue, the Second Ancestor of China, was admired even by gods and demons. He was a teacher of high virtue, a broad-minded person, respected equally by monks and lay people. He lived long in the capital city of Luoyang and read widely. Such a person is rarely encountered. His understanding was high and his virtue weighty. One day a spirit appeared in his dream and said to Huike, "This is not a place to stay if you want to harvest the fruit. The great road is not far away. You should go south."

The next day he had a piercing headache and asked his teacher, Zen Master Baojing of Mt. Xiang near Luoyang, to help relieve it. Then a voice from the sky was heard, "This is not a usual headache. Your bones are being replaced."

Huike told Baojing about his dream. Taking a look at his head, which had the appearance of five peaks sticking out, Baojing said, "You have an auspicious appearance, which shows that you are destined to have realization. The spirit's message for you to go south must mean that Bodhidharma, the great practitioner of the Shaolin Temple, is your teacher."

The spirit who had spoken to Huike was the guardian deity for his endless practice of the way. Following Baojing's instruction, Huike went to see Bodhidharma at Shaoshi Peak. It was a severely cold winter night, said to be the ninth day of the twelfth month. On such a winter night in the deep mountains it would be impossible for a person to stand outdoors, even without rain or snow. It was a horrendous season when bamboo cracks. A great snow covered the entire mountain. Huike searched in the snow for a trail. Who knows the extent of his hardship?

Finally Huike reached Bodhidharma's dwelling, but he was not allowed to enter. Bodhidharma did not turn around. Throughout the night Huike did not sleep, sit, or rest. He stood firmly until dawn. The night snow seemed to have no mercy, piling up and burying him up to his waist. Every drop of his tears froze. Seeing his frozen tears he shed even more tears. Looking at his own body, he thought to himself, "A seeker in the past crushed his bones, extracted his marrow, and squeezed his blood to feed the starving people. Another lay down his hair on the muddy road to let the Buddha pass. Another threw his body off the cliff to feed a tiger. They were like that. Then who am I?" Thus, his aspiration became stronger.

Those who study nowadays should not forget Huike's words, "They were like that. Then who am I?" If we forget, we will drown for numberless kalpas. Thus Huike addressed himself in this way, strengthening his aspiration for dharma. He did not mind being covered by snow. When we imagine the hair-raising ordeal of that night, we are struck with terror.

At dawn Bodhidharma took notice and asked, "What do you seek? Why have you stood in the snow for so long?"

Shedding more tears, Huike said, "All I wish is that you compassionately open the gate of sweet dew in order to awaken many beings."

Bodhidharma said, "The unsurpassed, inconceivable way of all buddhas must be practiced hard and consistently for vast kalpas. You must bear what is unbearable. But if you wish with small virtue, small wisdom, and casual, arrogant mind for the true vehicle, you will toil in vain."

Then Huike was encouraged. Unnoticed by Bodhidharma, he took a sharp knife, cut off his left arm, and offered it to him. Bodhidharma knew then that Huike was a dharma vessel, and he said, "When buddhas first seek the way, they give up bodily form for the sake of dharma. Now that I see your determination, you are invited to pursue the way here."

Thus Huike entered Bodhidharma's inner chamber, attending to him with great diligence for eight years. Huike was indeed an example and a great guide for humans and devas to follow. Such great diligence had not been heard of either in India or China. When it comes to "smiling" you should study Mahākāshyapa. And when it comes to attaining the marrow, you should study Huike.[2]

Reflecting quietly we know that even if Bodhidharma had come from India thousands of times, without the continuous practice of Huike there would not be a great number of students and practitioners today. Now as we see and hear the true dharma, we should express our gratitude to Huike. Most ways of expressing gratitude may miss the mark. Giving up the life of your body is not enough. A castle is not solid enough, as it can be taken by others or given away to a family. The life of the body can be given to impermanence, a lord, or a crooked way. Therefore none of these are suitable offerings. Continuous practice, day after day, is the most appropriate way of expressing gratitude. This means that you prac-

2. This refers to the following story: Bodhidharma said to his students, "The time has come. Can you express your understanding?" Daofu said, "My present view is that we should neither be attached to letters nor be apart from letters, and allow the way to function freely." Bodhidharma said, "You have attained my skin." Nun Zongchi said, "My view is that it is like the joy of seeing Akshobhya Buddha's land just once and not again." Bodhidharma said, "You have attained my flesh." Daoyu said, "The four great elements are originally empty and the five skandhas do not exist. Therefore I see nothing to be attained." Bodhidharma said, "You have attained my bones." Finally Huike bowed three times, stood up, and returned to his seat. Bodhidharma said, "You have attained my marrow."

tice continuously, without wasting a single day of your life, without using it for your own sake. Why is it so? Your life is a fortunate outcome of the continuous practice of the past. You should express your gratitude immediately. How sad and shameful to waste this body, that has benefited from the continuous practice of buddha ancestors, by becoming a slave of family, surrendering to their vanities, without noticing the fall! Or the body may be mistakenly given to that horrendous robber, the demon of fame and gain.

If ever you value fame and gain, then be compassionate to fame and gain. If you are compassionate to fame and gain, you will not allow them to break the body that can become a buddha ancestor. Being compassionate to family and relatives is also like this. Do not think that fame and gain are phantoms and illusions, but regard them as sentient beings. If you are not compassionate to fame and gain, you will accumulate unwholesome actions. The true eye of study should be like this.

Thoughtful people in the world express gratitude for receiving gold, silver, or rare treasures. They also express gratitude for receiving kind words. Who can forget the great gift of seeing and hearing the Tathāgata's unsurpassable true dharma? Being aware of this is itself the rare treasure of a lifetime. The bones and skulls of those who did not turn back from this continuous practice are enshrined in seven-treasure pagodas, given respect and offerings by humans and devas. When you become aware of such a great gift, you should attentively repay the mountain of benevolence, without allowing your life to disappear like a dewdrop on the grass. This is continuous practice. The power of this practice means that you yourself practice as an ancestor of buddhas.

The First and Second Ancestors of China did not found monasteries, nor did the Third and Fourth Ancestors. Thus they remained free of administrative duties. The Fifth and Sixth Ancestors did not build their own monasteries. Neither did Qingyuan nor Nanyue.

GREAT MASTER SHITOU did zazen on a large rock where he had a thatched hut. He sat continuously without sleeping day or night. Although he did not ignore work, he did not fail to do zazen throughout the day. Nowadays the descendants of his teacher Qingyuan are spread throughout China, benefiting humans and devas. This is all due to the solid continuous practice and the great determination of Shitou. The current Yunmen and Fayan lines are also descended from Shitou.

DAOXIN, the Fourth Ancestor of China, Zen Master Dayi, met Sengcan, the Third Ancestor, when he was fourteen and then labored for nine years. After inheriting the authentic teaching of buddha ancestors, Daoxin kept his mind gathered and did not sleep with his side on the mat for almost sixty years. In his guidance he did not discriminate between enemies and friends, so his virtue prevailed among humans and devas.

In the sixteenth year of the Zhenguan Era [642], Emperor Tai, in admiration of Daoxin's flavor of the way, invited him to the capital, wishing to test the hue of his dharma. Daoxin respectfully declined three times, claiming ill health. At the fourth summons, the Emperor ordered the messenger to cut off Daoxin's head if he declined again. The messenger saw Daoxin and relayed the imperial order to him. With complete composure Daoxin stretched out his neck and made ready for the sword. Extremely impressed, the messenger went back to the capital and wrote a report to the Emperor, who admired Daoxin even more. He expressed his appreciation by sending Daoxin a gift of rare silk.

Thus, the continuous practice of Daoxin, who was not attached to his bodily life as bodily life and tried to avoid becoming intimate with kings and ministers, is something rarely encountered in a thousand years. Because Emperor Tai was a just king, Daoxin had nothing against him. The Emperor admired Daoxin because he did not spare his own bodily life and was willing to die. Daoxin focused on his continuous practice, not without reason but with respect for the passage of time. Compared with the current tendency in this declining age when many people try to find favor with emperors, Daoxin's refusal of the three imperial requests is remarkable.

On the fourth day, the added ninth month, the second year of the Yonghui Era [651] during the reign of Emperor Gao, Daoxin gave instruction to his students, saying, "All things are liberated. You should guard your mind and teach future generations."

After saying this, he sat at ease and passed away. He was seventy-two years old. A stūpa was built for him on the mountain. On the eighth day of the fourth month of the following year, the door to the stūpa opened of itself, and inside it, his body looked as if he were alive. After that his students kept the door open.

You should understand Daoxin's words: "All things are liberated." It is not merely that all things are empty or all things are all things, but that all things are liberated. Daoxin had continuous practice before and after entering the stūpa. To assume that all living beings die is a narrow view. To assume that the dead do not perceive is a limited idea. Do not follow these views when you study the way. There may be those who go beyond death. There may be dead people who perceive.

XUANSHA, Great Master Zongyi, was from Min Prefecture, Fu Region. His family name was Xie and his dharma name was Shibei. From the time he was little he was fond of dropping a fishing line. Later he supported himself fishing from a tiny boat on the River Nantai. At the beginning of the Xiantong Era [860–874] of the Tang Dynasty, when he was thirty, he had an urge to leave the dusty world. So he gave up his boat, went to see Furong, Zen Master Lingxun, and dropped his hair. He received the monk precepts from Precept Master Daoxuan of the Kaiyuan Monastery in Jiangnan. He wore a simple cotton robe and straw sandals, ate barely enough to sustain life, and sat zazen all day long. People thought him extraordinary.

Xuansha was originally a dharma brother of Xuefeng Yicun, but studied with him closely as a student. Xuefeng called him Ascetic Bei [Shibei] because of his rigorous practice. One day Xuefeng asked, "Where is Ascetic Bei heading?"

Xuansha said, "He is not misleading anyone."

Later Xuefeng called Xuansha and asked, "Why doesn't Ascetic Bei travel all around to study?"

Xuansha said, "Bodhidharma didn't come to China. The Second Ancestor didn't go to India." Xuefeng approved his words.

When Xuefeng became abbot on Mt. Xianggu, later called Mt. Xuefeng, Xuansha accompanied him as his assistant. Because of their collaboration, many excellent students assembled in the monastery. Xuansha continued to enter the abbot's room to receive guidance from before dawn till late at night. Students who lacked decisive understanding would ask Xuansha to go with them to see Xuefeng. Sometimes Xuefeng would say to them, "Why don't you ask Ascetic Bei?" As caring as Xuefeng, Xuansha would not hesitate to respond to Xuefeng's request.

Without Xuansha's outstanding continuous practice, such dedication would not have been possible. The continuous practice of sitting zazen all day long is rare. While there are many who run around after sound and form, there are few who sit zazen all day long. Those of you who come later should fear wasting your remaining time and endeavor to sit zazen the whole day.

Changqing, Priest Huileng, was a revered teacher under Xuefeng. He visited and practiced with Xuefeng and Xuansha for almost twenty-nine years. During this time he wore out twenty sitting mats. Those who love zazen nowadays regard Changqing as an ancient, excellent example. There are many who long for him but few who measure up to him. His three-decade endeavor was not without results; he suddenly had great awakening when he was rolling up a bamboo shade.

He did not go back to his hometown to see his relations or chat with his fellow students for thirty years. He practiced single-mindedly and continuously, questioning over and over without negligence. What a sharp capacity! What a great root! We learn from sūtras about those who have solid determination. But those of you who seek what should be sought and are ashamed of what should be ashamed of need to encounter Changqing. Unfortunately, there are many who do not have way-seeking mind, are poor in conduct, and are bound by fame and gain.

*   *   *

GUISHAN, Zen Master Dayuan, went to the steep and rocky Mt. Gui immediately after receiving a prediction of enlightenment from Baizhang. He mingled with birds and beasts, erected a hut, and tempered his practice. While living on acorns and chestnuts, he was not intimidated by storms or snow. Without temple or property, he actualized continuous practice for forty years. Later this place became a monastery renowned throughout China, where excellent practitioners like dragons and elephants came to follow in his footsteps.

If you vow to establish a temple, do not be swayed by human concerns, but maintain the strict continuous practice of buddhadharma. Where the practice is tempered without having a hall is a place of enlightenment of old buddhas. The teaching given outdoors, under a tree, may be heard afar. Such a place can be a sacred domain for a long time. Indeed, the continuous practice of one person will merge with the way-place of all buddhas.

Foolish people in this declining age, you should not be consumed with erecting magnificent temple buildings. Buddha ancestors have never wished for such temple buildings. You uselessly decorate the halls before you clarify your own eye. Rather than dedicating a house of all buddhas, you are turning it into a pit of fame and gain. You should quietly ponder the continuous practice of the ancient Guishan. In order to do this, identify yourself with Guishan.

The sobbing rain of deep night pierces moss and pierces rock. On a snowy night of winter when even animals are rarely seen, how could the aromas from people's houses reach you? This kind of search is impossible without the continuous practice of taking your own life lightly and regarding dharma as precious. Without cutting grass or moving earth and lumber, Guishan was fully engaged in tempering practice of the way. What a deep feeling we have for him! With what great determination the authentic heir endured hardship, transmitting the true dharma on the steep mountain! It is said about Mt. Gui that there are a pond and a brook where ice accumulates and fog becomes dense. It is not an inviting place for retreat but it is where Guishan's practice of the buddha way and the depth of the mountains were merged and renewed.

Continuous practice is not something we should take casually. If we do not repay the gift of the hardship of Guishan's continuous practice, how can we, who aspire to study, identify with him as if he were sitting in front of us? Due to the power and the guiding merit of his continuous practice, the wind wheel is not upset, the world is not broken, the palace of devas is calm, and human lands are maintained.

Although we are not direct descendants of Guishan, he is an ancestor of the teaching. Later Yangshan went to study and attend him. Yangshan, who had studied with Baizhang, was like Shāriputra, who gave one hundred answers to ten questions. Attending Guishan, he spent three years watching over a buffalo.[3] This kind of continuous practice has been cut off and not seen in recent years. Such a statement by Yangshan as "spending three years watching over a buffalo" cannot otherwise be heard.

ANCESTOR DAOKAI of Mt. Furong is a true source of actualizing continuous practice. Offered a purple robe and the title of Zen Master Dingzhao by the Emperor, he did not accept them. His letter declining them upset the Emperor, but Daokai persisted in refusing these honors. When he had a hut on Mt. Furong, hundreds of monks and lay people gathered there. The flavor of his one daily bowl of watery gruel, which drove most of them away, is still talked about.

Once Daokai vowed never to go to a feast and said to the assembly, "Home-leavers should not avoid hardship. Seeking freedom from birth and death, rest your mind, stop worrying, and cut off dependence on relations. That's why you are called home-leavers. How can you receive luxurious offerings and be immersed in ordinary life? You should cast off this, that, and everything in between. Regard whatever you see and hear as a flower planted on a rock.

3. This refers to Guishan's words, "After a hundred years, I will become a water buffalo at the foot of this mountain."

When you encounter fame and gain, regard them as a dust mote in your eye.

"It is not that fame and gain haven't been experienced or known from beginningless time; rather they are like the head, which cannot help seeing the tail. Why should you struggle and long for them? If you don't stop longing now, when will you? Thus, the ancient sages teach you to let go right at this very moment. If you do so, what will remain? If you attain calmness of mind, buddha ancestors will be like something extra and all the things in the world will be inevitably flameless and plain. Only then can you merge with the place of suchness.

"Don't you see? Longshan did not see anyone throughout his life. Zhaozhou did not speak one phrase throughout his life. Biandan picked acorns for his meals. Fachang made a robe with lotus leaves. Ascetic Zhiyi only wore paper. Senior Monk Xuantai only wore cotton. Shishuang Qingzhu built a hall of dead trees and lived there with the assembly. What you need to do is to let your mind perish.

"Touji Datong asked his students to wash the rice that he cooked together with them. Thus what you need to do is to minimize your concerns. This is how the ancient sages encouraged themselves. Had they not thought their practices worthwhile, they would not have simplified their daily activities. Practitioners, if you have realization with your whole body, you will be a person of no lack. If you don't hit the mark, you will waste your effort."

Daokai continued: "I have become head of this monastery in spite of having achieved nothing worth mentioning. How can I sit on this seat and neglect the trust of the ancient sages? I want to follow the example of the teachers of old who were abbots of monasteries. After consulting with all of you, I have decided not to go out of the monastery, attend feasts, or ask for donations. We will divide one year's harvest from our fields into three-hundred-sixty-days and use them accordingly. But we will not reduce the number of monks in the assembly. When there is enough rice we will cook rice. When there is not enough, we will make gruel by adding water. When there is less rice, we will make watery gruel. When we accept new monks, we will serve tea that is nothing special. Tea will be made ready in the tea room for all to serve themselves. We will do only what is essential, eliminating all the rest, in order to concentrate on the endeavor of the way.

"Here, the livelihood is complete and the landscape is not dull. Flowers blossom and birds sing. Wooden horses whine and stone oxen run. Green mountains far away are faint, and spring water nearby is soundless. Monkeys on the mountain ridges chatter, and dewdrops wet the midnight moon. Cranes caw in the forests and the winds swirl around the dawn pines. When spring wind rises, a dead tree roars like a dragon. At the time of falling leaves, the shivering forest scatters blossoms. The jewel steps delineate moss patterns. Human faces take on shades of mist. Sounds are serene. Remote from worldly affairs, this one taste is subtle—nothing in particular.

"Today I am supposed to present the gate of the house to all of you. This is already off the track. Even so, I go on lecturing and giving instructions in the abbot's room. I take up a mallet and swing a whisk. I shout to the east and strike the west. My face grimaces as if I were having a seizure. I feel as if I were belittling you, students, and betraying the ancient sages.

"Don't you see? Bodhidharma came from India, got to the foot of Shaoshi Peak, and faced the wall for nine years. Huike stood in the snow and cut off his arm. What hardship! Bodhidharma did not say a word and Huike did not ask a question. But can you call Bodhidharma a person of not doing? Can you regard Huike as not seeking a master? Whenever I speak about examples of ancient sages, I feel there is no place to hide. I am ashamed that we who come later are so soft and weak.

"These days, people make offerings of a hundred flavors to others and say, 'As I have fulfilled the four types of offerings to monks, I feel ready to arouse the thought of enlightenment.' But I fear that such people do not know how to move their hands and legs and will be separated from the reality of birth and death of the world. Time flies like an arrow and their regret may be deep.

"There are times when others have awakened me with their

merit. But I am not forcing you to follow my advice. Have you seen this verse by a teacher of old?

> Rice without millet from fields in the mountains,
> yellow pickled vegetables—
> eat as you like.
> Otherwise, leave it to east and west.
> Please, fellow travelers, each of you make an effort.
> Take care."

These words of Daokai are the bones and marrow of the ancestral school, transmitted person to person. Although there are many examples of Daokai's continuous practice, I am only presenting this talk. Those of us who come after Daokai should long for and study the continuous practice he kneaded on Mt. Furong. It was the genuine form and spirit of Shākyamuni Buddha at Jeta Grove.

MAZU, Zen Master Daji of the Kaiyuan Monastery, Hong Region, Jiangxi, was from Shifang Prefecture, Han Region. His posthumous name is Daoyi. He studied with Nanyue and was his attendant for over ten years. Once he was about to visit his hometown and got halfway there, but turned around and went back to the monastery. When he returned, he offered incense and bowed to Nanyue, who wrote a verse for him:

> Let me advise you not to go home.
> At home the way is not practiced.
> Old women in the neighborhood
> would call you by your childhood name.

Respectfully receiving these dharma words, Mazu made a vow not to go in the direction of the Han Region in this or any other lifetime. Not taking one step closer to his old home, Mazu stayed in Jiangxi and traveled all over the region. Other than speaking of "Mind itself is buddha," he did not give any words of guidance.

However, he was an authentic heir of Nanyue, a life vein for humans and devas.

What is the meaning of "not to go home"? How does one not go home? Returning to east, west, south, or north is no more than the falling and rising of the self. Indeed, the way is not practiced by going home. Practice continuously, examining whether the way is practiced or not, either by going home or not going home. Why is the way not practiced by going home? Is the way hindered by not practicing? Is it hindered by the self?

Nanyue did not say ordinary words: "Old women in the neighborhood would call you by your childhood name." But he did say as dharma words: "Old women in the neighborhood would call you by your childhood name."[4] Why did he say so? Why did Mazu accept these dharma words? Because when you go south, the earth goes south. Other directions are also like this. It is a narrow view to deny this point by seeing Mt. Sumeru or the great ocean as merely large and separate from you, or to miss this point by using the sun, moon, and stars as a measure for comparison.

HONGREN, the Fifth Ancestor of China, Zen Master Daman, was a man from Huangmei. His lay name was Zhou, after his mother's family. Like Laozi, he had no father. From age seven when he was transmitted dharma until age seventy-four, he maintained the treasury of the true dharma eye of the buddha ancestors. During this time he discreetly entrusted the robe of dharma to Laborer Huineng [the Sixth Ancestor]. Hongren's was an incomparable continuous practice. Because he did not bring forth the robe of dharma for [his most learned student] Senior Monk Shenxiu but entrusted it to Laborer Huineng, the life of the true dharma has not been cut off.

MY LATE TEACHER Rujing, Priest Tiantong, was from Yue. At age nineteen, he abandoned scriptural studies, engaged in practice and

4. Dogen is contrasting hearing the teaching in an ordinary way and hearing it
   with true insight.

did not turn around even at age seventy. When offered a purple robe with the title of master from the Emperor Ning in the Jiading Era [1208–1224], he sent a letter politely declining it. Monks in the ten directions respected him for his action and those both near and far who were knowledgeable rejoiced over it. The Emperor was extremely impressed and sent him an offering of tea. Those who heard of this admired it as something rare at the time. Rujing's action is indeed a genuine continuous practice.

I say this because loving fame is worse than breaking a precept. Breaking a precept is a transgression at a particular time. Loving fame is like an ailment of a lifetime. Do not foolishly hold on to fame, or do not ignorantly accept it. Not to accept fame is continuous practice. To abandon it is continuous practice.

The titles of master for the first six ancestors were all given posthumously by emperors. These ancestors did not receive their titles due to love of fame. Likewise you should give up love of fame within birth and death and simply wish for the continuous practice of the buddha ancestors. Do not be like devouring creatures. To greedily love the self which is of slight significance doesn't take you above the level of creatures and beasts. To abandon fame and gain is rare for humans and devas, but all buddha ancestors have done so.

Some say, "I seek fame and love gain for the benefit of sentient beings." This is a greatly mistaken view held by heretics within the buddha-dharma, as well as by a troop of demons who slander the true dharma. Does this view mean that the buddha ancestors who do not seek fame and gain are unable to benefit sentient beings? What a laugh! What a laugh! Not-seeking can benefit beings. How is it so? Those who, without understanding this, promote what is not beneficial as beneficial are a troop of demons. Sentient beings helped by such demons are bound for hell. Such demons should deplore that their lives are in darkness. Do not regard such ignorant ones as beneficent beings.

Thus, declining the offer of a title of master has been an excellent custom since olden times. This is something that those of us in later generations should study. To see Rujing in person was to meet that person.

Leaving home at nineteen, looking for a teacher, Rujing engaged in the study of the way, without retreating or turning around. Until the age of sixty-five he still had not become close to or even seen an emperor, nor become intimate with ministers or government officials. Not only did he not accept a purple robe, he did not wear any brocade throughout his life. He only wore a black kashāya and a combined robe for formal talks and for giving instruction in the abbot's room.

Instructing the monks, Rujing said, "For the practice of Zen in pursuit of the way, maintaining the mind of the way is primary. It is deplorable that the ancestral way has declined in the last two hundred years. There have been few skin bags who have expressed a phrase of understanding.

"At the time when I hung my walking staff at Mt. Jing, Fuzhao Deguang was abbot. He said in his dharma talk, 'Studying buddhadharma, the path of Zen, you should not look for phrases by others. Each of you should have your own understanding.' Thus he did not oversee the monks' hall and did not guide the many monks who were studying there. He spent his time entertaining visiting dignitaries. Not understanding the essence of buddha-dharma, he was simply greedy for name and loved gain.

"If it were enough to merely have our own understanding of buddha-dharma, why have there always been determined practitioners who traveled around looking for teachers? Indeed Deguang had not yet mastered Zen. Nowadays the elders of monasteries in various places lack way-seeking mind as much as Deguang. How can they hold buddha-dharma in their hands? Regrettable, indeed!" Although Rujing said this to the assembly that included many of Deguang's students, none of them were resentful.

Rujing also said, "To study Zen is to drop off body and mind. You can actualize it by just sitting, without relying on burning incense, bowing, chanting Buddha's name, repentance, or reading sūtras."

In Song China, there are a great many skin bags, not merely

hundreds, who regard themselves as Zen practitioners, calling themselves descendants of the ancestral school. But those who encourage just sitting are rarely heard of. Within the country of four seas and five lakes, Rujing was the only one. Elders all over admired him, even though he did not admire them. There are leaders of large temples who do not know of him. Although born in China, they are like a herd of beasts. They have not studied what they should have studied, but merely wasted the passage of time. What a pity! Those who do not know about Rujing mistakenly regard idle chatter and confused talk as the teaching style of buddha ancestors.

Rujing said in his talks in the dharma hall, "Since I was nineteen, I have visited monasteries all over but have not met teachers to guide humans. Since then, I have not spent even one day or night without covering a zazen cushion. Since I became abbot, I have not chatted with people from my hometown. This is because I feel urgent about the passing of time. I have always stayed in the building where I hung my walking stick, without going to visit other huts or dormitories of the monastery. How could I have spent time enjoying the mountainside or admiring waterscapes?

"I have been doing zazen not only in the monks' hall and other communal places, but also alone in towers and screened-in places. I always carry a cushion so I can sit at the foot of a rock. My hope has been to thoroughly penetrate the diamond seat. Sometimes my buttocks get raw but still I sit harder.

"I am now sixty-five. Although my bones are aged and my head is dull, I don't yet understand zazen. But, because I care about my dharma brothers in the ten directions, I live in this monastery and transmit the way to the assembly, beginning with dawn instruction. I do this because I wonder, where is the buddha-dharma among the elders of other places?" Also, Rujing would not accept gifts from monks who arrived from other places.

Superintendent Zhao, a grandson of Emperor Ning, who was a commanding military officer and agricultural administrator of Ming Region, invited Rujing to the capital to give a dharma talk. At that time Zhao presented ten thousand silver coins to him. Rujing thanked him and said, "I have come to give a customary lecture on the treasury of the true dharma eye, wondrous heart of nirvāna. I am dedicating the merit to the well-being of the late Emperor. But I will not accept the silver coins. Monks have no need of these things. I greatly appreciate your kindness, but as usual I must decline your offer."

Zhao said, "Master, as a relative of His Imperial Majesty I am respected everywhere and I have wealth. On this memorial day of the late Emperor I would like to give him support in another world. Why can't you accept my offering? I feel greatly fortunate to have you here today. With your great compassion and great kindness, please accept my humble gift."

Rujing said, "Your Excellency, your request cannot be refused. But I have a question. When I expounded dharma, did you understand it?"

Zhao said, "I was simply delighted to hear it."

Rujing said, "You are brilliantly illuminating my words. I am honored. I just wish for the happiness of the late Emperor who was invoked today. Please explain to me what I said in my discourse. If you can, I will accept the silver. If you cannot, then please keep it for yourself."

Zhao said, "When I think about it, your composure and movement were excellent."

Rujing said, "That's what I did. How about what you heard?" Zhao hesitated. Rujing said, "The late Emperor's happiness is already fulfilled. Your gift should be left to his decision." Thus he bid farewell.

Zhao said, "I regret that you did not accept my offering. But I rejoice in seeing you." So saying, Zhao saw Rujing off.

Monks and laity on both sides of the Zhe River admired Rujing. This was recorded in the journal of Attendant Monk Ping, who said, "An old master like this is hard to meet. Where else could we possibly find someone so accomplished?"

Who in any direction would decline ten thousand silver coins? A teacher of old said, "Gold, silver, and jewels should be regarded as excrement. Even if you see them as gold and silver, it is customary for monks not to accept them." Rujing followed this teaching;

others did not. He would often say, "In the past three hundred years there have been few teachers like myself. Therefore, it is imperative that you practice diligently with me in the endeavor of the way."

In his assembly there was someone called Daosheng, from Mian Region in Shu, who was a Daoist. Five practitioners including him made a vow: "We will master the great way of buddha ancestors in our lifetime. We will not go back to our hometowns until we do." Rujing was delighted with their vow and allowed them to join walking and sitting meditation with the assembly. In the order of seating, he placed them right after the nuns. It was rare for Daoists to practice in a Zen monastery like this.

Also, a monk called Shanru from Fu Region made a vow: "I will not take a step toward my home in the south, but will single-mindedly study the great way of buddha ancestors." I personally witnessed many students like this in Rujing's assembly. There are few like them in the assemblies of other masters. The continuous practice at Rujing's assembly was outstanding amongst monks of Great Song China. Those who do not aspire to practice as they did should be sorrowful. Even when we meet the buddha-dharma, we don't necessarily respond to it. How much less fortunate our body-mind is if we don't meet the buddha-dharma at all!

Think quietly. Life does not last long. To realize even a few lines of the buddha ancestors' words is to realize the buddha ancestors. How is this so? Since buddha ancestors are body and mind as one, one phrase or two are the buddha ancestors' warm body-mind. Their body-mind comes forth and realizes your body-mind. At the very moment of realization, this realization comes forth and realizes your body-mind. This life realizes the life of many lifetimes. So, by becoming a buddha and becoming an ancestor, you go beyond buddhas and go beyond ancestors.

ACCOUNTS OF CONTINUOUS PRACTICE are like this. Do not run around after fame and gain in the realm of sound and form. Not to run around is the continuous practice that has been transmitted person to person by buddha ancestors. Mature hermits, beginning

hermits, one person, or half a person, I ask you to throw away myriad matters and conditions and to continuously practice the continuous practice of buddha ancestors.

*Written at the Kannondōri Kōshō Hōrin Monastery, on the fifth
day, the fourth month, the third year of the Ninji Era [1242].*

Within a Dream
Expressing the
Dream

THE PATH OF ALL BUDDHAS and ancestors arises before the first forms emerge; it cannot be spoken of in terms of conventional views. This being so, in the realm of buddha ancestors there is the active power of buddhas going beyond buddhas. Since this realm is not a matter of the passage of time, their lives are neither long nor short, neither quick nor slow. This cannot be judged in an ordinary manner. Thus the dharma wheel has been set to turn since before the first sign of forms emerged. The great merit needs no reward, and becomes the guidepost for all ages. Within a dream this is the dream you express. Because awakening is seen within awakening, the dream is expressed within a dream.

The place where the dream is expressed within a dream is the land and the assembly of buddha ancestors. The buddhas' lands and their assemblies, the ancestors' way and their seats, are awakening throughout awakening, and express the dream within a dream. When you meet such speech and expressions, do not regard them as other than the buddhas' assembly; it is buddha turning the dharma wheel.* This dharma wheel encompasses all the ten directions and the eight facets of a clear crystal, and so the great oceans, Mt. Sumeru, the lands, and all buddhas are actualized. This is the dream expressed within a dream, prior to all dreams.

Every dewdrop manifested in every realm is a dream. This dream is the glowing clarity of the hundred grasses.* What requires questioning is this very point. What is confusing is this very point. At this time, there are dream grasses, grasses within, expressive grasses, and so on. When we study this, then roots, stems, branches, leaves, flowers, and fruits, as well as radiance and color are all the great dream. Do not mistake them as merely dreamy.

However, those who do not wish to study buddha-dharma believe that expressing the dream within a dream means speaking of unreal dream grass as real, like piling delusion upon delusion. But this is not true. When you say, "Within confusion is just confusion," still you should follow the path in the vast sky known as "delusion throughout delusion." Just this you should endeavor to investigate thoroughly.

THE EXPRESSING of the dream within a dream is all buddhas. All buddhas are wind and rain, water and fire. We respectfully maintain these names of buddhas, and also pay homage to those names of other buddhas. To express the dream within a dream is the ancient buddhas; it is to ride in this treasure boat and directly arrive in the practice place. Directly arriving in the practice place is riding in this treasure boat. Meandering dreams and direct dreams, holding and letting go, all freely flow like the gusting breezes.

Turning the dharma wheel is just like this; turning the world of the great dharma wheel is immeasurable and boundless. It turns even within a single particle, ebbing and flowing ceaselessly within the particle. Accordingly, whenever such a dharma is turned, even an antagonist nods and smiles. Wherever such a dharma is turned, it freely circulates like the flowing breezes.

Thus, the endless turning of dharma traverses the entire land. In the all-embracing world, cause and effect are not ignored, and all buddhas are unsurpassable. You should know that the guiding way of all buddhas in the amassing of expressions of dharma is boundlessly transforming, being present in all situations. Do not search for the limits of dharma in the past and future.

All things emerge and all things arrive right here. This being so, one plants twining vines* and gets entangled in twining vines. This is the characteristic of unsurpassable enlightenment. Just as expression is limitless, sentient beings are limitless and unsurpassable. Just as cages and snares are limitless, emancipation from them is limitless. The actualization of the fundamental point is: "I grant you thirty blows." This is the actualization of expressing the dream within a dream.

Thus a tree with no roots, the ground where no light or shade falls, and a valley where no shouts echo are no other than the actualized expressions of the dream within a dream. This is neither the realm of humans nor of heavenly beings, and cannot be judged by ordinary people. Who could doubt that a dream is enlightenment, since it is not within the purview of doubt? Who could recognize this dream, since it is not related to recognition? As unsurpassable enlightenment is unsurpassable enlightenment, so the dream is called a dream.

THERE ARE INNER DREAMS, dream expressions, expressions of dreams, and dreams inside. Without being within a dream, there is no expression of dreams. Without expressing dreams, there is no being within a dream. Without expressing dreams, there are no buddhas. Without being within a dream, buddhas do not emerge and turn the wondrous dharma wheel. This dharma wheel is no other than a buddha together with a buddha, and a dream expressed within a dream. Simply expressing the dream within a dream is itself the buddhas and ancestors, the assembly of unsurpassable enlightenment. Furthermore, going beyond the dharma body is itself expressing the dream within a dream.

Here is the encounter of a buddha with a buddha. No attachments are needed to the head, eyes, marrow, and brain, or body, flesh, hands, and feet. Without attachment, one who buys gold sells gold. This is called the mystery of mysteries, the wonder of wonders, the awakening of awakenings, the headtop above the head. This is the daily activity of buddha ancestors. When you study this headtop, you may think that the head only means a human skull, without understanding that it is the crown of Vairochana Buddha.

How can you realize it as the tips of the bright, clear, hundred grasses? Who knows that this is the head itself?

Since ancient times the phrase "the headtop placed above the head" has been spoken. Hearing this phrase, foolish people think that it cautions against adding something extra. Usually they refer to something that should not occur when they say, "How can you add a head on top of a head?" Actually, isn't this a mistake?

The expression of the dream within a dream can be aroused by both ordinary people and sages. Moreover, the expression of the dream within a dream by both ordinary people and sages arose yesterday and develops today. You should know that yesterday's expression of the dream within a dream was the recognition of this expression as expressing the dream within a dream. The present expression of the dream within a dream is to experience right now this expression as expressing the dream within a dream. Indeed, this is the marvelous joy of meeting a buddha.

We should regret that, although the dream of the buddha ancestors' bright hundred grasstops is apparent, clearer than a hundred thousand suns and moons, the ignorant do not see it. What a pity! The head that is "the head placed above the head" is exactly the headtops of a hundred grasses, thousands of types of heads, the ten thousand kinds of heads, the heads throughout the body, the heads of the entire world unconcealed, the heads of the entire world of the ten directions, the heads of teacher and student that join in a single phrase, the headtop of a hundred-foot pole.[1] "Placing" and "above" in "placing the headtop above the head" are both heads. Study and investigate this.

Thus, the passage "All buddhas and their unsurpassable, perfect enlightenment all emerge from this *[Diamond] Sūtra*" is exactly expressing the dream within a dream, which has always been the head placed atop the head. This sūtra, while expressing the dream within a dream, brings forth buddhas with their unsurpassed enlightenment. These buddhas, with their enlightenment, in turn speak this

1. *a hundred-foot pole:* This refers to Changsha's words: "If you take one step beyond the top of a hundred-foot pole, the world in the ten directions will reveal its entire body."

sūtra, which is the established expression of the dream within a dream.

As the cause of a dream is not obscure, the effect of the dream is not ignored. This is indeed one mallet striking one thousand or ten thousand blows, one thousand or ten thousand mallets striking one blow or half a blow. As it is so, a thing of suchness* expresses the dream within a dream; a person of suchness expresses the dream within a dream. A thing of no suchness expresses the dream within a dream; a person of no suchness expresses the dream within a dream. This understanding has been acknowledged as crystal clear. What is called "talking all day long about a dream within a dream" is no other than the actual expression of the dream within a dream.

AN ANCIENT BUDDHA SAID, "Now I express the dream within a dream for you. All buddhas in the past, present, and future express the dream within a dream. The six generations of Chinese ancestors expressed the dream within a dream." Study and clarify these words. Shākyamuni Buddha holding up the flower and blinking is exactly the expression of the dream within a dream. Huike doing prostrations and attaining the marrow is also the expression of the dream within a dream.

Making one brief utterance, beyond understanding and beyond knowing, is the expression of the dream within a dream. As the expression of the dream within a dream is the thousand hands and eyes of Avalokiteshvara that function by many means, the power of seeing colors and sounds, and hearing colors and sounds, is fully maintained. The manifesting body is the expression of the dream within a dream. The expressions of dreams and of myriad aspects of dharma are the expression of the dream within a dream. Taking hold and letting go are the expressions of the dream within a dream. Directly pointing is expressing the dream; hitting the mark is expressing the dream.

When you take hold or when you let go, you need to study the common balancing scale.[2] As soon as you understand it, the

2. *balancing scale:* The dream within a dream is compared to a scale. A stick is

measuring of ounces and pounds will become clear, and will express the dream within a dream. Without knowing ounces and pounds, and without reaching the level balance, there is no actualization of the balance point. When you attain balanced equilibrium, you will see the balance point. Achieving balance does not depend on the objects being weighed, on the balancing scale, or on the activity of weighing, but just hangs on emptiness. Thus, deeply consider that without attaining balance you do not experience solidity. Just hanging on its own in emptiness, the expression of the dream within a dream allows objects to float free in emptiness. Within emptiness, stable balance is manifested. Stable balance is the great way of the balance scale. While suspending emptiness and suspending objects, whether as emptiness or as forms, expression of the dream within a dream joins settled balancing.

There is no liberation other than expression of the dream within a dream. The dream is the entire great earth; the entire great earth is stable. Thus, the inexhaustibility of turning the head and pivoting the brain [actualizing freedom] is just your awakening of the dream within a dream—identifying with and actualizing the dream within a dream.

Shākyamuni Buddha said in a verse [in *The Lotus Sūtra*]:

All buddhas, with bodies of golden hue,
splendidly adorned with a hundred auspicious marks,
hear the dharma and expound it for others.
Such is the fine dream that ever occurs.
In the dream you are made king,
then forsake palace and household entourage,
along with utmost satisfaction of the five sense desires,
and travel to the site of practice
under the bodhi tree.
On the lion's seat
in search of the way, after seven days

---

suspended horizontally from a hook at a point in between the movable weight and the object to be weighed. The scale by itself looks unstable and not grounded, but becomes stable and manifests its full function when balanced.

you attain the wisdom of the buddhas,
completing the unsurpassable way.
Arising and turning the dharma wheel,
you expound the dharma for the four groups of
     practitioners*
throughout thousands of millions of kalpas,
expressing the wondrous dharma free of flaws,
and liberating innumerable sentient beings.
Finally you enter pari-nirvāna,*
like the smoke dispersing as the lamp is extinguished.
If later in the wicked world
one expounds this foremost dharma,
one will produce great benefit,
like the merit just described.

You should study this discourse of the Buddha, and thoroughly investigate this buddha assembly of the buddhas [in *The Lotus Sūtra*]. This dream of buddhas is not an analogy. As the wondrous dharma of all buddhas is mastered only by a buddha together with a buddha, all dharmas awakened in the dream are genuine forms. In awakening there are aspiration, practice, enlightenment, and nirvāna. Within the dream there are aspiration, practice, enlightenment, and nirvāna. Every awakening within a dream is the genuine form, without regard for large or small, superior or inferior.

However, on hearing the words in the passage, "In the dream you are made king," people in the past and present mistakenly think that, thanks to the power of expounding "this foremost dharma," mere night dreams may become like this dream of buddhas. Thinking like this, one has not yet clarified the Buddha's discourse. Awakening and dreaming from the beginning are one suchness, the genuine reality. The buddha-dharma, even if it were an analogy, is the genuine reality. As it is not an analogy, "made king in the dream" is the genuine truth of the buddha-dharma. Shākyamuni Buddha and all the buddhas and ancestors each arouse mind, cultivate practice, and attain universal true awakening within a dream. This being so, the Buddha's path of transforming the sahā world throughout his lifetime is indeed created in a dream. "In search of the way, after seven days" is the measure of attained buddha wisdom. As for what is described, "Turning the dharma wheel . . . throughout thousands of millions of kalpas . . . liberating innumerable sentient beings," these fluctuations within a dream cannot be traced.

"All buddhas, with bodies of golden hue, splendidly adorned with a hundred auspicious marks, hear the dharma and expound it for others. Such is the fine dream that ever occurs." These words clearly show that this "fine dream" is illuminated as "all buddhas." There is the "ever occurring" of the Tathāgata's words; it is not only hundreds of years of dreaming. "Expounding it for others" is manifesting the body. "Hearing the dharma" is hearing sounds with the eye, and with the mind. It is hearing sounds in the old nest, and before the empty kalpa.

As it is said, "All buddhas, with bodies of golden hue, [are] splendidly adorned with a hundred auspicious marks," now we can directly realize beyond any doubt that this "fine dream" is itself "all buddhas with bodies." Although within awakening the buddhas' transformations never cease, the buddha ancestors' emergence is invariably the creation of a dream within a dream. You should be mindful of not slandering the buddha-dharma. When we practice not slandering the buddha-dharma, this path of the tathāgatas is immediately actualized.

On the twenty-first day, the ninth month, the third year of the Ninji Era [1242], this was presented to the assembly at the Kannondōri Kōshō Hōrin Monastery, Uji County, Yamashiro Province.

Undivided Activity

THE GREAT WAY OF ALL BUDDHAS, thoroughly practiced, is emancipation and realization.

"Emancipation" means that in birth you are emancipated from birth, in death you are emancipated from death. Thus, there is detachment from birth-and-death and penetration of birth-and-death. Such is the complete practice of the great way. There is letting go of birth-and-death and vitalizing birth-and-death. Such is the thorough practice of the great way.

"Realization" is birth; birth is realization. At the time of realization there is nothing but birth totally actualized, nothing but death totally actualized.

Such activity makes birth wholly birth, death wholly death. Actualized just so at this moment, this activity is neither large nor small, neither immeasurable nor measurable, neither remote nor urgent. Birth in its right-nowness is undivided activity. Undivided activity is birth in its immediacy.

Birth neither comes nor goes. Birth neither appears nor is already existing. Thus, birth is totally manifested, and death is totally manifested. Know that there are innumerable beings in yourself. Also there is birth, and there is death. Quietly think over whether birth and all things that arise together with birth are inseparable or not. There is neither a moment nor a thing that is apart from birth. There is neither an object nor a mind that is apart from birth.

Birth is just like riding in a boat. You raise the sails and row with the pole. Although you row, the boat gives you a ride, and without the boat you couldn't ride. But you ride in the boat and your riding makes the boat what it is. Investigate a moment such as this. At just such a moment, there is nothing but the world of the boat. The sky, the water, and the shore are all the boat's world, which is not the same as a world that is not the boat's.

When you ride in a boat, your body and mind and the environs together are the undivided activity of the boat. The entire earth and the entire sky are both the undivided activity of the boat. Thus birth is nothing but you; you are nothing but birth.

JIASHAN KEQIN, Zen Master Yuanwu, said, "Birth is undivided activity. Death is undivided activity."

Clarify and investigate these words. What you should investigate is: While the undivided activity of birth has no beginning or end and covers the entire earth and the entire sky, it hinders neither birth's undivided activity nor death's undivided activity. At the moment of death's undivided activity, while it covers the entire earth and the entire sky, it hinders neither death's undivided activity nor birth's undivided activity. This being so, birth does not hinder death; death does not hinder birth.

Both the entire earth and the entire sky appear in birth as well as in death. However, it is not that one and the same entire earth and sky are fully manifested in birth and also fully manifested in death: although not one, not different; although not different, not the same; although not the same, not many.

Similarly, in birth there is undivided activity of all things, and in death there is undivided activity of all things. There is undivided activity in what is not birth and not death. There is birth and there is death in undivided activity. This being so, the undivided activity of birth and death is like a young man bending and stretching his arm, or it is like someone asleep searching with his hand behind his back for the pillow. This is realization in vast wondrous light.

About just such a moment you may suppose that because realization is manifested in undivided activity, there was no realization prior to this. However, prior to this realization, undivided activity was manifested. But the undivided activity manifested previously does not hinder the present realization of undivided activity. Because of this your understanding can be manifested moment after moment.

Presented to the assembly at the residence of the former governor of Izumo Province, next to the Rokuharamitsu Temple, Kyōto, on the seventeenth day, the twelfth month, the third year of the Ninji Era [1242].

Great Awakened Ones

1243–1246

Intimate Language

ACTUALIZING THE FUNDAMENTAL POINT, you realize the great road maintained by all buddhas. "You are like this. I am like this. Keep it well," is revealed.

Yunju, Great Master Hongjue, was asked by an imperial minister who brought an offering, "The World-honored One had intimate language and Mahākāshyapa did not conceal it. What was the World-honored One's language?"

Yunju said, "Your Excellency."

"Yes," he responded.

Yunju asked, "Do you understand it?"

The minister said, "No, I don't."

Yunju said, "If you don't understand it, the World-honored One had intimate language. If you understand it, Mahākāshyapa did not conceal it."

Yunju, a teacher of gods and humans, is the fifth-generation direct heir of Qingyuan. A great sage of all the ten directions, he guides sentient beings and insentient beings. The forty-sixth generation heir of the buddhas [including the Seven Original Buddhas], Yunju spoke dharma for buddha ancestors. Celestial beings sent offerings to his Three Peaks Hut, but after he received dharma transmission upon attaining the way, he went beyond the realm of devas and no longer received offerings from them.

"The World-honored One had intimate language and Mahākā-shyapa did not conceal it" had been transmitted by the forty-six buddhas through Yunju. Still, these words were the original face of Yunju. This understanding cannot be grasped by ordinary humans. It does not come from outside. It has not existed from the beginning. It is not newly acquired.

The intimate language spoken of here was not only put forth by Shākyamuni Buddha, the World-honored One, but also by all buddha ancestors. When there is the World-honored One, there is intimate language. When there is intimate language, Mahākāshyapa does not conceal it. Since there are hundreds and thousands of World-honored Ones, there are hundreds and thousands of Mahākāshyapas. You should study this point without fail, as if cutting through what is impossible to cut through. Investigate it in detail little by little, hundreds and thousands of times, instead of trying to understand it all at once. Do not think that you understand it right away. Yunju was already a world-honored one, so he had intimate language and Mahākāshyapa did not conceal it. But do not assume that the minister's response to Yunju was intimate language.

YUNJU SAID TO THE MINISTER, "If you don't understand it, the World-honored One had intimate language. If you understand it, Mahākāshyapa did not conceal it."

You should aspire to investigate these words for many eons. Yunju's words, "If you don't understand it," are the World-honored One's intimate language. Not understanding is not the same as going blank. Not understanding does not mean that you don't know.

By saying, "If you don't understand it," Yunju is encouraging practice without words. You should investigate this. Then Yunju said "If you understand it." He did not mean that the minister should rest on his understanding.

Among the gates to the study of buddha-dharma, there is a key to understanding buddha-dharma and to going beyond understanding buddha-dharma. Without meeting a true teacher, you wouldn't even know there is a key. You might mistakenly think that what cannot be seen or heard is intimate language.

Yunju did not mean that Mahākāshyapa had not concealed it

just because the minister understood it. Not concealing can happen with not understanding. Do not think that anyone can see and hear not concealing. Not concealing is already present. You should investigate the very moment when nothing is concealed. Do not think that the realm you don't know is intimate language. At the very moment when you do not understand buddha-dharma, that is a moment of intimate language. That is when the World-honored One has intimate language. That is when the World-honored One is present.

However, those who have not heard the teachings of the true masters, although they sit in the teaching seat, have not even dreamed of intimate language. They mistakenly say: "The passage, 'The World-honored One has intimate language' means that he held up a flower and closed and opened his eyes to the assembly of innumerable beings on Vulture Peak. The reason for this is that the teaching by words is shallow and limited to forms, so the Buddha used no words, took up a flower and blinked. This was the very moment of presenting intimate language. But the assembly of innumerable beings did not understand. That is why this is secret language for the assembly of innumerable beings. 'Mahākāshyapa did not conceal it' means that he smiled when he saw the flower and the blinking, as if he had already known it; nothing was concealed from him. This is a true understanding, transmitted from person to person."

There are an enormous number of people who believe in such a theory. Sometimes they comprise whole communities all over China. What a pity! The degeneration of the buddha way has resulted from this. Those who have clear eyes should turn these people around one by one.

If the World-honored One's words were shallow, his holding up a flower and blinking would also be shallow. Those who say that the World-honored One's words are limited to forms are not students of buddha-dharma. Although they know that words have form, they do not yet know that the World-honored One does not have form. They are not yet free from ordinary ways of thinking. Buddha ancestors drop off all experience of body and mind. They use words to turn the dharma wheel. Hearing their words many people are benefited. Those who have trust in dharma and who practice dharma are guided in the realm of buddha ancestors and in the realm of going beyond buddha ancestors.

Did the innumerable beings in the assembly understand the intimate language of the flower and the blinking? You should understand that they stand shoulder to shoulder with Mahākāshyapa. They are born simultaneously with the World-honored One. The innumerable beings are no other than the innumerable beings. Arousing the thought of enlightenment at the very same moment, they take the same path and abide on the same earth.

The teaching with words is heard with wisdom that is known and with wisdom that is not known. Seeing one buddha, they see as many buddhas as grains of sand in the Ganges. At the assembly of each buddha, there are millions and billions of beings. Understand that each buddha demonstrates the moment when the flower and the blinking emerge. What is seen is not dark; what is heard is clear. This is mind eye, body eye, mind ear, and body ear.

How do you understand Mahākāshyapa's smile? Speak! Those with mistaken views have called it secret language. And they have called it "unconcealed." That is stupidity piled upon stupidity.

Upon seeing Mahākāshyapa smile, the World-honored One said, "I have the treasury of the true dharma eye, the wondrous heart of nirvāna. I entrust this to Mahākāshyapa." Are these words or no words? If the World-honored One avoided words and preferred holding up a flower, he would have held up the flower again and again. How could Mahākāshyapa have understood him, and how could the assembly of beings have heard him? You should not pay attention to people's mistaken explanations.

Actually the World-honored One has intimate language, intimate practice, and intimate realization. But ignorant people think "intimate" means that which is known by the self and not by others. Those east and west, past and present, who think and speak this way are not following the buddha way. If what they think were true, those who do not study would have much intimacy, while those who study would have little intimacy. Would those who study extensively have no intimacy? What about those who have the celestial eye, celestial ear, dharma eye, dharma ear, buddha eye, or buddha ear? Would they have no intimate language or intimate heart?

Intimate language, intimate heart, and intimate action in the buddha-dharma are not like that. When you encounter a person, you invariably hear intimate language and speak intimate language. When you know yourself, you know intimate action. Thus, buddha ancestors can thoroughly actualize this intimate heart and intimate language. You should know that where there are buddha ancestors, intimate language and intimate action are immediately manifest. "Intimate" means close and inseparable. There is no gap. Intimacy embraces buddha ancestors. It embraces you. It embraces the self. It embraces action. It embraces generations. It embraces merit. It embraces intimacy.

When intimate language encounters an intimate person, the buddha eye sees the unseen. Intimate action is not known by self or other, but the intimate self alone knows it. Each intimate other goes beyond understanding. Since intimacy surrounds you, it is fully intimate; it is beyond intimate.

You should clearly study this. Indeed, intimacy comes forth at the place where the person is, at the moment when understanding takes place. Thus the person becomes a correct heir of buddha ancestors. Right now is the very moment, when you are intimate with yourself, intimate with others. You are intimate with buddha ancestors, intimate with other beings. This being so, intimacy renews intimacy. Because the teaching of practice-enlightenment is the way of buddha ancestors, it is intimacy that penetrates buddha ancestors. Thus intimacy penetrates intimacy.

OLD MASTER XUEDOU said to his assembly:

The World-honored One has intimate language.
Mahākāshyapa does not conceal it.

Night rain causes the blossoms to fall.
The fragrant water reaches everywhere.

"Night rain causes the blossoms to fall," and "the fragrant
water reaches everywhere," spoken here by Xuedou are intimate.
You should study this and examine the eyeballs and nostrils of buddha ancestors. This is not somewhere Linji or Deshan can arrive.
You should open the nostrils within the eyeballs, and sharpen the
nose tip within the ears. With the entire body and mind, study the
realm where the ear, nose, and eye are neither old nor new. This is
how blossoms and rain open up the world.

"The fragrant water reaching everywhere," spoken of by
Xuedou, conceals the body and reveals light. This being so, in the
daily practice of the buddha ancestors' school, the passage "The
World-honored One has intimate language. Mahākāshyapa does
not conceal it" is studied and penetrated. Each of the Seven Original Buddhas has studied intimate language like this. Thus, Mahākāshyapa and Shākyamuni Buddha have completely manifested
intimate language.

*Presented to the assembly of the ancient Yoshimine Monastery of
Yoshida County, Echizen Province, on the twentieth day, the
ninth month, the first year of the Kangen Era [1243].*

Insentient Beings
Speak Dharma

SPEAKING DHARMA by means of speaking dharma actualizes the fundamental point that buddha ancestors entrust to buddha ancestors. This speaking dharma is spoken by dharma.

Speaking dharma is neither sentient nor insentient. It is neither creating nor not creating. It is not caused by creating or not creating. It doesn't depend on conditions. Therefore, just as birds fly in the air, speaking dharma leaves no trace. It is just given to Buddhist practitioners.

When the great road is complete, speaking dharma is complete. When the dharma treasury is entrusted, speaking dharma is entrusted. When a flower is held up, speaking dharma is held up. When a robe is transmitted, speaking dharma is transmitted. In this way all buddhas, all ancestors have maintained speaking dharma since before the King of the Empty Eon. Expounding dharma has been their fundamental practice since the time before all buddhas.

Do not think that buddha ancestors have brought forth speaking dharma. Speaking dharma has brought forth buddha ancestors. This speaking dharma is not limited to the teachings of eighty-four-thousand dharma gates,* but opens up the teachings of immeasurable, boundless gates. Do not think that dharma spoken by later buddhas was spoken by earlier buddhas. Just as earlier buddhas don't become later buddhas, earlier speaking dharma does not become later speaking dharma. Thus, Shākyamuni Buddha said, "Just as all buddhas in the three worlds spoke dharma, I now speak wondrous dharma."

In this way, just as each buddha employs speaking dharma, all buddhas employ speaking dharma. Just as each buddha transmits speaking dharma, all buddhas transmit speaking dharma. Insentient beings' speaking dharma was transmitted from the ancient buddhas to the Seven Original Buddhas, and it has been transmitted from the Seven Original Buddhas to the present day. In this speaking dharma by insentient beings there are all buddhas, all ancestors. Do not think that the dharma I am speaking now is something new that has not been transmitted. Do not think that what has been transmitted since ancient times is the empty pit of an old demon.

NANYANG HUIZHONG, National Teacher Dazheng of the Guangzhai Monastery in the city of Xijing, in the Great Tang Dynasty, was asked by a monk, "Do insentient beings understand dharma when it's spoken?"

Nanyang replied, "Obviously, insentient being always speak dharma. The speaking never stops."

The monk asked, "Why don't I hear it?"

Nanyang said, "You don't hear it, but that doesn't mean others don't hear it."

The monk said, "Tell me, who hears it?"

Nanyang responded, "All the sages do."

The monk asked, "Do you hear it, sir?"

"No, I don't hear it."

The monk persisted, "If you don't hear it, how do you know that insentient beings understand this dharma?"

Nanyang responded, "This fortunate person doesn't hear it. If I did, I would be equal to all sages. Then you could not hear me expound dharma."

The monk said, "If so, human beings would be left out."

Nanyang said, "But I speak to humans, not to sages."

The monk asked, "What happens to sentient beings after they hear you?"

Nanyang responded, "They are no longer sentient beings."

* * *

Nanyang said, "Obviously, insentient being always speak dharma. The speaking never stops." "Always" includes all time. "The speaking never stops" means there is no break in speaking dharma. Just because insentient beings do not use the voice or the manner of sentient beings in speaking dharma, you should not suppose that the way insentient beings speak dharma is different from the way sentient beings speak dharma. The buddha way does not appropriate the voice of sentient beings and apply it to the voice of insentient beings. Insentient beings do not necessarily speak dharma with a voice heard by the ears. Similarly, sentient beings do not speak dharma with the voice heard by the ears. Now ask yourself, ask others, and inquire, "What are sentient beings? What are insentient beings?"

In this way you should concentrate and study closely what "insentient beings speaking dharma" is. Foolish people may think that the sound of trees, or the opening and falling of leaves and flowers, is insentient beings speaking dharma. Such people are not studying buddha-dharma. If it were so, who would know and hear insentient beings speaking dharma? Reflect now: are there grasses, trees, and forests in the world of insentient beings? Is the world of insentient beings mixed with the world of sentient beings? Furthermore, to regard grasses and trees as insentient beings is not thoroughgoing. To regard sentient beings as grasses, trees, tiles, and pebbles is not enough.

Even if you hold a human view that regards grass, trees, and so on as insentient, you cannot grasp them by ordinary thinking. The reason is that there is a distinct difference between trees in heaven and trees in the human world. Those that grow in China and those that grow elsewhere are not the same. Plants in the ocean and those on mountains are completely different. Furthermore there are trees that spread in space and there are trees that spread in clouds. Among hundreds of grasses and myriad trees that grow in air or in fire there are those that should be understood as sentient, and those that should not be seen as insentient. There are grasses and trees that are like humans and beasts. They cannot be classified as either sentient or insentient. In sorcery, the trees, stones, flowers, fruits, and water are difficult to speak of even if you believe what you see. It is impossible to generalize about things in all corners of the world only by seeing and knowing about grasses and trees in Japan.

Nanyang said, "All sages do." That means that in the assembly where insentient beings speak dharma, all sages stand and listen. All sages and insentient beings actualize listening and actualize speaking. All sages speak dharma for all sages. Is this sacred or ordinary? If you experience with your body the way insentient beings speak dharma, you will grasp with your body how all sages hear. As soon as you grasp this with your body, you can comprehend the realm of sages. In this way you should practice the celestial path of going beyond ordinary and going beyond sacred.

Nanyang said, "I don't hear it." Do not suppose that these words are easy to understand. Does he "not hear" as he goes beyond ordinary and sacred? Or does he "not hear" because he tears apart the old convention of ordinary and sacred? Investigate this and let the words come through.

Nanyang said, "This fortunate person doesn't hear it. If I did, I would be equal to all sages." This presentation is not one or two phrases. The fortunate person is neither ordinary nor sacred. Is this a buddha ancestor? Because buddha ancestors go beyond ordinary and go beyond sacred, what all sages hear is not the same.

Nanyang said, "Then you could not hear me expound dharma." You should work on these words and cook the enlightenment of all buddhas and sages. The essence is that insentient beings speak dharma, and all sages hear it; Nanyang speaks dharma, and this monk hears it. Day by day and month by month you should make this matter the focus of your study. Now you should ask Nanyang, "I am not asking you what happens after sentient beings hear it. But what happens at the precise moment that sentient beings hear dharma expounded?"

DONGSHAN, High Ancestor Great Master Wuben, studied with his teacher Great Priest Yunyan, Early Ancestor. Dongshan asked Yunyan, "Who can hear insentient beings speak dharma?"

Yunyan said, "Insentient beings hear insentient beings speak dharma."

Dongshan asked, "Do you hear it, sir?"

Yunyan said, "If I heard it, you could not hear me speak dharma."

Dongshan responded: "Being so, I don't hear you speak dharma."

Yunyan replied, "You haven't been hearing me speak dharma. How could you hear insentient beings speak dharma?"

Dongshan responded by presenting this poem:

How splendid! How wondrous!
Inconceivable! Insentient beings speak dharma.
The ears never hear it.
Only the eyes do.

Dongshan asked, "Who can hear insentient beings speak dharma?" You should investigate this question in detail throughout your life, throughout many lives. The question can also work as a statement. This statement is the skin, flesh, bones, and marrow. It is not merely transmitting mind with mind. This "transmitting mind with mind" is a common notion of beginning and advanced students. However, the key to practice is taking up the robe and transmitting it, taking up dharma and transmitting it. How can people nowadays master this matter in three or four months?

Dongshan had heard about the words of Nanyang, "Insentient beings speak dharma. . . . All sages can hear it." But he inquired further: "Who can hear insentient beings speak dharma?" Is Dongshan agreeing with or not agreeing with Nanyang's words? Is this a question or a statement? If Dongshan was not agreeing with Nanyang, why did he speak this way? If he was agreeing with Nanyang, why did he speak this way?

Yunyan said, "Insentient beings hear insentient beings speak dharma." You should transmit this blood vein and experience body and mind dropping off. Insentient beings hearing insentient beings speak dharma is essentially all buddhas hearing all buddhas speak dharma. In the assembly of beings, those who hear insentient beings speak dharma are insentient, whether they are sentient beings or insentient beings, ordinary or sacred.

With these essentials you should determine if past or present teachings are true or false. Even if a teaching was brought from India, if it has not been correctly transmitted by genuine masters, you should not adopt it. Even if the lineage of teaching has lasted for thousands of years, if there is not an authentic succession from heir to heir, you should not inherit it. Today correctly transmitted teaching has already spread across the eastern lands. You can easily distinguish what is genuine or false.

When you hear, "Sentient beings hear sentient beings speak dharma," you should accept this as the bones and marrow of all buddhas and ancestors. When you hear the words of Yunyan and Nanyang and wrestle with them, the sages who speak what all sages hear are insentient. Insentient beings who speak what insentient beings hear are sages. Since insentient beings speaking dharma are insentient, what they speak is insentient. This is how sentient beings speak dharma. This is how speaking dharma is insentient.

Dongshan responded: "Being so, I don't hear you speak dharma." "Being so" here refers to Yunyan's words, "Insentient beings hear insentient beings speak dharma." Because insentient beings hear insentient beings speak dharma, Dongshan said, "I don't hear you speak dharma." At this moment Dongshan not only became part of the audience, but also revealed his towering determination to speak dharma for insentient beings. He not only experienced insentient beings speaking dharma, but he thoroughly took hold of hearing and of not hearing insentient beings speak dharma. From there he experienced sentient beings speaking, not speaking, already having spoken, now speaking, and just speaking dharma. Further more, he clarified the hearing and the not hearing of the dharma spoken by sentient beings and insentient beings.

Actually, hearing dharma is not limited to ear sense and ear consciousness. You hear dharma with complete power, complete mind, complete body, and complete way from before your parents

were born, before the empty eon, through the entire future, the
unlimited future. You can hear dharma with body first and mind
last.

Such ways of hearing the dharma are all effective. Don't think
that you are not benefited by hearing the dharma if it does not
reach your mind consciousness. Effacing mind, dropping body, you
hear the dharma and see the result. With no mind and no body you
should hear dharma and benefit from it. Experiencing such moments is how all buddha ancestors become buddhas and attain an-
cestorhood.

Ordinary people cannot understand that dharma power transforms body and mind. The boundary of body and mind cannot be
encompassed. When the effect of hearing dharma is planted in the
field of body and mind, it never decays. It is bound to grow and
bear fruit. Foolish people may think that when we hear dharma,
if we do not advance in understanding and cannot remember the
teaching, there will be no benefit from it. They say it is essential to
learn broadly and to memorize extensively with our entire body
and mind. They think that forgetting the teaching, absentmindedly
leaving the place of instruction, creates no benefit and no accomplishment. They think this way because they have not met a genuine teacher and encountered themselves. One who has not received
correct transmission face to face cannot be a genuine teacher. A
genuine teacher is one who has received transmission correctly
from buddha to buddha.

Indeed, to memorize in mind consciousness and not to forget is
exactly how the power of hearing the dharma encompasses the
mind and encompasses consciousness. At the very moment when
this is done, you realize the power of encompassing body; encompassing past body; encompassing mind; encompassing past mind;
encompassing future mind; encompassing cause and effect, action
and result; encompassing nature and form, essence and activity; encompassing buddha; encompassing ancestor; encompassing self and
other; encompassing skin, flesh, bones, and marrow. The power of
encompassing speech and encompassing sitting and lying down is

manifest throughout the entire earth and sky. The power of hearing dharma is not easy to know. But when we join the great assembly of buddha ancestors and study their skin, flesh, bones, and marrow, there is no instant when the power of speaking dharma does not work, and there is no place where the power of hearing dharma does not extend. The tides of timelessness bring forth sudden or gradual effects. Thus, learning broadly and memorizing extensively is not to be abandoned. However, it is not the key. Students should know about this. Dongshan understood it.

Yunyan replied, "You haven't been hearing me speak dharma. How could you hear insentient beings speak dharma?" This is how Yunyan pulled open his robes and certified with the bones and marrow of the ancestors that Dongshan had actualized enlightenment on top of enlightenment. "You haven't been hearing me speak dharma." Ordinary people can't say this. He was assuring Dongshan that however variously insentient beings speak dharma, he should not be lost in thought about it. The transmission at this moment was truly subtle and pivotal. Ordinary sages cannot easily understand it.

Dongshan responded by presenting this poem: "How splendid! How wondrous! Inconceivable! Insentient beings speak dharma." Thus, insentient beings and their speaking dharma are both difficult to think about. What are the so-called insentient beings? They are neither ordinary nor sacred, neither sentient nor insentient. Ordinary and sacred, sentient and insentient can be reached by thinking whether they are speaking or not speaking. Now it is inconceivable, splendid, and wondrous. But what is splendid and wondrous cannot be reached by the wisdom and consciousness of the ordinary or the sacred. Heavenly beings and ordinary humans cannot assess it.

"The ears never hear it." Even with heavenly ears or with dharma ears of all realms and all times, we don't understand what we are hearing. Even with an ear on the wall or an ear on a stick, insentient beings speaking dharma cannot be heard, because it is not a sound that is the object of the ear. It is not that hearing with ears does not happen, but that it is impossible to hear even if we try for hundreds and thousands of kalpas. Insentient beings speaking dharma is the awesome manifestation of the single way beyond sound and form. Insentient beings speaking dharma is beyond the pit ordinary beings and sages fall into.

"Only the eyes do." Some people may think that this statement means that the coming and going of grass, trees, flowers, and birds viewed by humans are what eyes hear. This view is mistaken. It is not at all buddha-dharma. There is no such understanding in the buddha-dharma. When we study Dongshan's words, "Only the eyes do," it means we hear the voice of insentient beings speaking dharma with the eyes. We manifest the voice of insentient beings speaking dharma with the eyes. You should investigate the eyes extensively. Because the voice heard by the eyes should be the same as the voice heard by the ears, the voice heard by the eyes is not the same as the voice heard by the ears. Do not think that eyes have ear organs. Do not think that eyes are ears. Do not think that voice appears in the eyes.

AN ANCIENT TEACHER [Xuansha] said, "The entire world of the ten directions is no other than a monk's single eye."

Don't suppose that you can understand Dongshan's words, "Only the eyes do," by hearing this with your eyes. Although you study the ancient teacher's words, "The entire world of the ten directions is no other than a monk's single eye," the entire world of the ten directions is no other than a monk's single eye.[1] Furthermore, there are eyes on one thousand hands, one thousand true dharma eyes, one thousand ear eyes, one thousand tongue eyes, one thousand mind eyes, one thousand eyes throughout the mind, one thousand eyes throughout the body, one thousand eyes on top of sticks, one thousand eyes on the extremities of the body, one thousand eyes on the extremities of the mind, one thousand dead eyes in the midst of death, one thousand living eyes in the midst of life, one thousand eyes of self, one thousand eyes of other, one thousand

1. Dogen is contrasting hearing the teaching in an ordinary way and hearing it with true insight.

eyes on top of eyes, one thousand eyes of study, one thousand verti-
cal eyes, and one thousand horizontal eyes.

This being so, even if you study these entire eyes as the entire
world, still it's not the embodiment of eyes. You should urgently
investigate hearing with the eyes insentient beings speaking
dharma. The meaning of Dongshan's words is that insentient beings speaking dharma cannot be understood by ears. The eyes can
hear the voice. Furthermore, there is hearing voice throughout the
body and there is hearing voice wherever the body can reach. Even
if you do not embody hearing the voice with the eyes, you should
master with your body "insentient beings hear insentient beings
speaking dharma," and you should let go of "insentient beings hear
insentient beings speaking dharma."

As this teaching has been transmitted, my late teacher Rujing,
Old Buddha Tiantong, said, "Gourd with its tendrils is entwined
with gourd."

This is the speaking dharma of insentient beings that transmits
Yunyan's true eye and his bone and marrow. Because all speaking
dharma is insentient, insentient beings speak dharma. This is a venerable example. Insentient beings are those who speak dharma for
insentient beings. What do you call insentient beings? You should
know, those who hear insentient beings speak dharma are thus.
What do you call speaking dharma? You should know, those who
do not know insentient beings are thus.

TOUZI, Great Master Ciji of Shu Province, was an heir of Zen
Master Cuiwei Wuxue, and his posthumous name was Datong.
Touzi was called Old Buddha Touzi by Mingjue. He was once asked
by a monk, "What is insentient beings speaking dharma?"

Touzi replied, "Don't bad-mouth them."

What Touzi says here is indeed the dharma standard of the old
buddha, an accomplishment of the ancestral teaching. Insentient
beings speaking dharma and the speaking dharma of insentient beings are equally beyond bad-mouthing. You should know that insentient beings speaking dharma is the totality of buddha ancestors.

It is not known by followers of Linji or Deshan. Only buddha ancestors penetrate this completely.

Presented to the assembly of the ancient Yoshimine Monastery, Yoshida County, Echizen Province, on the second day, the tenth month, the first year of the Kangen Era [1243].

1244, Echizen

Turning the
Dharma Wheel

MY LATE TEACHER RUJING, Old Buddha Tiantong, ascended the teaching seat and declared: "The World-honored One
said, 'When one person opens up reality and returns to the source,
all space in the ten directions disappears.'

"My teacher, Xuedou Zhijian, said, 'Since this is a statement
by the World-honored One, it cannot help being an extraordinary
formulation.'

"But I, Rujing, would say it otherwise. When one person opens
up reality and returns to the source, a mendicant smashes his rice
bowl."

Priest Wuzu Fayan said, "When one person opens up reality
and returns to the source, pounding and crackling resounds
throughout space in the ten directions."

Priest Fuxing Fatai said, "When one person opens up reality
and returns to the source, the space in the ten directions is just the
space in the ten directions."

Jiashan Keqin, Zen Master Yuanwu, said, "When one person
opens up reality and returns to the source, in the space in the ten
directions flowers are added on brocade."

Daibutsu [Dōgen himself] says, "When one person opens up
reality and returns to the source, space in the ten directions also
opens up reality and returns to the source."

* * *

THE WORDS "When one person opens up reality and returns to the source, all space in the ten directions disappears" come from *The Shūrangama Sūtra*. This saying has been commented on by these several buddha ancestors. It is indeed the bones, marrow, and eyeballs of buddha ancestors.

There is a debate whether *The Shūrangama Sūtra*, which consists of ten scrolls, is an authentic sūtra or not. The argument has lasted until now. Among the existing translations, the newest one from the Xinlong Era [705–707] is particularly suspect. However, Fayan, Fatai, and Rujing have all commented on this saying. Thus these words have already been turned by the dharma wheel of buddha ancestors. The buddha ancestors are turning this dharma wheel. In this way, these words turn the buddha ancestors, and these words have already expounded the buddha ancestors. Because these words have been turned by buddha ancestors and have turned buddha ancestors, even if this sūtra was spurious, it has become a genuine buddha sūtra and ancestor sūtra, an intimate and familiar dharma wheel. Even a tile or a pebble, a fallen leaf, an udumbara flower, or even a brocade robe, when taken up and turned by buddha ancestors, is the buddha-dharma wheel and the buddha treasury of the true dharma eye.

Know that when sentient beings leap beyond and attain true awakening, they are buddha ancestors, disciples and teachers of buddha ancestors, and skin, flesh, bones, and marrow of buddha ancestors. They are no longer the siblings of any ordinary sentient beings, but siblings of buddha ancestors. Likewise, even if the words in the ten-scroll *Shūrangama Sūtra* are inauthentic, the saying discussed above is an extraordinary buddha saying and ancestor saying that cannot be compared with usual words. But even if these words go beyond, do not regard the entire text of the sūtra as buddha words and ancestor words; do not regard the entire text as the eyeball of study.

There are many reasons that the saying should not be compared with usual words. I will present some of the reasons. What is called turning the dharma wheel is the activity of buddha ancestors. There have been no buddha ancestors who do not turn the dharma wheel.

How the dharma wheel is turned is by taking up sound and form and smashing sound and form, by leaping out of sound and form and turning the dharma wheel, by gouging out the eyeballs and turning the dharma wheel, or by raising a fist and turning the dharma wheel. The dharma wheel also turns by itself when the nostrils are grabbed and empty space is grasped. Taking up the saying discussed above at this immediate moment is to take up the morning star, grasp nostrils, peach blossoms, or empty space. This is no other than taking up buddha ancestors and taking up the dharma wheel. This is the essence of clearly turning the dharma wheel. Turning the dharma wheel is to practice without separating from the monastery for a whole lifetime, to ask for instructions, and to whole-heartedly engage the way on the sitting platform.

Presented to the assembly of the Yoshimine Monastery, Echizen Province, on the twenty-seventh day, the second month, the second year of the Kangen Era [1244].

In Honor
of Master Rujing

I use this wooden dipper to stir up wind and waves.
The profound power of his great teaching asks an equal
    response.
Even when the plum has wilted and winter has reached its
    deepest cold,
do not let your body be numb or your mind absent.

*Written in Japan on the seventeenth day, the seventh month, the
second year of the Kangen Era, on the occasion of the memorial
day of my late teacher Rujing, thirtieth abbot of the Tiantong
Monastery, Qingyuan Prefecture, Great Song China. As we are
unable to hold a full memorial ceremony for him today [the day
before the official opening of the Daibutsu Monastery], I can only
repay his nurturance by conveying to my disciples his teaching of
"body and mind dropping off."*

On Carving the Buddha Image for the Daibutsu Monastery

IT IS AUSPICIOUS that today the work of laying out the site for the buddha hall has been completed. The officer of the local government supervised the work. Now that the layout is finished I want to have a temporary building constructed on this site and have a purification ceremony for the Buddha. After this we will gradually build the buddha hall.

As a vow of my lifetime, I am determined to carve a statue of Shākyamuni Buddha with my own hands. I am not certain how long I will live, but this is my intention. It might not be exquisitely crafted but my intention is to carve it with my own hands, even if it takes many years.

In reverence,
Dōgen

THE FOURTEENTH DAY, THE EIGHTH MONTH, THE SECOND YEAR OF THE KANGEN ERA

1245, Echizen

Space

PROVOKED BY THE QUESTION "What is right here?"[1] the way is actualized and buddha ancestors emerge. The actualization of the buddha ancestors' way has been handed down heir by heir. Thus the whole body of skin, flesh, bones, and marrow hangs in empty space.

Space is not classified within the twenty types of emptiness.* Indeed emptiness is not limited merely to the twenty types of emptiness. There are eighty-four thousand types of emptiness and more.

SHIGONG, Zen Master Huizang of Fu Region, asked his younger dharma brother Zen Master Zhizang of Xitang, "Do you know how to grasp space?"

Zhizang said, "Yes, I do."

Shigong said, "How do you grasp it?" Zhizang stroked the air with his hand.

Shigong said, "You don't know how to grasp space."

Zhizang responded, "How do you grasp it, elder brother?" Shigong poked his finger in Zhigong's nostril and yanked his nose.

Zhizang grunted in pain and said, "You're killing me! You tried to pull my nose off."

Shigong said, "You can grasp it now."

* * *

1. *What is right here?*: A question by Huangbo to a novice, Emperor Xuan to be. See p. 134.

SHIGONG SAID, "Do you know how to grasp space?" He was asking whether the entire body is hands and eyes. Zhizang said, "Yes, I do." Space is one piece but is defiled with a touch. As soon as it is defiled, space has fallen to the ground.

Shigong said, "How do you grasp it?" Even if you call it thusness, it changes quickly. Although it changes, it slips away as thusness. Zhizang stroked the air with his hand. He knew how to ride on a tiger's head, but didn't know how to grab its tail.

Shigong said, "You don't know how to grasp space." Not only did Zhizang not know how to grasp it, but he had never dreamed of space. The gap between them was profound, yet Shigong did not want to speak for the other. Zhizang responded: "How do you grasp it, elder brother?" Thus Zhizang wanted Shigong to speak for himself, not depending on Zhizang to say it all. Shigong poked his finger in Zhigong's nostril and yanked his nose. You should know that Shigong hid his body in Zhigong's nostril. This is the same as Shigong poking his own nostril. Thus, space is one ball that bounces here and there.

Zhizang grunted in pain and said, "You're killing me! You tried to pull my nose off." He thought he had met another person, but right there he actually met himself. At this moment defiling himself was not possible. This is how you should study the self.

Shigong said, "You can grasp it now." This is certainly a way to grasp space. It is not that Shigong and another Shigong reached out together with one hand; it is not that space and other space reached out together with one hand. No effort was needed [for grasping space].

There is no gap in the entire world to let space in, but this story has been a peal of thunder in space. From the time of Shigong and Zhizang there have been many practitioners regarded as masters in the five schools, but few of them have seen, heard, and understood space. Some of those before and after Shigong and Zhizang touched upon space, but there are few who have reached it. Shigong brought up space but Zhizang did not see it.

Let me respond to Shigong. You grabbed Zhigong's nose. If this was grasping space, you should grasp your own nose. You should have grasped your own finger with a finger. You have some understanding of grasping space. Even if you have a good finger to grasp space, you should penetrate the inside and outside of space. You should kill space and give life to space. You should know the weight of space. You should trust that the buddha ancestors' endeavor of the way, in aspiration, practice, and enlightenment, throughout the challenging dialogues is no other than grasping space.

My late teacher Rujing, Old Buddha Tiantong, said, "The entire body of a windbell is a mouth hanging in emptiness." Thus we know that the entire body of space is hanging in emptiness.

ONCE LECTURER LIANG of Mt. Xi, Hong Region, studied with Mazu, who said, "Which sūtra do you teach?"

Liang said, *"The Heart Sūtra."*

Mazu said, "How do you teach it?"

Liang said, "I teach it with the heart."

Mazu said, "The heart is like a main actor. The will is like a supporting actor. The objects of the six senses are like their company. How do they understand your teaching of the sūtra?"

Liang said, "If the heart doesn't understand it, does emptiness understand it?"

Mazu said, "Yes, it does." Liang flipped his sleeves and started to walk away.

Mazu called, "Lecturer." Liang turned his head around.

Mazu said, "Just this, from birth till death." At this moment Liang had realization. He hid himself at Mt. Xi and no one heard about him any longer.

In this way buddha ancestors all teach sūtras. Empty space is teaching sūtras. Without being empty space, no one can teach even one single sūtra. Teaching *The Heart Sūtra* and teaching the body sūtra are both done with empty space. With empty space, thinking is actualized and beyond thinking is actualized. Empty space is wisdom with a teacher, wisdom without a teacher, knowing by birth, knowing by learning. Becoming a buddha, becoming an ancestor is also empty space.

* * *

VASUBANDHU, the Twenty-first Ancestor, said:

> Mind is like the world of space
> constantly bringing forth empty things.
> When you realize space
> There are no good or bad things.

Now the wall that faces the person meets the person who faces the wall. Here is the mind of a wall, the mind of a decayed tree. This is "the world of space." Awakening others with this body, manifesting this body to speak dharma is "constantly bringing forth empty things." Being used by the twelve hours and using the twelve hours is, "When you realize space." If the rock's head is large, its base is large. If the rock's head is small, its base is small. This is, "There are no good or bad things."

Right now investigate the fact that that empty space is the treasury of the true dharma eye, the wondrous heart of nirvāna.

This was presented to the assembly of the Daibutsu Monastery, Echizen Province, on the sixth day, the third month, the third year of the Kangen Era [1245].

Formal Talk on the First Day of the Practice Period

RECORDED BY EJŌ,
ATTENDANT MONK

MASTER DŌGEN ARRIVED at this Daibutsu Monastery on the eighteenth day, the seventh month, the second year of the Kangen Era [1244]. In the following year students from four directions assembled like clouds.

On the first day of the summer practice period he ascended the teaching seat, held up a whisk, drew a circle in the air, and said, "Our practice period—peaceful dwelling—goes beyond this."

He drew another circle and said, "Peaceful dwelling is to study this thoroughly. So it is taught that the buddha who is King of the Empty Eon received this life vein, becoming a buddha, becoming an ancestor. The fist and the staff embody this point. They transmit dharma and transmit the robe.

"During each summer practice period, make each moment the top of your head. Don't regard this as the beginning. Don't regard this as going beyond. Even if you see it as the beginning, kick it away. Even if you see it as going beyond, stomp on it. Then you are not bound by beginning or going beyond. How is it?"

Dōgen took up the whisk, drew a circle, and said, "Dwell peacefully in this nest."

Given to Hironaga Hatano

The whole universe
shatters into a hundred pieces.
In the great death
there is no heaven, no earth.

Once body and mind have turned over
there is only this to say:

Past mind cannot be grasped,
present mind cannot be grasped,
future mind cannot be grasped.

Dōgen
THE FIFTH MONTH,
THE THIRD YEAR
OF THE KANGEN ERA

Eternal Peace

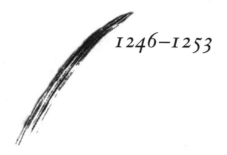

1246–1253

Formal Talk upon Naming the Eihei Monastery

RECORDED BY EJŌ,
ATTENDANT MONK

O N T H E F I F T E E N T H D A Y, the sixth month, the fourth year of the Kangen Era, when the Daibutsu Monastery was renamed the Eihei [Eternal Peace] Monastery, Dōgen ascended the teaching seat and said, "Heaven's way is high and pure. The earth's way is rich and serene. Humans have a way that is easy and calm. So, when the World-honored One was born, he took seven steps and, with one hand pointing to heaven and the other hand pointing to the earth, he said, 'In the heavens above and on the earth below, I alone am the honored one.' The World-honored One's way is like this. And my way is witnessed by this great assembly."

After a pause, Dōgen said, "In the heavens above and on the earth below, this very place is Eihei."

Guidelines for Officers of the Eihei Monastery

1246, Echizen

THE OFFICERS IN A MONASTERY are precious and venerable. Those who maintain the way and whose virtue is mature ought to be selected. Here are some examples.

Prince Nanda, a lay brother of the Tathāgata, realized arhathood when he was serving as an officer. When the World-honored One was in the city of Kapilavastu, he went to visit Nanda. Standing in the doorway, he lit up the house to let Nanda know that the time for him to receive the precepts was at hand.

Nanda thought, "This must be the World-honored One." He sent someone to look, and sure enough, it was the World-honored One. Nanda wanted to go out to see him. His wife thought, "If I let him go, he might be suddenly moved to leave the household." So she tugged on his robe, and Nanda said, "I'll be right back."

She said, "Please come back before my makeup dries."

Nanda said, "Of course I will."

The Buddha handed Nanda his bowl and asked Nanda to serve him rice. But when Nanda came back with the rice, the Buddha was gone. So Nanda offered it to his own brother, Monk Ānanda.

Ānanda said, "Who gave you this bowl?"

Nanda said, "The Buddha did."

Ānanda said, "Then you should go find the Buddha and give it

to him." So Nanda went out, found the Buddha, and offered him
the bowl. There, the Buddha asked a disciple to shave Nanda's
head.

Nanda said to the disciple, "You can't hold a razor to the head
of a prince of Jambudvīpa." Then he said to himself, "Even though
I obey the World-honored One in the morning, I can still go home
in the evening." The Buddha understood his thought and transformed the place where Nanda was standing into a deep pit so that
he was unable to return home. Then Buddha said to Ānanda,
"Make Nanda an officer."

Ānanda conveyed the Buddha's word to Nanda. Nanda said,
"What is an officer?"

Ānanda said, "That's a position of responsibility in a temple."

Nanda said, "What kind of work is it?"

Ānanda said, "After the monks go out to do their begging, you
sweep the garden, sprinkle water on the grounds, collect firewood,
remove cow dung, clean up, see that nothing is stolen, and close the
gates and doors for the sangha. In the evening you open up the
gates and clean the toilets."

When this conversation was over, the monks went out to beg
and Nanda went to close the gates. When he closed the west gate,
the east gate flapped open. When he closed the east gate, the west
gate opened. And this went on and on. Nanda said to himself, "If
anything is stolen, I will build hundreds and thousands of beautiful
temples after I become king. That should be more than enough to
compensate for the loss." So he went home.

Fearful that he would run into the Buddha if he took the main
road, he took a back road. Nevertheless he ran into the Buddha on
the way home. He hid himself in a bush, but when the wind blew,
his body was revealed. The Buddha said, "What are you doing
here?"

Nanda replied, "I am worried about my wife."

The Buddha took him to a garden called the Deer Park outside
the city and said, "Have you ever seen Intoxicating Fragrance
Mountain?"

Nanda said, "No, I haven't."

The Buddha put Nanda in the seam of his robe and flew with
him, instantly arriving at the mountain. There were fruit trees on
the mountain, and under the trees there was a female monkey with
burnt-out eyes. The Buddha said, "How is this monkey compared
with a celestial deva?"

Nanda said, "Devas are desireless. How can one compare this
monkey with a deva?"

The Buddha said, "Have you seen a deva?"

Nanda answered, "No, I haven't."

Then the Buddha, putting Nanda in his robe again, took him
to the Thirty-three Heavens* and showed him around. He then
brought him to Pleasure Park and showed him many beautiful
women. He also showed him the Garden of Intercourse and let him
hear the various pleasurable sounds. At one spot there was a celestial woman without a partner. Nanda asked the Buddha about her
and the Buddha suggested that he speak to her directly. When
Nanda asked why she was alone, she responded, "Nanda, the Buddha's brother, will be reborn here as a result of keeping the precepts
and he will become my husband."

The Buddha said to Nanda, "What do you think of this woman
compared with your wife Sundarī?"

He replied, "My wife is like that blind monkey compared with
this celestial woman."

Then the Buddha said, "If you hold to pure practice, you will
receive much merit. By maintaining the precepts now you will be
reborn in this celestial realm."

Then Nanda accompanied the Buddha back to the Jeta Grove.
After that, Nanda maintained pure practice, longing for this heavenly palace. But the Buddha told the community of monks, "Don't
follow Nanda's practice." So none of the monks mingled with
Nanda or stayed in the same place where Nanda was sitting.

So Nanda said to himself, "Ānanda is my younger brother; he
wouldn't abandon me." So he went to Ānanda, and when he sat
down, Ānanda stood up and was about to leave. Nanda said, "You
are my brother. How can you abandon me?"

Ānanda replied, "Because your practice is different from mine."

"What do you mean by that?"

"Your ultimate wish is to be born in the deva's world, and my wish is nirvāna." When Nanda heard this he became more and more worried.

The Buddha later asked him, "Have you seen the Naraka Hell?"

Nanda said, "No, I haven't."

The Buddha put him back into the sleeve of his robe and took him to the various hells. Each place had prisoners, but there was one place without anybody, so Nanda asked the Buddha why. The Buddha told him to speak directly to the keeper. The keeper said, "Nanda, the Buddha's brother, is practicing in order to be in the deva's world. He will stay there for a while and then will come here to receive his torture."

Nanda was frightened and, shedding tears like rain, told the Buddha of his fear. The Buddha said, "If you practice for the pleasure of being in the deva's world, you will have this problem."

Nanda went back to the Jeta Grove together with Buddha, who expounded the overall principles to the community. Consequently, Nanda for the first time aroused the wish for emancipation. He maintained the precepts and in the end attained the fruit of arhatship (from *The Womb Storehouse Sūtra*).

Venerable Nanda belonged to the warrior class and as a son of King Suddhodana was half-brother of the Tathāgata. He filled the position of a monastic officer and became an arhat. His merit of seeing the Buddha, and his example of realizing the fruit should be revered and longed for. Only those who aspire to the way and long for ancient examples should fill such a monastic position.

The attentiveness of the officers should be the same as that of the abbot. You should make understanding and fairness priorities, as well as flexibility and harmony. You should have great compassion and great empathy toward the assembly of clouds and water,* serve the monks who come from the ten directions, and contribute to the flourishing of the monastery. Such positions have been filled by those who do not seek worldly benefits, but are solely engaged in the work of the way. The permeating fragrance and kneading practice in the way by these officers cannot be surpassed.

HERE IS AN EXAMPLE of an encounter between an officer of the monastery and the teacher. One day Guishan called the administrator* of the monastery. When he came, Guishan said, "I called the administrator. Why did you come?" The administrator remained silent. Guishan asked his attendant monk to call the head monk. Guishan said, "I asked for the head monk. Why did you come?" The head monk remained silent.

Caoshan at a later time, putting himself in the place of the administrator, said, "I know you didn't call me." Putting himself in the place of the head monk, Caoshan said, "If you had asked the attendant monk to call me, perhaps I wouldn't have come."

Much later, Master Fayan said, "Just now the attendant monk called." In taking up these matters, investigate thoroughly the life vein of the monastery officers.

HERE ARE EXAMPLES of those who served as the administrator and who clarified the great matter:

Zen Master Xuanze of the Baoen Monastery, Jinling City, once filled the position of administrator in the community of Fayan. One day Fayan said, "Administrator, how long have you been with us?"

Xuanze said, "I've been in your community for three years."

Fayan said, "You are a junior person in the monastery. How come you never ask questions?"

Xuanze said, "I don't want to mislead you. I must confess. When I was with Master Qingfeng, I attained the peaceful bliss."

Fayan said, "By what words did you enter that place?"

Xuanze replied, "When I asked Qingfeng, 'What is the self of the practitioner?' he said, 'The fire child seeks fire.' "

Fayan said, "Good words, but I'm afraid you didn't understand them."

Xuanze said, "The fire child belongs to fire; fire seeking fire is just like self seeking self."

Fayan said, "Indeed, you didn't understand. If the buddha-

dharma was like that, it wouldn't have come down to this day."
Xuanze was so upset that he stood up and left. But on his way he
thought, "Fayan is the teacher of five hundred monks. Although he
didn't approve me, what he said should be correct." So he went
back and apologized.

Fayan said, "Why don't you ask me?"

Xuanze then said, "What is the self of the practitioner?"

Fayan said, "The fire child seeks fire." At that, Xuanze experienced great awakening.

YANGQI, Zen Master Fanghui of Yuan Region, was studying with
Ciming, who became abbot of monasteries at Mt. Nanyuan, Mt.
Daowu, and Mt. Sishuang. Yangqi assisted him and directed the
monastic affairs in all these places. Although he was with Ciming
for a long time, he had not yet developed insight.

Every time Yangqi went to ask questions, Ciming said, "There
is a lot of work to do in the kitchen. Please go." One time Ciming
said, "Administrator, your dharma descendants are bound to fill the
world any way. Why do you rush?"

There was an old woman who was living near the monastery.
People could not measure her. She was only known as Ciming's old
woman friend. Whenever Ciming had time, he would visit her. It
rained one day when Ciming was on his way to visit the old woman.
Yangqi hid on the narrow path and waited. Seeing Ciming, Yangqi
grabbed him and said, "Old man, today you must explain to me, or
I'll hit you!"

Ciming said, "Administrator, if you understand this, you can
take a break."

Before Ciming had finished speaking, Yangqi had a great awakening. He threw his body on the muddy ground and made a prostration. He stood up again and said to Ciming, "What is this
meeting on a narrow path?"

Ciming said, "Move over, I want to go somewhere."

So Yangqi went back to the monastery. The following day he
dressed formally, went up to the abbot, and made a full bow to
thank him. Ciming scolded him and said, "You don't yet have it."

On another day there was a gathering for dharma instruction in the abbot's room. The monks waited for a long time after the morning meal for the sound of the drum signaling the gathering, but it was not heard. Yangqi asked the abbot's assistant, "This is the day for dharma instructions. Why aren't you hitting the drum?"

The assistant said, "Master went away and has not come back yet."

Fanghui followed Ciming's path, and when he got to the old woman's hut, he saw Ciming burning firewood and cooking gruel. Yangqi said, "Master, this is a day for dharma instruction. The entire community has been patiently waiting for you. Why don't you come back?"

Ciming said, "If you can give me a turning word, I will come back. Otherwise everyone should go east, west, or wherever they choose."

Yangqi put his hat on his head and took a few steps. Ciming was greatly pleased, and they went back together. From this time on, whenever it looked like Ciming was leaving the monastery, Yangqi would have the drum hit to assemble the monks.

One time Ciming stopped as he was leaving and angrily said, "Where did you get a guideline on giving dharma instructions at night in a small monastery like this?"

Yangqi said, "We got it from [your teacher] Master Fenyang. Please don't say that this is against guidelines."

Nowadays in the monasteries, dharma instructions are given at the end of the evening chanting ceremony on the days ending with a three and an eight. This is the origin of the custom.

In ancient times, the only administrative officer was the administrator, who did the work that is done nowadays by the director and treasurer.* As there has come to be a lot of work to do in a monastery, a few such administrative positions have been created.

Xuanze and Yangqi each clarified the great matter of birth and death while working as administrator. Know that their effort has indeed been rewarded. An abbot like Yangqi is hard to find in the ten directions these days.

*   *   *

AN EXAMPLE of someone advanced in the way who filled the position of practice leader* is Xiujing, Great Master Baozhi of the Huayan Monastery in Jingzhao, an heir of Dongshan. While he was at Luotu's assembly, he became practice leader. One day he called the assembly to work by hitting the *han** with the mallet, and said, "Those of you whose seats are on the right side of the monks' hall, please take care of firewood, and those on the left, please plow the field."

The head monk said, "What about the holy monk [Manjushrī, who is enshrined in the center]?"

Xiujing replied, "He is not seated on either side. Where is there for him to go?" Not a minor teacher, Xiujing was a fine example of someone accomplished in the way. The elders of today do not reach to his stature.

ONE WHO HAD great awakening while serving as practice leader was Shigui, Zen Master Zhuan of Wen Region, an heir of Fuyan Qingyuan of Longmen. On his first visit to Fuyan, Shigui expressed his understanding of everyday matters. Fuyan said, "You have reached the limit of your discriminating mind. What you lack is exertion in practice and the open eye."

Shigui was then put in charge of the meditation hall. One day, while standing and waiting on Fuyan, he asked, "What about the moment of going beyond duality?"

Fuyan said, "It's the sound of hitting the han with a mallet in the hall." Shigui did not stop pursuing his inquiry. In the evening Fuyan came to the hall, and Shigui asked the same question again. Fuyan said, "Playing with words." At that Shigui attained great awakening. Fuyan said, "There is nothing more to say."

Fuyan was an excellent disciple of Wuzu Fayan. Shigui received the blood spirit of the ancestral school and met the opportunity mentioned above while he was serving as practice leader. Nowadays he is called Gushan. Few people can be compared with the reputable Shigui when it comes to commenting and writing both prose and verse on the ancestors.

* * *

AN EXAMPLE of one who clarified the great matter while serving as head cook* is Guishan Lingyou. He was in Baizhang's community when he became head cook. He went to the abbot's quarters to attend to the abbot.

Baizhang said, "Who is there?"

Guishan said, "Lingyou."

Baizhang said, "Please poke around in the fireplace and see if there is still anything burning."

After checking, Guishan said, "There is no fire."

Baizhang stood up and went to the fireplace with the poker. After searching around he found a small ember. Showing it to Guishan, he said, "Isn't this fire?" Guishan understood, and after thanking the master, expressed his understanding.

Then Baizhang said, "You have only come to the crossroads. A sūtra says, 'If you want to see buddha nature, you should contemplate time, causes, and conditions.' When the time comes, delusion immediately turns into enlightenment and forgetting turns into remembering. If we contemplate buddha nature, we realize that buddha nature is ours. It doesn't come from somewhere else. An ancestor said, 'When you're enlightened, it's not different from not enlightened. With no-mind you attain no-dharma.' These words are not false. Both ordinary people and sages equally make the original mind their own. Dharma is complete by itself. You are already as you are. Maintain this well."

Later the ascetic Sima came from Hunan. Baizhang said to him, "I want to move to Mt. Gui. Do you think it's a good thing to do?"

Sima said, "Mt. Gui is an extraordinary place. You could assemble fifteen hundred people there, but it's not a place for you to live."

Baizhang said, "Why?"

Sima answered, "You are a bone person and it's a flesh mountain. If you resided there, you would have less than a thousand students."

Baizhang said, "Is there anyone in this community who could reside there?"

Sima replied, "Let me look them over."

Baizhang asked the attendant monk to call in the head monk and asked the ascetic, "What about this one?"

Sima cleared his throat and, after asking the monk to walk several steps, said, "This monk is not suitable."

Then Baizhang sent for the head cook, Lingyou.

Sima said, "This is indeed the master of Mt. Gui."

That evening Baizhang invited Lingyou to his room and entrusted him with these words: "My place of teaching is here. Mt. Gui is an excellent spot. I want you to reside there to continue my teaching and bring across many latecomers."

Then Hualin, the head monk, heard about this and said, "I have the honor of being the head monk. I wonder why Lingyou has been selected to be an abbot."

Baizhang said, "If you can say a word in front of the assembly that demonstrates your excellence, you, too, can be an abbot." Then he pointed at a water jar and said, "If you don't call this a jar, what do you call it?"

Hualin said, "You can't call it a wooden stick."

Baizhang did not approve it. Then he asked the same question to Lingyou. Lingyou turned over the jar with his foot. Baizhang laughed and said, "The head monk is defeated by this mountain fellow." Then he sent Lingyou to Mt. Gui.

The mountain was steep and there was no sign of humans there. Guishan joined the monkeys and ate chestnuts. Monks at the foot of the mountain gradually learned about him, formed an assembly, and established a monastery. Later Li Jingrang recommended to the Emperor that the place should be given the name of the Tongqing Monastery. Minister Peixiu visited to inquire about the profound mystery. After that, Zen students from all over assembled there.

ZHONGXING, Zen Master Jianyuan, was once head cook in the assembly of Daowu of Tianhuang. One day he accompanied his teacher Daowu to a lay member's house to pay a condolence call on the death of a family member.

Zhongxing knocked on the coffin and said, "Alive or dead?"

"I don't say alive, I don't say dead," replied Daowu.

Zhongxing asked again, "Why won't you say something?"

Daowu said, "I won't say it, I won't say it."

On their way back from the funeral, Zhongxing said, "Master, please say something. If you don't, I will hit you."

Daowu said, "Hit me if you will, but I will not say alive, I will not say dead." Zhongxing gave Daowu a few blows. After returning to their temple, Daowu asked Zhongxing to leave, saying, "If the other officers of the temple know that you hit me, they will retaliate." So Zhongxing thanked him and bid him farewell.

Later, after Daowu's death, Zhongxing went to see Shishuang and told him the story. Zhongxing told him that he had hit Daowu. He then asked Shishuang what he would have said to Daowu. Shishuang said, "Don't you see that Daowu said, 'I won't say alive, I won't say dead'?" At that point Zhongxing had great awakening. He then prepared a memorial meal for Daowu and offered his repentance.

HONORABLE WUZHUO was head cook on Mt. Wutai. While he was cooking one day, Manjushrī appeared on the top of a pot. Wuzhuo hit him with his ladle and said, "Even if Old Man Shākyamuni comes, I will hit him."

PRIEST SHEXIAN GUIXING was a stern and aloof old teacher who was respected by the monks. A group of monks, including Fayuan of Fushan in Shu Region, and Yihuai of Mt. Tianyi in Yue Region, came to practice in his community.

It was a cold and snowy day. On their first meeting Shexian shouted and drove them out. Not only that, he threw water around in the visitors' room,* so everyone's clothes got wet. All the visiting monks fled except Fayuan and Yihuai. They arranged their robes and continued sitting in the visitors' room. Shexian came and, in a scolding voice, said, "If you two monks don't leave, I'll hit you."

Fayuan approached Shexian and said, "The two of us came hundreds of *li* to study your Zen. How could a dipper full of water drive us away? Even if we get beaten to death, we will not leave."

Shexian laughed and said, "You both need to practice Zen. Go to the monks' hall and hang up your bags."

Later Shexian asked Fayuan to serve as head cook. At that time, the assembly was suffering from Shexian's aloof style and unappetizing food. One day Shexian went out to the nearby village and while he was away, Fayuan took the key to the storehouse without permission, got some noodles and oil, and made a delicious morning meal for the community. Shexian returned earlier than expected and, without saying anything, joined in the meal at the monks' hall. After the meal was over he sat outside the monks' hall. He sent for Fayuan and said, "Did you get the noodles and oil from the storehouse?"

Fayuan said, "Yes, I did. Please punish me."

Shexian told him to estimate the price of the noodles and oil and to compensate the community by selling his robes and bowl. Shexian then gave him thirty blows and expelled him from the monastery. Fayuan stayed in a nearby city and asked his dharma brother to plead with Shexian to pardon him, but Shexian would not. Fayuan also pleaded: "Even if I am not readmitted, I would like to request permission to visit and practice in the community." But Shexian did not approve it.

One day Shexian went to the city and saw Fayuan standing in front of a travelers' shelter. Shexian said to him, "This shelter belongs to the monastery. How long have you been living here? Have you paid your fees?" He told Fayuan to calculate his fees and make the payment. Fayuan was not disturbed. He carried his bowl in the city, collecting food. He sold the food and made his payment to the monastery. Later Shexian went to the city and saw Fayuan begging. He returned to the monastery and told the assembly that Fayuan had a true intention to study Zen and finally called him back.

AFTER LINGYOU was appointed head cook on Mt. Baizhang, he carried water and hauled firewood without minding all the toil, without noticing the passing of all the years, and finally he was asked by Baizhang to become the master of Mt. Gui. The life there was modest and simple. Offerings from the human world and from heaven had not reached there. He fed himself on nuts and acorns. Monks had not yet gathered there. He kept company with the mountain monkeys. This was the difficult practice of an ancient sage, which has served as encouragement for later students. Those who fill the position of head cook should revere Guishan's example like their own eyeballs, and hold him in as high esteem as their own heads.

Zhongxing is also an excellent example. You should long for his ancient deed. Wuzhuo is also a great spiritual guidepost. You, present-day followers of the way, should not neglect his example. In particular, the heart of head cook Fayuan needs to be studied. Someone like him is encountered once in a thousand years. Neither the wise nor the unsuited can come up to him. If those of you who are head cooks do not have the aspiration of Fayuan, how can you arrive at the inner chamber of buddha ancestors? The head cooks mentioned above are all dragons and elephants of the buddha ocean, extraordinary people in the ancestral realm. When we look for such people nowadays, we cannot find them anywhere.

HERE IS ANOTHER EXAMPLE of a person accomplished in the way serving as head cook: Jiashan was head cook in the community of Guishan. Guishan said, "What is the community eating in the monks' hall?"

Jiashan said, "The last two years, one and the same spring."

Guishan said, "Continue to practice that way."

Jiashan said, "A dragon resides in the phoenix nest."

Zen Master Daokai of Furong at Mt. Dayang saw Touzi Yiqing and had thorough realization. When Daokai was head cook, Touzi said, "You must be finding your responsibility in the kitchen difficult."

Daokai said, "Not at all."

Touzi said, "Do you boil and cook gruel, or do you steam rice?"

Daokai said, "Helpers wash the rice and start the fire; cooks make gruel and steam rice."

Touzi said, "What do you do?"

Daokai said, "Please be compassionate and leave me alone." Touzi fully appreciated this response.

Touzi and Daokai are both outstanding figures of the ancestral gate. Touzi entrusted the position of head cook to Daokai, and Daokai served as head cook for Touzi. This is an excellent example of the ancestral seat. Thus, the position of head cook should not be given to a mediocre person. One who is appointed should be a dragon or an elephant. Nowadays, there are not many who can compare with Daokai. Those who hear about him are few. Those who understand him are even fewer. If you want to inherit the bones and marrow of buddha ancestors, you should study the body and mind of Daokai.

Jiashan is an heir of Huating, who is an heir of Yaoshan. Thus, Jiashan's lineage is venerable. He was appointed head cook by Guishan. Guishan is an heir of Baizhang. While Baizhang was leading his community on Mt. Baizhang, Guishan started his own community on Mt. Gui with true and clear eye.

The flow of the way and actualization of dharma of these head cooks was as deep as an abyss and as broad as an ocean. Thus their communal heart should be seen and heard through the generations. They are all bright and clear ancestral teachers. Those who are wise revere them. Those who are ignorant disregard them.

AN EXAMPLE OF SOMEONE accomplished in the way while serving as work leader is Baofu, Zen Master Benquan of Zhang Region, a dharma heir of Huitang. He penetrated the source when he saw Huitang raise his fist. Baofu was distinguished for his spontaneous way of expressing understanding.

Shangu, Lord Huang, had just begun to have some understanding and asked Huitang, "Whom can I talk to among your students?"

Huitang said, "Baofu from Zhang Region."

Baofu was directing the work of plowing the fields. Shangu went together with Huitang and asked Baofu, "Work leader, did you know that a wooden pillar gave birth to a child?"

Baofu said, "Boy or girl?" Shangu hesitated. Baofu was about to hit him.

Huitang said, "Don't be discourteous."

Baofu said, "If I don't hit this wooden head, when will he get it?" Shangu burst into laughter.

FOR CHOOSING monastic officers and their assistants, purity and honesty are not enough qualification. You should always choose those who are fully accomplished in the way. Here are some examples of assistant officers who were accomplished in the way: Zhaozhou was in charge of the kitchen furnace in Nanquan's community. One day he locked the kitchen doors and windows and, filling the kitchen with smoke, screamed, "Fire! Fire! Help!"

The entire community came. Zhaozhou said, "If anyone of you can say it, I'll open the door." No one could respond. Nanquan passed a chain to Zhaozhou through a hole in the window. Zhaozhou opened the door.

Xuefeng became the head rice cook at the community of Dongshan, while he was going back and forth between Dongshan's and Deshan's communities. When Xuefeng was washing rice, Dongshan said, "Are you washing the sand out of the rice, or washing the rice out of the sand?"

Xuefeng said, "I am getting rid of both at once."

Dongshan said, "What will the community eat?" Xuefeng turned over the rice basket. Dongshan said, "If you are like this, you will be well-suited to Deshan's community."

Shishuang, Zen Master Qingzhu, became the rice steward in the community of Guishan. One day when he was shifting rice in the granary, Guishan said, "Don't scatter any of this donated stuff."

Shishuang said, "I'm not scattering any."

Guishan picked up a grain from the ground and said, "You said you are not scattering any rice. Where does this come from?" Shishuang could not say a word. Guishan said, "Don't be deceitful about one grain of rice. Hundreds and thousands of grains come from one grain."

Shishuang said, "I still don't know where this grain comes from."

Guishan had a great laugh and returned to the abbot's room. In the evening he ascended the seat and addressed the community, "There is a worm in the rice."

ZHIXIAN, Zen Master Guanxi, after attaining realization at Linji's community, left Linji and wandered on. He went to Moshan, Nun Liaoran, and said, "If we fit, I'll stay here. Otherwise, I'll turn over the meditation platform."

Then he went into the meditation hall. Moshan sent her personal attendant to ask Zhixian, "Did you come here for enjoyment or buddha-dharma?"

Zhixian said, "For buddha-dharma."

Moshan ascended the high seat to give a dharma talk. Zhixian sat in the assembly and listened. After the dharma talk, Zhixian asked a question. Instead of answering, Moshan asked, "Where did you come from today?"

Zhixian said, "I came from the mouth of the road."

Moshan said, "Why don't you cover it?"

Zhixian could not answer. He bowed to her and said, "What is Moshan [Last Mountain]?"

She said, "The peak is not revealed."

He said, "Who is the master of Moshan?"

She replied, "Neither male nor female."

Zhixian shouted, "Then why don't you go back and forth?"

Moshan said, "Being neither divine nor demonic, how is it possible to go back and forth?"

Zhixian made a full bow. After this, he served as head gardener in her community for three years. Later, when Zhixian was abbot of his community, he said to the assembly, "I got half a scoop at Old Man Linji's and got another half at Old Woman Moshan's. All together I ate one full scoop. Even now, I'm still full."

THE POSITION of head gardener is most toilsome and should be filled by someone who has a heart for the way, and not by anyone without such a heart. You must work year-round in the garden, sowing and cultivating according to the season. By this work, you manifest your buddha face, ancestor face, donkey feet, and horse feet. Like a farmer or a peasant, all day long you plow and hoe. You carry excrement and urine for fertilizing. Free from self-concern, you await the moment of ripening for harvest, being careful not to miss the right time.

When plowing the ground and sowing the seeds, you don't wear a combined robe or a kashāya, but a white under-robe and a work robe. However, at the time when the other monks gather to chant the Buddhas' names or sūtras, hear dharma talks, or receive personal instructions, you join the community. You are not supposed to miss any of these activities. In the garden every morning and evening, you offer incense, bow, chant the names of Buddhas, and make a dedication to the dragon spirit and earth spirit, without ever being negligent. The work leader provides you materials and workers as needed. You sleep in a cottage in the garden at night.

Indeed, the position of gardener has always been served by those who have a heart for the way, including those who have reputation. Those who have small capacity or are ill-suited have not been put in this position. In the community of my late teacher Rujing, a monk called Pu from Shu, a western province, was appointed to this position for the first time when he was over sixty years old. During the period of almost three years when he was gardener, the positions in the community were stable. So the monks were joyful and Rujing was deeply pleased. If we compare the abbots of many monasteries with Old Man Pu, their practice cannot come up to that of this head gardener.

WUZU FAYAN of Qi Region studied with Haihui, Priest Shouduan of Mt. Boyun. He inquired about the great matter and deeply penetrated bone and marrow. Haihui appointed him miller. Every year Fayan collected money by selling rice bran and wheat bran, and earned interest by lending the money. He hired workers with some of this money to do temple improvements, and he put the rest in the monastery treasury.

But one day, someone brought an accusation against him to Haihui, saying, "Fayan drinks wine, eats meat, and entertains young women at the mill every day." So the entire community was stirred up. Hearing this, Fayan purposely bought meat and wine and hung them on the wall of the mill. He bought cosmetic powder and gave it to the women, and asked them to paint their faces. When some monks came to the mill, Fayan took the women's hands, teasing them and laughing, without any sign of shyness.

Haihui then called him to the abbot's room and asked him why he was doing it. Fayan said nothing but, "Yes, yes."

Haihui slapped his face, but Fayan did not flinch. He bowed and started to leave. Haihui yelled at him and said, "Get out! Quick!"

Fayan said, "I need to settle my account and find someone to take over my position." Later he said, "I paid for the wine and for the meat that is hanging in the mill and put one thousand three hundred *qian* in the monastery treasury." Haihui was greatly surprised and realized that the accusations had come from the jealousy of petty minds.

In Haihui's community at that time, Fashen, Zen Master Yuantong, was head monk. He accepted an offer to be abbot of Mt. Simian and asked Fayan to be head monk there.

The mill is a place for pounding rice and grinding flour. It is usually located five, six, or ten *ting* [160–330 feet] away from the monastery buildings. The miller works there by himself. This was Fayan's position. In the past, those with a heart for the way filled this position, and those who were unsuited did not. But nowadays it is difficult to find people with a heart for the way, so both those who are suited and ill-suited are used. What a pity that the world has become crude and coarse!

When we reflect on Old Buddha Fayan's practice, there is nothing that can compare with it, either in the past or in the present. It is like the colors of peach and plum, the purity of pine and cypress. Winter wind does not break it. Frost and snow do not impinge on it. We can see how diligent his study of the way was and how lofty his sincerity was. Those of you who come later should not give up your determination for the practice of the way, should not back off even if you are faced with this kind of misfortune. You should take a look at Fayan's extraordinary practice and try to make an effort in this direction. The depth of the ancient way-mind teachers can be actualized through this kind of determination. The more we reflect, the higher and more solidly we know it. This is what we should yearn for.

THE FOLLOWING is an example of toiling within study, practicing thoroughly after attaining the way.

Linji, Great master Huizhao, was planting pine trees on Mt. Huangbo. Huangbo said to him, "Why are you planting so many pines in the deep mountains?"

Linji said, "First, for the landscaping of the monastery, and second, as a landmark for future generations."

Huangbo said, "Remember the thirty blows you got from me?"

Linji hit the ground with the hoe twice, and breathed out a long sigh. Then Huangbo said, "My teaching will flourish greatly through you."

Some time later Guishan told this story to his student Yangshan and asked, "Do you think Huangbo entrusted his teaching to Linji alone at that time, or did he also entrust it to other students?"

Yangshan said, "The time of this event is beyond my reach. I can't answer your question."

Guishan said, "Even so, I want to know. Why don't you tell me?"

Yangshan said, "Linji may send his students this way and to the farthest southern provinces, but they may be stopped here by a fierce storm."

Linji was at Huangbo's community for twenty years and toiled through his practice of the way. Sometimes he planted pine, sometimes he planted cedar. Wasn't this inconceivable language and wondrous practice? The landscape of one mountain is a guidepost for myriad years.

It is said in the world that the wise don't forget virtuous deeds. The small-minded do not repay a debt of gratitude. Children of this house of buddha ancestors owe a deep debt of gratitude for the dharma heart they have received. Repaying a debt means planting pine, planting cedar. It means being contented with the morning meal and with the midday meal. Although the time of the original event is distant from us, we, too, are planting trees in the deep mountains and hitting the ground with the hoe. This is receiving the thirty blows and "My teaching will greatly flourish through you." If you wish to be a bridge for the buddha way, you should learn from Linji through his practice.

EVEN A MINOR POSITION was not given lightly. One day Huitang saw his teacher, Huanglong, who looked concerned. So he asked him what was wrong. Huanglong said, "The position of monastery accountant is not filled."

Huitang recommended Cigan, who was the treasurer. Huanglong said, "Cigan's personality is somewhat coarse, and he may easily be cheated by small-minded people."

Then Huitang said, "Attendant Hua is quite honest and diligent."

Huanglong said, "Although Hua is honest and diligent, he is not as suitable as head gardener Huaixiu, who is more open-minded and faithful."

Lingyuan later asked Huitang, "Why did Master Huanglong take so much consideration in appointing just an accountant?"

Huitang said, "Those who are responsible for this house should be given the same consideration as those who are responsible for the nation. Not just Huanglong but all the sages cautioned about this."

Zen Master Huaixiu of Guishan, Zen Master Hua of Shuanglin, and Iron Face Cigan, mentioned here, were all excellent teachers in the world, who once served as accountant, head gardener, or assistant director. If we look for such people now, it will be just like looking for legendary horses—Flying Rabbit and Black Ears. Those who serve as monastery accountants nowadays have crude faces and unrefined bearing. It might seem that Huanglong was withholding the way and the dharma, but these positions were not to be given lightly. Otherwise a bad result might occur.

*   *   *

MONASTIC OFFICERS should not construct a fine building or a
large hall that has a great view. Wuzu Fuyan said to the community:
"When my old teacher Yangqi became abbot of Mt. Yangqi, the
monastery buildings were old and decayed, barely able to keep out
the wind and rain. In the evening, snow and hail covered the sitting
platform and the monks could not stay there. The monks, expressing their sincerity, volunteered to repair the building. Yangqi re-
jected this offering, saying, 'According to the Buddha's teaching,
this is the time when the human life-span is decreasing, and the
high lands and the deep valleys are always changing. How can we
achieve complete satisfaction in all things? Sages in the past sat
under trees and did walking meditation on bare ground. You have
left the household to study the way and are not yet accustomed to
the daily activities with hands and legs. You are only forty or fifty
years old. How can you have the leisure to enjoy a comfortable
building?'

"He would not accept their wish. The following day he ascended the teaching seat and presented this poem:

When I began living here in this building with crumbling
     walls,
all the platforms were covered by jewels of snow.
Scrunching up my shoulders to my neck, I exhaled into
     darkness,
reflecting on the ancient one abiding under a tree."

In general, creating magnificent buildings, towers, and ponds is
equally cautioned against in both worldly and unworldly realms.
The *Shizhi* says: "If you want to know the deeds of the Yellow Emperor, you should see his abode called the He Palace. If you want
to see the deeds of Emperors Yao and Shun, you should see their
Courts of the Affairs of State, roofed with grass."

By these descriptions we know that the ancient rulers who were
regarded as wise and saintly did not value fine fences, rooms, or
roofs. They laid thatch on their roofs but did not bother to trim it.

Even more so, why should we, descendants of buddha ancestors, wish for fine or elaborate red towers and jeweled buildings? The span of our lifetime is not long. Do not spend it in vain.

For over twenty years in China and Japan I have seen that many people, old and young, do not value their time, but toil away their lives constructing buildings with mud and wood. They get confused and lose their composure. What a pity! How painful! They throw away pure dharma and don't let go of defiled karma. If they understand the shortness of their remaining lives, how can they spend time to build a house as tall as a tree? This is what Ancestor Fayan meant.

The Administrator

The responsibility of the administrator is to oversee the administration of the monastery. This includes responding to government notifications and inquiries and making the community available to new monks. The administrator gathers the assembly for ceremonies, sees donors, and takes care of celebrations and condolences. The administrator is in charge of the communal budget, lending, and borrowing. He makes sure that there is financial reserve and enough stock of grain in accordance with the cash flow and the annual purchase of rice and barley. The administrator supervises seasonal making of soy sauce and vinegar, pressing of oil, pounding of rice, and grinding of grains.

You should exercise caretaking heart in supervising the monks' morning and midday meals. Entertain visitors from all directions with hospitality. Circumstances allowing, you should take direct charge in preparing ceremonial meals for the monks. Ceremonial midday meals are offered on the following occasions: the winter solstice, New Year's Day, the beginning and end of summer practice period, the Lotus Festival,[1] the Fifth Day of the Fifth Month Festi-

1. *Lotus Festival:* Details unknown. Possibly the Buddha's Birthday on the eighth day of the fourth month.

val, the Seventh Day of the Seventh Month Festival, the Ninth Day
of the Ninth Month Festival, the starting up and closing down of
the charcoal brazier, the Twelfth Month [the Buddha's Enlightenment Day on the eighth day], and Nirvāna Day [the sixteenth day
of the second month]. If you are unable to handle all these by yourself, you should ask other officers to share the responsibility.

Personally take care of minor matters as well as the daily rou-
tines of the monastery. Regarding important and unprecedented
matters, consult with the other officers and monks in charge, and
then with the abbot, before deciding what to do. In case the abbot
or other officers appear to be out of line according to the guidelines
of the monastery, or are not in accord with the feelings of the assembly, you should quietly bring your observation to their attention, regardless of the importance of the matter. You should not
keep silent, or use coarse or abusive language.

When you instruct or admonish new trainees, use skillful
means, without using extreme measures such as beating, to make
them understand. When punishment is needed, administer it pub-
licly in the kitchen with no more than ten blows. Be cautious, so
that no unexpected things will happen. In case a trainee needs to be
expelled, make sure that the fault is severe enough to warrant the
punishment, and see that the trainee understands the seriousness
of the charge. Consult with the abbot first. If someone is expelled
improperly, it may cause interference by the local authorities.

Make appointments to the following positions and jobs so as to
benefit all the residents of the monastery: street monks [who collect
offerings in town], head of the fields, caretaker of the charcoal [for
fuel], keeper of the soy sauce, one in charge of the morning meal,
caretaker of a subsidiary temple, keeper of the *Prajñā Pāramitā**
Sūtra archive, keeper of the *Avatansaka Sūtra* archive, house attendant, steward of the water supply, head gardener, head of the mill,
caretaker of the lamps. In making appointments to these positions,
you should consult with the abbot. The appointments should not
be neglected or delayed.

When donors visit the monastery, arrange suitable seats for
them and entertain them in a proper manner. When preparing a

meal offering, discuss the arrangement with the other officers and those in charge so that you can avoid unexpected errors.

The essence of the administrator's work is to revere the wise and include the many, to be harmonious to seniors and friendly with juniors. You should give comfort to the community of monks who share the same practice, and let them have joyful hearts. Do not depend upon personal power or authority, nor belittle the members of the community. Do not act willfully or make the members of the community insecure. Follow the zazen schedule unless you are sick or meeting with government officials. Make sure that the serving of the morning and midday meals goes smoothly. If the stock in the storehouse falls short, make every effort to solve the problem without overburdening the abbot or broadcasting it to the community.

Encourage and praise those colleagues who have ability and virtue, and give advice privately to those who cannot carry on their duties or whose practice is doubtful. Make an effort to uplift and refresh the monks' spirits so that they may continue their effort in dharma. If any of them has a great fault and is doing damage to the community, report this confidentially to the abbot. Watch quietly on other matters you are responsible for.

The administrator has an obligation to the community. To have an obligation to the community means not to have selfish motives. Not to have selfish motives means to long for the way of the ancients. To long for the way means to follow the way.

Before performing your duties, first refer to *The Guidelines for Zen Monasteries* by Changlu Zongze. Get a grasp of the general ideas, and keep the way in mind in conducting your duty. When carrying out a task, make sure to consult with the rest of the officers and then do your work. It is the communal way to consult with others whether the matters are important or unimportant. But if you do consult with others and do not accept their suggestions, it is worse than not consulting at all. It should be your major concern to be open and accessible to the community of monks, and to try to make them feel at ease.

Don't put a lot of weight on having a large community. And

don't make light of having a small community. Remember that at one time the demon Devadatta attracted five hundred monks who joined his community, but, after all, they were out of line with the dharma. Teachers outside of the way may have many followers, even though their views may be crooked. Yaoshan was an ancient buddha whose community was fewer than ten monks. Zhaozhou was also an ancient buddha, whose community was fewer than twenty monks. Fenyang had only seven or eight students. Buddha ancestors, great dragons, were not limited by the number of monks they had. Without seeking an abundance of students in the community, just revere those who maintain the way. Those who maintain the way with virtue, now and in the future, are the descendants of Yaoshan, and the offspring of Fenyang. We should honor and long for their authentic practice.

Even if we have one hundred, one thousand, or myriad students, if they are without a heart for the way and do not follow the ancients, they are less than toads or worms. Even if there are only seven, eight, or nine students, if they have the aspiration for enlightenment and follow the ancient examples, they will surpass dragons and elephants, the sages and the wise. To have a heart for the way is not to neglect the great road of buddhas and ancestors, but to treasure and protect it. For the sake of the way, you stop wanting name, fame, and profit, and leave your hometown. You regard gold as dung and fame as snot. Not betraying the truth and not accepting the false, you honor the guidelines and align your life with the prevailing customs of the community. In this way, you don't sell off the daily tea and rice of the buddhas and ancestors. This is what it means to have a heart for the way. To be aware that the breath that comes in does not anticipate the breath that goes out is the aspiration for enlightenment. This is right endeavor.

To follow ancient examples means to allow the eye of the ancestral school to see directly, and to allow the ear beyond time to hear with humility. It is to gouge out the vast open sky and settle your body in it, to pierce through the skull of the world and just sit. You open the fist and you stay with the nostril. You dye the white cloud within the blue sky, stir up autumn water, and wash the bright moon. This is following the ancient examples. When you do this, even seven or eight make a large monastery. So, if you want to see all buddhas in the ten directions, just see one Buddha Shākyamuni. Those who are not like him, even if there are hundreds of thousands of them, will not make a monastery, as they are not an assembly of the Buddha's followers.

YOU SHOULD AROUSE respect and love when you see those with a heart for the way or those who follow ancient examples. When you encounter scholars of scriptures who do not have faith in the three treasures and do not follow them, or those who do not have a heart for the way and do not follow ancient examples, you should regard them as demons or *icchantikas** and not admit them to the monastery.

The Buddha said, "Those who do not have faith are like broken jars." Thus, sentient beings who do not believe in buddha-dharma cannot be vessels of buddha-dharma. The Buddha also said, "Faith makes it possible for people to enter the great ocean of buddha-dharma." It is clear that those who do not have faith cannot be included in the community of practitioners.

Zen Master Huanglong said, "In this Age of Imitation Dharma, many people arrogantly indulge themselves in vain things and exclude the real." We should know that if we indulge ourselves in vain things, the false prevails.

Sanghanandi recognized the arrogance of people of his time when he said, "It has been over eight hundred years since the Buddha entered pari-nirvāna between the two shala trees. People nowadays have little correct thought, no dedicated faith, and no respect for thusness. They only love magical powers. Just eight hundred years after the Buddha's time, long before the two thousand years that the Buddha predicted, people already lack faith. How can we be worthy of those in the Buddha's time? How can we deal with the four types of confusion* and be liberated from the three poisons?"

Even if you seek for students of the way in mountains and fields, it is not easy to find those suited for the monastery. When choosing students, make sure not to block the road for the wise. If you see a true person, open the way. But if you open the way and a person does not come forward, do not feel regretful. Do not give priority to short-sighted considerations, but make long-range considerations your art of the heart.

DON'T REJOICE over receiving benefit or feel deprived over the lack of it. Honor and profit are the biggest obstacles to the way. That's why people who longed for the way in ancient times, both lay persons and home-leavers, abandoned honor and profit. You descendants of buddha ancestors who wish to establish the community seats should not be avaricious for fame, gain, or property.

Long ago, Zen Master Yanjun of the Guanyin Monastery in Dongjing was a student of Touzi, Zen Master Daitong. Yanjun visited ancestral seats far and wide, some of which were located in Chang, Lu, Min, and Shu. When Yanjun and his companions were passing through the deep valley of Fenglin, they came across a valuable jewel. The travelers looked at one another, wondering whether or not they should pick it up.

Yanjun said, "In ancient times a man found a piece of gold when he was plowing in the garden, but treated it like a tile or pebble. Wait until I build a monastery on a mountain; then I may use this as an offering to monks from the four directions." Thus, Yanjun urged his companions to leave the jewel behind.

From this anecdote, we should know that finding a piece of gold while plowing and treating it like a tile or pebble is the path of wisdom in the dusty world. Finding a rare jewel in the deep valley and leaving it behind is an excellent example in the path of buddha ancestors. In order to continue the life vein of buddha ancestors, we should not go toward profit in the common world, such as offerings from humans and devas, or the patronage of kings and ministers. Don't violate the spirit of dharma by seeking worldly profit. Aspire to be a teacher for home-leavers rather than a teacher for kings and ministers. Home-leavers come first and lay people come next. The emphasis should be heavier on monks and lighter on lay people.

When Huailian, Zen Master Dajue, was abbot of the Guangli

Monastery on Mt. Ayuwang, two monks were arguing over donations given to them. The administrator of the monastery could not
make a decision. Then Huailian called the monks before him and
cautioned them, "Some years ago when Lord Bao was the judge in
Kaifeng, someone made an appeal: 'I borrowed one hundred *liang*
of silver coins from a friend who died soon after. I went to his son
to return the money, but he would not accept it. I would like Your
Honor to order him to accept the money.'

"Admiring the attitude of the borrower, the judge called the
son and asked him if he would accept the money. But he declined,
saying, 'I don't remember my father lending silver coins to anyone.'
Neither the borrower nor the son would give in. So the judge ruled
that the money be donated to a temple nearby to hold rites for the
deceased man. I personally witnessed this incident. Thus, people in
the dusty world can shun wealth and long for righteousness. You
two monks became disciples of the Buddha and are acting shame-
lessly." Huailian expelled the two monks according to the rules of
the monastery. Later, Zen Master Mingjia told this story, and it was
quoted in *The Treasure Teaching of the Zen Gate* from *Xihu Guangji*.
When we reflect on this story, the son who would not accept the
money was a model householder who protected the decency of his
father. This story is a jewel ornament not only in the dusty world
but also in the monks' world.

Shuguang of the Han Dynasty said, "If you are wise and have
wealth, your aspiration is damaged. If you are foolish and have
wealth, your shortcomings will increase." Even a lay person understands this. How could a monk be greedy for wealth? Both the wise
and the foolish are equally cautioned against having wealth. The
ancient sage's words should be valued more than a thousand pieces
of gold.

It is said in *Lushi Chunqi*, "Emperor Yao summoned the wise
man Xuyou, who was living in a swamp, and asked him to take over
the throne. Xuyou declined and moved away to the foot of Mt. Ji."

From this story we should know that even a lay person can make
light of ruling the world and lean heavily on the way. You, a disciple
of the Buddha's, should be even less concerned about large or small

property, knowing that accepting wealth will hurt yourself and others. In practicing the buddha way, you should regard wealth as a serpent, poison, drool, or excrement. This is a pure attitude.

The Guidelines for Zen Monasteries says, "Do you expound the dharma for profit or not?" Sometimes people come to the administrator to make an offering to the community or to propose a construction project. In this case you should examine carefully whether the donor has faith and pure intention. Consult with the abbot and discuss the matter together. If you decide that this offering is based on pure dedication and right view, accept the offering. Otherwise, do not. Right faith is like the dedication of Elder Sudatta or the patronage of Prince Jeta to the Buddha. What made Sudatta Sudatta was not merely his great wealth. What made Jeta Jeta was his honorable poverty. Because of their right faith, their offering was accepted by the Tathāgata. However, in case people without right faith in the three treasures wish to give small meritorious gifts while they are lying on their death beds, these gifts should be immediately accepted.

The Buddha spoke to all the monks practicing in Jeta Grove, "You should respect donors just as you would respect and care for your parents. Donors are greatly beneficial for your fulfillment of the precepts, samādhi, and understanding. Your respect for the donors does not hinder respect for the three treasures. Donors provide four types of offerings. You should have a compassionate heart toward the donors. If you remember small generosity, how can you not appreciate great support?

"You should make a wholehearted effort in your practice of body, speech, and mind, so that their blessings may not be wasted. Let them receive the fruit of their generosity and let their reputations spread. You should help the donors in the same way that you give shelter to those who have no place to go, give food to those who are hungry, or give sight to the blind" (the third section of *The Ekottarāgama Sūtra*).

Thus, to respect donors and to have a compassionate heart toward them is an admonition of the Tathāgata, the World-honored One. A small action can result in great fruition in the field of blessings of the three treasures. Ancestor Nāgārjuna said, "A small wholesome action can be the cause of great fruition. Those who, seeking the fruit of buddhahood, chant one verse of admiration to the Buddha, recite one line of taking refuge, burn one pinch of incense, or offer a flower, invariably attain buddhahood."

THE MONKS' MEALS should not contain food obtained by the four inappropriate means and the five unacceptable means. Monastic meals should follow these guidelines. The administrator and the abbot should make sure that these guidelines are observed. The four inappropriate means for monks to obtain food are: the external fault, to be hired for a mission by the state; the internal fault, to practice medicine and necromancy; the upward fault, to practice astrology and numerology; and the downward fault, to engage in commercial farming. These four are also called the four wrong ways of feeding monks, or the four impure ways of eating. Food obtained through any of these means should not be served to the community.

The five unacceptable means of obtaining food are: to demonstrate miraculous qualities as a means to obtain profit, to boast about your own merit as a way to obtain profit, to use fortune telling while expounding dharma, to frighten people with a forceful voice in order to gain respect, and to discuss the results of offerings in order to motivate people. Food obtained through any of these five means should not be eaten. The Buddha's disciples and teachers of the way should avoid these five means and follow the path of right livelihood.

The Guidelines for Zen Monasteries says, "Are you not harming the monastic environment?" What is said here is that monks should not accept materials that come through the four inappropriate means and the five unacceptable means. The reason is that those who obtain meals through any of these means will have difficulty in maintaining right views.

YOU SHOULD REFRAIN from the company of those who do not follow the ancient path and should associate with those who do. If you become intimate with the former, this will become an obstacle of the way, as negligence of the way will immediately emerge. One with a heart for the way is a noble character in the buddha way. One without it is a minor character in the buddha way.

It is said in *Zhuangzi*, "Everyone in the world follows something. One who follows love and righteousness is a noble character. One who follows a material way is a minor character." Chen Xiuwen said, "So-called 'noble character' and 'minor character' are merely ways of classifying. When one follows the path, one becomes a noble character. When one goes against it, one becomes a minor character." The buddha way is also like this. You master the way by responding to a heart for the way. Listen to these words and observe the practice of those in olden days who had a heart for the way. Make their teachings the heart and eyeball of your practice of today.

You should help maintain the established practice and rejuvenate the solemn manners of the community, which have been declining. *The Guidelines for Zen Monasteries* says, "Outwardly follow the laws of the nation and inwardly follow the guidelines of the monastery." Your monastery is an auspicious assembly of buddha ancestors, a forest of fine teachers. The guidelines should be strictly observed, and the formal practice should be well established. Where the formal practice is not maintained, the buddha way declines. Not to follow the formal practice is to follow what is not practice. When the way is in decline, what is outside the way is practiced as the way.

Chenjin of the Later Han Dynasty became the governor of Nanyang. For three years he only sat and mumbled. But nevertheless his influence transformed the land he was governing. This is an excellent example of governing. What makes great achievement does not depend on speaking or not speaking, or even on endeavor or the lack of endeavor. What Chenjin did was not to do anything that was in discord with the way, and that was the best thing to do.

According to *The History of the Han Dynasty*, Emperor Cheng said, "Heaven created humans but they were unable to govern themselves. So, an emperor was chosen to govern with justice." It

is the same in the Buddhist monastery. Because monks are unable
to govern themselves, an abbot is chosen to lead them. The *Mozi*
said, "In olden times the justice of state was modeled after heavenly
principles. A wise person was chosen to be emperor as the represen-
tative of heaven. Because the emperor could not govern the entire
world under the heaven by himself, other wise ones were chosen to
be the three chief ministers." In my understanding, buddha inherits
from buddha, and ancestor transmits to ancestor, establishing host
and guest—bowing between teacher and disciple. This seems to
correspond to the words of those in the ancient times. *The Guidelines for Zen Monasteries* says, "Becoming host and guest for one day,
you can be teacher and disciple for the rest of your life." This is
what it means to be host and guest.

You SHOULD REJOICE in your heart every time you see the faces
of monks from the ten directions. *The Guidelines for Zen Monasteries*
says, "One who does not have a broad capacity to accept monks and
a deep heart to love them is not suited for the job of administrator."

The Buddha said to Ānanda, "Bodhisattvas and mahāsattvas*
who live together should look upon one another just as they look
upon me, because they are my true company. We are all riding on
the same boat. Their learning is my learning."

The abbot, officers, crew heads, and monks of the monastery
should apply these words of the Buddha to their everyday activities.
There is nothing beyond this for the essential way of emancipation.

The administrator should give instruction to the newly arriving
monks. *The Sūtra of Three Thousand Guidelines for Monks* says, "The
newly arrived monks should be provided with the following ten
types of care: shelter, necessary articles for daily life, daily inquiry
after their well-being, information about local customs, information about posthumous names in order to avoid using personal
names of the deceased, information about where to practice begging, monastic rules, information about food, local government
regulations, and information about safe places to go in case of
robbery.

The Sūtra of Three Thousand Guidelines for Monks says, "If a donor comes and offers to provide food for the monks, do not tell the other monks before seeing what he offers."

The sūtra also says, "There are five cautions to give to lay workers when you send them to town on errands: no fighting, buy only pure things, do not take advantage of others in purchasing goods, do not hire someone else to do this work, and be sensitive to the feelings of others." In this way you should give detailed instructions to the workers before they go to town.

The Guidelines for Zen Monasteries says, "Offering meals on the fifth day of the fifth month and the seventh day of the seventh month is a custom in the buddha ancestors' house, as well as a custom in the common world. It may not be possible to do this thoroughly in a monastery with thatched roofs and brushwood gates, in the deep mountains or the dark valley. In that case you should use art to create offerings, without dwelling on the lack of material things, and do what gives joy and comfort to the monks.

The country of Japan is on these remote islands, one hundred thousand *li* away from the country where the Buddha was born. It has been twenty-two hundred years since the Buddha's parinirvāna. We are far away from the time of the sage. It is sad indeed, but we should be most joyful when we see the sangha and hear the dharma. You should be grateful for your own effort in the way. Again you should be grateful for the beneficial virtue of the ancestral school, when you examine the high practice of Fayan and the deep aspiration of Fushan.

The Practice Leader

The Chinese word for practice leader, *weino*, is based on a Sanskrit word meaning "one who causes the community to rejoice." The one who holds this position is in charge of all affairs concerning monks' practice. The practice leader should take special care of new arrivals. Those who were officers in other places or those who are reputable monks should be offered better accommodations. A former abbot should be offered one of the three special seats in the

monks' hall according to seniority, based on the dates of the certificate of his appointment or his inauguration ceremony. Well-
known or highly virtuous monks from other monasteries should be
offered seats next to them according to seniority.

It is also the practice leader's responsibility to install light or
heavy mats in the monks' hall, to maintain the curtains and bamboo
screens, and to start up and close down the furnace, regulating the
heat, according to the season and weather. You arrange the name
plaques of those who participate in the summer practice period in
the order of the monks' seniority, based on their dates of ordination, which you post before the practice period begins.

You supervise the Manjushrī attendant in offering incense,
lighting lamps, and cleaning the altar utensils in preparation for the
assembly entering the monks' hall. You and your assistant monk
take care of the doors, windows, curtains, screens, and utensils of
the study hall,* keeping them in good order. If there is anything
missing or damaged, consult with the head cook or the work leader.
You oversee meals, furnishings, and the caretakers for the sick
monks in the infirmary. You and the monk in charge of the infirmary work together so that the sick are not neglected. You appoint
various officers, including attendant to the abbot, head of infirmary,
monk in charge of the furnace, head of study hall, head monk, and
head of the buddha hall. Where there are abundant offerings of
coins in the buddha hall, the abbot appoints a monk to collect them.

You are responsible for dismissing from the community serious
offenders of the monastic practice, after consultation and agree-
ment with the abbot. Less serious offenders may be moved to another practice space in the community. If you come across monks
who are fighting with each other, offer courteous mediation and
help them be reconciled. If they will not listen, you may need to
punish them in accordance with the guidelines. If something is
missing in the community and the owner insists on an investigation,
inform the community and make a search. If nothing is found, the
owner of the object may be dismissed or transferred to another
practice space. If the missing object is not so valuable, you should

dissuade the owner from troubling the community and disturbing the practice of the monastery.

Use the money offered to the sacred monk, Manjushrī, in the monks' hall only for the purchase of incense, lamps, and other items for the altar, and not for any other purposes. Take out the money from the collection cylinder, keep the account together with the Manjushrī attendant, and spend it.

You should follow government regulations concerning the official registry of monks. Post the list of those whose registrations are accepted. The outlined background of each monk should be reported to the government bureau of religious institutions. Pay the registration fees to the government. Although the administrator is responsible for registering the monks, if their documents are brought to your attention, examine them carefully. The official documents of newly arrived monks should be checked for their authenticity. This should not be neglected or taken lightly. When a monk is seriously ill, report it to the government. Pay for a monk's funeral by auctioning his robes and other articles. You are solely responsible for collecting the deceased monk's documents, including a purple robe with certificate of a title [of Zen Master given by the Emperor]. Ask the administrator to report his death and return the documents to the government bureau within the required time limit.

When contributions are given to the sangha, hit the wooden block in the monks' hall and announce to the assembly the contributions along with the intentions of the donors, in order to help them receive the wholesome fruits of their generosity.

Serve welcoming tea for new arrivals with courtesy and respect. Then, relay their names and ordination ages to the abbot's attendant, officers, and crew heads. You need to know their ordination ages for seat assignments, which are based on ordination seniority. Post two plaques for each monk in the study hall. One has the date of entry into the monastery, and the other the date of ordination. These plaques are occasionally rearranged. Make sure not to make a mistake about the order of tea being served in the study hall, and the order of assigning the head of the study hall, so as not to confuse the community.

All members of the community must participate in communal work except those who are assigned by rotation—the head of the study hall and the one on watch in the monks' hall. Even the abbot must participate, except when he is sick or hosting a government official. If he fails to participate, his attendant will be held responsible for his absence and must leave the community.

The term "practice leader" is sometimes called in Chinese *yue-zhong*, meaning "the delight of the community." The practice of one in this position is exemplified by Shākyamuni Buddha's disciple, Mandgalyāyana, but it is in fact the practice of all buddha tathāgatas. With compassion you care for those who arrive, and you nurture the monks in the community. You make the community's heart your heart, and their thought of the way your thought. You make parental heart your heart and the heart of children your heart. If you practice in this way you will be like a boat with a rudder on a wide river, or like rain in a time of drought.

The Sūtra of Three Thousand Guidelines for Monks lists the following seven types of hospitality that should be extended to new arrivals: to inquire about their present condition, to assign them seats, to provide them with a vacant living space, to provide them with mat and pillow, to provide them with a lamp, to explain the monastic guidelines, and to explain the local customs. Thus, when you see newly arrived monks, ask them if they lack any of the monks' necessities, where they are from, whether their teachers are still alive, and where they have practiced before coming. And get them settled, following the established procedure of the monastery.

The Head Cook

According to *The Guidelines for Zen Monasteries*, the duty of the head cook is to supervise the cooking of meals for the community. Activating a heart for the way and responding to each situation, make sure that the community enjoys the meals they receive. Be careful not to waste the communal food, see that the supplies are not in disarray, and keep lay assistants who are capable. Do not be too strict with the assistants in your application of the guidelines. If you are too strict, the assistants will become tense. On the other hand, if you are too loose, the work will not be accomplished.

You should personally make sure that the food is clean. In determining the menu and the number of servings for the morning and midday meals, talk with the administrator and other main officers. You are solely responsible for keeping the supply of soy sauce, vinegar, pickles, and dried vegetables. Don't miss the proper timing in obtaining these items. Manage the furnaces and lamps in the kitchen as needed. When distributing donated materials, do so equitably. Discuss with the administrator and work leader all the administrative matters concerning them, and be careful not to intrude on their areas of responsibility.

Remove and replace damaged furnaces, pots, utensils, and other kitchen articles whenever necessary. Guide the kitchen assistants in following the rules for the kitchen. Let monks know in detail about serving procedures in the monks' hall and carrying meals to the dormitories. The servers should respectfully bow and stand aside if they meet a teacher while carrying the food. Choose capable and sensitive monks to bring meals to the abbot, the officers, and crew heads. To prevent problems, check on those you send to the dormitories and make sure that they are competent. If an officer or crew head wants to retain a server for an extended period, consider granting their wish, without being rigid about job rotation. Take your meals in the kitchen, but don't eat anything different from the rest of the community.

When a morning or midday meal is ready to be served, offer incense, make bows in the direction of the monks' hall, and send off the food. *The Guidelines for Zen Monasteries* says, "In order to make offerings to the monks, there is a head cook." Since olden times, advanced monks with a heart for the way have filled this position. Those who are unsuitable have not filled this position. In ancient days such masters as Guishan, Jiashan, Wuzhuo, and Jianxuan served as head cook.

Concerning meal offerings to the community of monks, *The Guidelines for Zen Monasteries* says, "Monks, beyond ordinary or wise, penetrate the ten directions." Thus, monks in the monastery coming from all over, both ordinary and wise, are equally worthy of offerings of finely prepared and sufficient meals. The food you prepare, even one grain of rice or one leaf of greens, should come from the touch of your hand, and the motion of your fist. You prepare it as an offering for buddhas and ancestors, as an offering for clouds and water.

Do not see what is created with the eye of flesh. Do not measure what is there with ordinary thought. The bliss of Indra or the wheel-turning king does not surpass that of the head cook. The rice and vegetables you prepare do not arise in the realm of past, present, or future. They do not come from heaven, earth, or humans. But they are actualized when you raise your hand, and they are intimately present when you handle them. Thus, your work as head cook dedicates the way to the way. It is an opportunity to offer the heart to the heart. This is how you dedicate each meal to the community.

In regard to this, *The Guidelines for Zen Monasteries* states, "Responding to the effort of the head cook, we accept this meal for the attainment of the way." Thus giver and recipient attain the way together. We receive each meal with this spirit. The meal you prepare provides an incomparable opportunity to be free from various obstacles and to conduct wholesome actions. This is why the Tathāgata advised Mahākāshyapa to participate in the meals of the sangha. This indicates that even the pure practice of begging could be a hindrance for the practice of the way. Among the meals taken by monks, morning and midday meals served in the monasteries of buddha ancestors are the finest, as their merit is equal to that of meals obtained by the pure practice of begging.

After you obtain materials for the next day's morning and midday meals, take care of them as if they were your own eyeballs. Zen Master Renyong of the Baoning Monastery said, "Take care of the belongings of the monastery as your own eyeballs." In my view, taking care of the monastery belongings is even more important than taking care of our own eyeballs. The practice of Shāriputra receded in his former life, by giving away his eyeballs to a Brahman. Don't deviate by giving monastery belongings to those outside of the way.

Prepare food for the monks with respect, as if you were preparing it for the Emperor. As you are preparing food for the three treasures, do not eat portions of it to check the taste of salt, soy sauce, or vinegar. When referring to rice or vegetables, use honorific expressions, instead of insulting the food by using informal, vulgar, insensitive, or jocular ways of referring to it.[2]

The Guidelines for Zen Monasteries says, "The head cook should consult in advance with the administrator and other officers on the amount of food for every meal as well as on the menu." Don't make a decision on these matters by yourself, but consult with other officers. Menus and quantities should be discussed at length, without haste. This attitude should be followed by the other officers as well. Discussions must be carried on with a heart for the community and a heart for the way. When a decision is made, the menus should be posted on the announcement boards in the abbot's quarters, study hall, aged monks' quarters, retired officers' quarters, and so forth. The menus can be written out by a novice. Make detailed descriptions of the food to be served for both meals, which you should post before dawn. Then cook the morning meal. You should personally check and clean the ingredients with diligence and sincerity. Don't be mindless even for a moment. Don't be careful about one thing and careless about another. Why is this so? You are adding just one speck to the mountain of wholesomeness. Do not miss even one drop of water in the ocean of merit.

The Sūtra of Three Thousand Guidelines for Monks says, "There are five guidelines for instructing others in setting up rice for the monks: to measure it yourself, not to mix debris such as grass with the rice, to take out mouse droppings, not to let the bran remain with the rice, and to prepare it in a clean place." *The Guidelines for*

2. *honorific:* For example *okome* instead of *kome* (uncooked rice) and *osu* instead of *su* (vinegar).

Zen Monasteries says, "The head cook should not offer food to the community that lacks excellence in six tastes and is not filled with three virtues." The six tastes are: bitter, sour, sweet, spicy, salty, and mild. The three virtues, according to *The Mahā Pari-nirvāna Sūtra*, are: simplicity, purity, and appropriateness.

During the preparation of rice for cooking, be careful of both the sand and the rice. Xuefeng was once head cook at Dongshan's monastery. One day he was sorting the sand from the rice. Dongshan asked him, "Are you separating the sand from the rice, or are you separating the rice from the sand?"

Xuefeng said, "I'm separating the rice and sand at the same time."

Dongshan said, "Which will the community eat, the rice or the sand?"

Xuefeng turned over the rice pot. Then Dongshan said, "You may meet someone who will be able to help you in the future."

Old buddhas who attained the way still practiced with their hands diligently. How then can ordinary people who come later be lax in their practice? If you make an effort to follow the true dharma, you are one of those who is within the way. When preparing rice, first wash the pot and put the ingredients into it. Then wash the rice and make sure that everything is clean.

In *The Sūtra of the Three Thousand Guidelines for Monks* it says, "There are five guidelines for washing rice: to use a solid container, to use clean water, to rinse five times, to keep the container in an out-of-the-way place, and to cover the top tightly." *The Guidelines for Zen Monasteries* says, "While preparing food, you should examine it carefully and make sure that everything is washed clean. Then put the rice and vegetables in the pot and guard the pot with care. Don't let the ingredients be touched by rats or be casually examined by people." Direct the kitchen crew in examining the ingredients and take personal responsibility for the process. *The Sūtra of the Three Thousand Guidelines for Monks* says, "There are five guidelines for washing the pot: not to scrape the bottom of the pot with a utensil, to use a sieve for separating the water from the solid parts when pouring out dirty water, to keep the pot filled with water, to clean the wooden lid and place it on top of the pot, and to make sure that the lid is kept tight at night."

The necessary utensils for preparing meals for the day should be made ready. The wooden pot for serving rice, the soup pot, the large serving plates, and other utensils should be rinsed and dried. Those things that are suited to high places should be put in high places, and those suited for low places should be put in low places. What is stable in a high place should be made stable in a high place and what is stable in a low place should be made stable in a low place. Wooden ladles, iron ladles, and bamboo chopsticks should be laid out all together. Protect them with a sincere heart and handle them lightly and effortlessly.

You should start preparation for the meals a day ahead. First, see if there are worms in the rice. Remove any beans that are mixed in with the rice. Remove the bran and any weeds or sand. After carefully cleaning the rice, put it in a clean and pure place and keep it there. Then select the vegetables for the next day's meals. *The Sūtra of Three Thousand Guidelines for Monks* says, "There are five guidelines for preparing vegetables: to remove the roots, to arrange them neatly, not to mix green and yellow leaves, to wash them clean, and to stir them well while cooking." Be aware of these guidelines and follow them.

When the rice and vegetables for the next day have been cleaned, ask someone experienced to chant a dedication to the guardian spirit of the furnace. Possible chants, according to the occasion, are the "Ease and Bliss" chapter of *The Lotus Sūtra*, *The Diamond Prajñā Pāramitā Sūtra*, the "Universal Gate" chapter of *The Lotus Sūtra*, the Lankāvatāra Dhāranī, the Great Compassionate Heart Dhāranī, the "Emptiness" chapter of *The King Suvarnaprabhāsottama Sūtra*, "Enlightenment of the Way" by Yongjia, *Awakening Stick* by Guishan, or "Song of Faith in Mind" by Sengcan. Any of these can be chanted according to the appropriate situation as an offering to the guardian spirit of the furnace. Then the person chants the dedication: "Having offered this chanting, we dedicate the merit to the guardian spirit of the furnace of this monastery. May you protect the dharma and give peace to all buddhas throughout time and space. All venerable beings, bodhisattvas and mahāsattvas, great prajñā pāramitā."

You should personally supervise the cleaning of the rice and vegetables. Don't be swayed by the scarcity, abundance, or quality of the materials to be prepared in the kitchen, but just wholeheartedly work with the materials you are given. You are strongly cautioned against creating an emotional scene or complaining about the scarcity of the materials. Be diligently engaged in the endeavor of the way throughout the day. Don't leave the kitchen when the gruel is being boiled, the rice being steamed, the soup being made, or the vegetables being cooked. Oversee the procedure with clear eyes and don't let one grain of rice be wasted or one blade of greens be spoiled.

The Sūtra of Three Thousand Guidelines for Monks states, "There are five guidelines for making soup: to add ingredients in the proper order, to cook them well, to balance the various tastes, to make sure personally that the soup is clean, and to put out the fire and cover the pot when it is done." Have an assistant tend the fire when steaming rice or making soup.

The Sūtra of Three Thousand Guidelines for Monks states, "There are five guidelines for burning wood in the furnace: not to lay the firewood flat, not to burn wet firewood, not to turn the burning wood around, not to use the mouth to blow out the fire, and not to put out the fire with hot water."

When the rice is steamed and the soup is made, put the rice in the bamboo basket and the soup in the serving pot. Then put the food on the counter. By properly venerating the sources that have brought this food, you see buddhas, you see ancestors, you penetrate Guishan and Shishuang [who talked about one grain of rice]. By picking up one blade of grass, the treasure king's kingdom is constructed, and by moving one particle of dust, the great wheel of dharma is turned. In this way, getting a pail of water or a bowl of rice is also turning the wheel of a meal, turning the wheel of dharma.

At a proper time after setting the food on the counter with reverence, burn incense, spread the bowing mat on the floor in front of the food counter, and make nine full bows in the direction of the monks' hall. Then fold up the bowing mat, make a standing bow, and stand with hands held together on the chest, as the wooden fish-shaped board is hit. Make a standing bow and send out the food. Follow those who are carrying the food to the monks' hall. If the midday meal gathering is large, join the servers. For serving, don't wear the kashāya, but tie the sleeves of your robe with a cloth belt. If the assembly is of moderate size, you don't need to serve.

While preparing meals, don't be careless even when you are given coarse ingredients. Rather, make a greater effort than when you are given fine ingredients. Thus, you can rejoice in completing the work day and night. Without the compassionate intention of the Great Master Shākyamuni, how can we prepare the monks' daily meals in a remote country like Japan? How gratifying it is to be able to learn the art of the way in a proper manner! How would this be possible if the ocean of virtue of the three treasures were not flowing? How fortunate it is to be able to keep the position of head cook for as long as one year! You should rejoice each moment in the merit you receive. To rejoice in the merit you receive is to rejoice in the merit of all buddhas, whose light illuminates you. Always keep in mind the ancient words [from *The Guidelines for Zen Monasteries*]: "The way to offer meals to monks should be based on reverence." Thus reflect on the meaning of the head cook working in the kitchen.

The Work Leader

The work leader is responsible for all the labor in the monastery. You are responsible for repair and maintenance of buildings, gates, windows, and fences. You replace missing tools and utensils and are responsible for their upkeep. You keep the mill in working order, oversee the work in the fields, and manage the workers' quarters and the building where the oil is pressed and stored. You are responsible for the maintenance and cleaning of the toilets, the horses and saddles, the boats, and the carts, as well as for planting and harvesting. You are responsible for the fire watches and for the security of the monastery, protecting it from thieves. You supervise the workers and make their rotation schedules.

You should have a heart for service and dedication, being aware of the proper timing and the best way to make things work harmoniously. In case of a major construction or a large work project, consult with the abbot, draft a plan, and discuss it with your colleagues, without trying to force your own view on others.

Although you are based in the compound with the other officers, you usually work outside, supervising the workers and overseeing the quality of their work. If your work space is set up independently, it may be placed outside of the eastern walkway so that the sound of hatchets chipping wood does not reach the monks' quarters, the dharma hall, the abbot's quarters, or the officers' quarters. *The Sūtra of Three Thousand Guidelines for Monks* says, "There are five guidelines for instructing others to cut firewood: not to work in the passageway, to make sure the ax handle is secure, not to use wood with green leaves, not to use tomb plaques, and to stack the firewood in a dry place." In all monasteries two workers are in charge of the water-drip clock in the work leader's office. Make the rounds of the monastery, supervising the work, without slackening your effort. Keep the tools and utensils in good repair and the stock well supplied. Put service of the community before your own welfare. *The Guidelines for Zen Monasteries* says, "Working for the benefit of the monastic community is the main objective of the work leader." Thus, make an effort to notice any damaged equipment, and repair or replace it even before you are informed of it.

The Guidelines for Zen Monasteries says, "To abide mindfully in the monks' quarters and be attentive to the articles used daily is a way to show respect and appreciation to the work leader." *The Guidelines for Zen Monasteries* also says, "To make use of a room or tools without considering those who will use them later shows a lack of respect to the work leader." Thus your duty is everyone's duty. Everyone's gratification is your gratification. How could your work be equated with ordinary work in the world? How could your work be merely a step toward something else?

THESE POINTS are the head and tail of the ancient buddhas and the pupils of the eyes of the olden sages. Don't ignore them at any time, as they are not outside the practice of the realization of the way. If you ignore arms and legs, you betray the top of the head. Then with what face and eyes could you see buddha ancestors?

Written on the fifteenth day, the sixth month, the fourth year of the Kangen Era [1246] at the Eihei Monastery, Echizen Province. Dōgen, founding monk.

1247, Echizen

Auspicious
Beginning of Spring

Homage to the buddha, dharma, sangha treasures! How
    auspicious!
The beginning of spring! How auspicious!
The one house of the ancestral teachers and lineage! How
    auspicious!
The buddha-dharma prevailing widely! How auspicious!
    How auspicious!
The monastery gate prospers! How auspicious!
When many disciples assemble to meet themselves and to
    encounter the moment,
the world comes and honors our way.
How auspicious! How auspicious! How auspicious!
The beginning of spring! How auspicious!
How auspicious! The founding of this monastery!
Eihei! How auspicious!

Dōgen

THE FIRST DAY OF SPRING,

THE FIFTH YEAR

OF THE KANGEN ERA

How auspicious! How auspicious!

1247, Kamakura

Original Face

Flowers in spring
cuckoos in summer
moon in autumn
snow in winter
serene and cool

Transmission
Outside Scripture

On this wind-swept shore
waves batter ceaselessly—
but on the high rocks of the dharma
not even the clinging oysters
can leave a mark.

*Written in the first year of the Kangen Era at the request of the
Lady of the Lord Saimyōji [Regent Tokiyori Hōjō].*

Formal Talk upon Returning from Kamakura

RECORDED BY EJŌ, ATTENDANT MONK

ON THE FOURTEENTH DAY, the third month, the second year of the Hōji Era, Dōgen ascended the teaching seat and said, "I left here on the third day of the eighth month of last year for Kamakura, Sagami Province, to expound the dharma to lay students. Having returned yesterday, I am giving a talk this morning. Some of you may think that crossing countless mountains and rivers to teach lay students is giving priority to lay people over monks. Others may wonder if I taught them dharma that has never been expounded and has never been heard. However, there is no dharma that has never been expounded and has never been heard.

"I just expounded this dharma to guide people: Those who practice wholesome actions rise and those who practice unwholesome actions fall. You practice cause and harvest the effect. It's just like picking up jade and throwing away gravel. Thus I try to clarify, speak, identify with, and practice this teaching of cause and effect. Do you all understand it?"

After a pause he said, "Please bear with me. My tongue speaks of cause and effect with no reason. Plowing the way, how much is mistaken? Today take pity on me for becoming a water buffalo.

This is my sense of expounding dharma. Now, how shall I express my feeling about returning to the monastery?

> I was away over half a year,
> a lonely moon in a great void.
> Today I am back.
> The clouds seem joyful.
> I love this mountain more than before."

1249, Echizen

Omens of the Sixteen Arhats

THIS IS THE RECORD of the appearance of auspicious flowers on the first day of the first month, the third year of the Hōji Era, between the hours of Serpent and Ox [around 11 AM] during a service for the Sixteen Arhats in the abbot's quarters of the Eihei Monastery on Mt. Kichijō [Auspiciousness]. In front of the Buddha statue there appeared especially wonderful and beautiful flowers. They also appeared in front of all the wooden images of the Sixteen Arhats, as well as all the painted images of them.

The only precedent for the appearances of auspicious flowers was at the Rock Bridge on Mt. Tiantai in the Tai Region of Song China. Appearance of such flowers on other mountains has not yet been heard of. But they have already appeared several times on this mountain. These are truly auspicious signs that the honored ones are protecting with compassion the people and the dharma of this mountain monastery.

Mendicant Kigen [Rare Profundity]
Founder of this monastery

1249, Echizen

On a Portrait of
Myself

Fresh, clear spirit covers old mountain man this autumn.
Donkey stares at the sky ceiling; glowing white moon floats.
Nothing approaches. Nothing else included.
Buoyant, I let myself go—filled with gruel, filled with rice.
Lively flapping from head to tail,
sky above, sky beneath, cloud self, water origin.

1251, Echizen

Three Auspicious Signs at the Eihei Monastery

LET ME RESPOND to your question about the sounds of a bell on this mountain. I have often heard them during this eight-year period. Around midnight on the fifth day, the first month of this year, when the honorary monk Prime Minister Kasan'in and I were discussing the buddha-dharma in the Ryōzen Hermitage, we heard around two hundred strokes of the bell. As its loudness was like the bell of the Kiyomizu Temple in Higashiyama, Kyōto, or that of the Hōshō Temple, I listened with great joy, struck with awe. Kasan'in, also filled with a great joy, said that this is an extraordinary place. The Middle Commander Minister Kanetomo, who came with Kasan'in, did not hear the bell even though he was in the same room. Nor did the honorary monk Secretary Ukon, the son of the imperial wet nurse, also known as the dharma teacher Keishi. Also, two or three court ladies, and seven or eight samurai did not hear it.

On another occasion when I was explaining the precepts to the assembly on the fifteenth day, the first month, the fifth year of the Kangen Era [1247], a five-colored cloud rose in front of the abbot's quarters and floated there for about half an hour. Many monks and lay people saw it.

Also, from the fourth month until the twelfth day of the elev-

enth month of the second year of the Hoji Era [1248], an unusual
and wondrous scent spread inside and outside the monks' hall.

These three occurrences are indeed auspicious signs of this
spiritual place. The ringing of the bell is like sounds heard on Mt.
Tiantai in China.

Identifying with Cause and Effect

Every time Baizhang, Zen Master Dahui, gave a dharma talk, a certain old man would come to listen. He usually left after the talk, but one day he remained behind. Baizhang asked, "Who is there?"

The man said, "I am not actually a human being. I lived and taught on this mountain at the time of Kāshyapa Buddha. One day a student asked me, 'Does a person who practices with great devotion still fall into cause and effect?' I said to him, 'No, such a person doesn't.' Because I said this I was reborn as a wild fox for five hundred lifetimes. Reverend master, please say a turning word for me and free me from this wild fox body." Then he asked Baizhang, "Does a person who practices with great devotion still fall into cause and effect?"

Baizhang said, "Don't ignore cause and effect."

Immediately the man had great realization. Bowing, he said, "I am now liberated from the body of a wild fox. I will stay in the mountain behind the monastery. Master, could you perform the usual services for a deceased monk for me?"

Baizhang asked the head of the monks' hall to inform the assembly that funeral services for a monk would be held after the midday meal. The monks asked one another, "What's going on? Everyone is well; there is no one sick in the Nirvāna Hall." After their meal, Baizhang led the assembly to a large rock behind the monastery and showed them a dead fox at the rock's base. Following the customary procedure, they cremated the body.

That evening during his lecture in the dharma hall Baizhang talked about what had happened that day. Huangbo asked him, "A teacher of old gave a wrong answer and became a wild fox for five hundred lifetimes. What if he hadn't given a wrong answer?"

Baizhang said, "Come closer and I will tell you." Huangbo went closer and slapped Baizhang's face. Laughing, Baizhang clapped his hands and said, "I thought it was only barbarians who had unusual beards. But you too have an unusual beard!"

This story is in *The Expansive Lamp Record of the Tiansheng Era.* Still, students do not understand the principle of causation and mistakenly deny cause and effect. What a pity! Things are deteriorating, and the ancestral way has degenerated. Those who say "one does not fall into cause and effect" deny causation, thereby falling into the lower realms. Those who say "one cannot ignore cause and effect" clearly identify with cause and effect. When people hear about identifying with cause and effect, they are freed from the lower realms. Do not doubt this. Many of our contemporaries who consider themselves students of Zen deny causation. How do we know? They confuse "not ignoring" with "not falling into." Thus we know that they deny cause and effect.

VENERABLE KUMĀRALABDHA, the Nineteenth Ancestor in India, said, "We see both wholesome and unwholesome results occurring in the world throughout time. Ordinary folks deny cause and effect when they see kind and fair-minded people suffer and die young while those who are violent and unjust prosper into old age. Such ordinary folks say neither crime nor beneficial acts bring consequences. They do not realize that the consequences of our actions follow us for one hundred, one thousand, or ten thousand eons."

We clearly know from this that Kumāralabdha does not deny cause and effect. But students nowadays do not understand this. They do not revere or follow the ancient way. Calling themselves teachers of humans and devas, they are robbers, enemies of practitioners. Followers of the ancestral teaching should not instruct later generations to deny causation, because that is a crooked view, not the dharma of buddha ancestors. People fall into this crooked view because their studies are shallow.

Nowadays monks in China say, "Those of us who have received human bodies and encountered buddha-dharma don't remember even one or two past lives, but the wild fox on Mt. Baizhang remembered as many as five hundred past lives. He did not become a fox because of past actions. Trapped by a limited view of enlightenment, he was transmigrating only in the animal realm." Many who are regarded as great teachers talk like this, but such a view is not acceptable among buddha ancestors.

In the realms of humans, foxes, and others, some may be born with the capacity to see past lives. Such a capacity may be the result of unwholesome action and not necessarily a seed of enlightenment. The World-honored One has cautioned us in detail about such a point. Not to understand it reflects a lack of study. Regrettably, to know as many as one thousand or ten thousand lifetimes is not necessarily to understand buddha-dharma. There are those outside the way who remember eighty thousand eons. But, again, this is not the way to understand buddha-dharma. Compared with such capacities, this fox who could recall five hundred lifetimes is not significant.

The most serious mistake made by those who study Zen in China is to believe that a person who practices with great dedication does not fall into cause and effect. What a pity! There have been an increasing number of those who deny cause and effect, even though they witness the Tathāgata's true dharma being transmitted from ancestor to ancestor. Therefore, those who study the way should urgently clarify this teaching. The point of Baizhang's words "don't ignore cause and effect" is that we should not be ignorant of causation.

Thus, the significance of studying cause and realizing effect is clear. This is the way of buddhas and ancestors. Those who themselves have not yet clarified buddha-dharma should not superficially explain it to humans and devas.

*   *   *

ANCESTOR NĀGĀRJUNA SAID, "If you deny cause and effect in the worldly realm, as some people outside the way do, you negate this present life as well as future births. If you deny cause and effect in the realm of practice, you reject the three treasures, the four noble truths,* and the four fruits of shrāvakas."

You should clearly know that those who deny cause and effect are outside the way, whether they are living a worldly or a renunciate life. They say that the present life is unreal and that their transient body is in this world, but their true nature abides in enlightenment. They believe their true nature is mind, and that mind and body are separate.

There are also those who say that people return to the ocean of true nature when they die. Without having studied buddha-dharma, they say that transmigration through birth and death ends and there are no future births after they return to the ocean of enlightenment. Those who hold this view of annihilation are outside the way. They are not the Buddha's disciples even if they look like monks. They are indeed outside the buddha-dharma. Because they deny cause and effect they deny present and future lives. They deny causation because they have not studied with true teachers. Those who have studied deeply with true teachers should abandon mistaken views that deny causation. You should have faith in, and pay respects to, the compassionate teaching of Ancestor Nāgārjuna.

YONGJIA, Great Master Zhenjue, Priest Xuanjue, was a senior student of Huineng, the Sixth Ancestor, who taught on Mt. Caoxi. He had initially been a student of the Lotus School on Mt. Tiantai, and a dharma brother of Zuoxi Xianlang. While he was reading *The Mahā Pari-nirvāna Sūtra*, a golden light filled the room and he awakened beyond birth and death. He went to Mt. Caoxi to present his realization to Huineng, who gave him his seal of approval. Yongjia later composed a verse called "The Song of Actualizing the Way," in which he wrote: "Superficial understanding of emptiness ignores cause and effect and invites calamity."

It is true that ignoring causation invites disaster. Past sages clarified cause and effect, but students have become confused in recent

times. Those of you who have pure aspiration for enlightenment
and want to study buddha-dharma for the sake of buddha-dharma
should clarify causation as past sages did. Those who reject this
teaching are outside the way.

OLD BUDDHA HONGZHI wrote a poem about the wild fox:

> A foot of water has expanded to a wave ten feet tall.
> Helplessly wandering through five hundred births
> the fox who struggles with not-falling, not-ignoring
> remains entangled in twining vines.
> Ha ha, do you get it?
> If you are not stuck
> you will let me continue my "goo goo wa wa."
> Shrine songs and dance emerge spontaneously
> during clapping and cheering.

The lines "The fox who struggles with not-falling, not-ignoring
remains entangled in twining vines" sounds as if Hongzhi understands not-falling to be the same as not-ignoring.

This story of the fox is not complete. It says that the old man did
become free from a wild fox's body but it does not say whether he
was then born in the world of humans, devas, or elsewhere. If the
old man is reborn in a wholesome realm, free from a wild fox's
body, it must be either the realm of devas or humans. Otherwise he
would be reborn in one of the four unwholesome realms.* There is
no shortage of locations for rebirth. But those outside the buddha
way mistakenly believe that sentient beings return to the ocean of
permanence or to the great self after death.

YUANWU KEQIN of Jiashan commented in verse on this ancient
case:

> A fish swims and makes the water murky.
> A bird flies, shedding its feathers.

The ultimate mirror is difficult to escape.
The great void is boundless.
Once you go, you go endlessly.
By virtue of causation, the one who practices with great
    dedication
lives five hundred lifetimes.
Thunder cracks the mountains and storms shake the ocean.
The color of purified gold does not change.

This poem still has a view of permanent self and a sense of denying cause and effect.

Zen Master Dahui Zonggao, of Mt. Jing, Hang Region, wrote:

Not falling and not ignoring
are like a pebble and a lump of clay.
When they show up together on a footpath
the silver mountain opens up.
Seeing it, the silly Priest Budai of Ming
claps his hands and bursts out laughing.

People in China nowadays regard Dahui as an established ancestor. However, his view does not equal even the expedient teachings in the buddha-dharma. It resembles a view of spontaneous enlightenment by people outside the way.

More than thirty masters wrote poems or commentaries on this story. Not one of them understands the saying "a person who practices with great dedication does not fall into cause and effect" as a denial of causation. What a pity! Such people waste their lives by not clarifying cause and effect. In studying buddha-dharma you should first understand causation. By denying causation you generate crooked views and cut off wholesome roots.

GENERALLY SPEAKING, causation is self-evident. There are no exceptions. Those who create unwholesome actions decline and those who practice wholesomeness evolve. There is not a hair's-breadth's discrepancy. If cause and effect had been ignored or denied, buddhas would not have appeared and Bodhidharma would not have come from India. Sentient beings would not have seen buddha or heard the dharma. The principle of cause and effect is not clarified by Confucius or Laozi. Buddhas and ancestors alone have transmitted it. Students in these decadent times seldom meet a genuine teacher or hear the true dharma. That is why they do not clarify cause and effect.

When you deny causation, endless harm results. Even if you do nothing more than deny cause and effect, this is a disastrous, poisonous view. If you want to make the aspiration for enlightenment your priority and so repay the boundless gift of buddha ancestors, you should immediately clarify all causes and all effects.

During the summer practice period in the seventh year of the Kenchō Era [1255] I copied Dōgen's draft. There must be a second or final version edited by him, but I have used his draft for the time being. Ejō

Eight Awakenings
of Great Beings

ALL BUDDHAS ARE GREAT BEINGS. What great beings practice is called the eight awakenings. Practicing these awakenings is the basis for nirvāna. This is the last teaching of our original teacher Shākyamuni Buddha, which he gave on the night he entered pari-nirvāna.

The first awakening is to have few desires. To refrain from widely coveting the objects of the five sense desires is called "few desires."

The Buddha said, "Monks, know that people who have many desires intensely seek for fame and gain; therefore they suffer a great deal. Those who have few desires do not seek for fame and gain and are free from them, so they are without such troubles. Having few desires is itself worthwhile. It is even more so, as it creates various merits. Those who have few desires need not flatter to gain others' favor. Those who have few desires are not pulled by their sense organs. They have a serene mind and do not worry, because they are satisfied with what they have and do not have a sense of lack. Those who have few desires experience nirvāna. This is called 'few desires.' "

The second awakening is to know how much is enough. Even if you already have something, you set a limit for yourself for using it. So you should know how much is enough.

The Buddha said, "Monks, if you want to be free from suffering, you should contemplate knowing how much is enough. By knowing it you are in the place of enjoyment and peacefulness. If you know how much is enough, you are contented even when you sleep on the ground. If you don't know it, you are discontented even when you are in heaven. You can feel poor even if you have much wealth. You may be constantly pulled by the five sense desires and pitied by those who know how much is enough. This is called 'to know how much is enough.' "

The third awakening is to enjoy serenity. This is to be away from the crowds and stay alone in a quiet place. Thus it is called "to enjoy serenity in seclusion."

The Buddha said, "Monks, if you want to have the joy of serene nondoing, you should be away from the crowds and stay alone in a quiet place. A still place is what Indra and other devas revere. By leaving behind your relations as well as others, and by living in a quiet place, you may remove the conditions of suffering. If you are attached to crowds, you will receive suffering, just like a tree that attracts a great many birds and gets killed by them. If you are bound by worldly matters, you will drown in troubles, just like an old elephant who is stuck in a swamp and cannot get out of it. This is called 'to enjoy serenity in seclusion.' "

The fourth awakening is diligent effort. It is to engage ceaselessly in wholesome practices. That is why it is called "diligent effort." It is refinement without mixing in other activities. You keep going forward without turning back.

The Buddha said, "Monks, if you make diligent effort, nothing is too difficult. That's why you should do so. It is like a thread of water piercing through a rock by constantly dripping. If your mind continues to slacken, it is like taking a break from hitting stones before they spark; you can't get fire that way. What I am speaking of is 'diligent effort.' "

The fifth awakening is "not to neglect mindfulness." It is also called "to maintain right thought." This helps you to guard the dharma so you won't lose it. It is called "to maintain right thought" or "not to neglect mindfulness."

The Buddha said, "Monks, for seeking a good teacher and good help, there is nothing like not neglecting mindfulness. If you practice this, robbers of desire cannot enter you. Therefore, you should always maintain mindfulness in yourself. If you lose it, you will lose all merits. When your mindfulness is solid, you will not be harmed even if you go into the midst of the robbers of the five sense desires. It is like wearing armor and going into a battlefield, so there is nothing to be afraid of. It is called 'not to neglect mindfulness."

The sixth awakening is to practice meditation. To abide in dharma without being confused is called "stability in meditation."

The Buddha said, "Monks, if you gather your mind, it will abide in stability. Then you will understand the birth and death of all things in the world. You will continue to endeavor in practicing various aspects of meditation. When you have stability, your mind will not be scattered. It is like a well-roofed house or a well-built embankment, which will help you maintain the water of understanding and keep you from being drowned. This is called 'stability in meditation.' "

The seventh awakening is "to cultivate wisdom." It is to listen, contemplate, practice, and have realization.

The Buddha said, "Monks, if you have wisdom, you are free from greed. You will always reflect on yourself and avoid mistakes. Thus you will attain liberation in the dharma I am speaking of. If you don't have wisdom, you will be neither a follower of the way nor a lay supporter of it, and there will be no name to describe you. Indeed, wisdom is a reliable vessel to bring you across the ocean of old age, sickness, and death. It is a bright lamp that brings light into the darkness of ignorance. It is an excellent medicine for all of you who are sick. It is a sharp ax to cut down the tree of delusion. Thus, you can deepen awakening through the wisdom of listening, contemplation, and practice. If you are illuminated by wisdom, even if you use your physical eyes, you will have clear insight. This is called 'to cultivate wisdom.' "

The eighth awakening is not to be engaged in hollow discussions. It is to experience realization and be free from discriminatory thinking, with thorough understanding of the true mark of all things. It is called "not to be engaged in hollow discussions."

The Buddha said, "Monks, if you get into hollow discussions, your mind will be scattered. Then, you will be unable to attain liberation even if you have left the household. So, you should immediately leave behind scattered mind and hollow discussions. If you wish to attain the joy of serenity, you need to cure the sickness of hollow discussions. This is called 'not to be engaged in hollow discussions.' "

These are the eight awakenings. Each awakening contains all eight, thus there are sixty-four awakenings. When awakenings are practiced thoroughly, their number is countless. When they are practiced in summary, there are sixty-four.

These are the last words of Great Teacher Shākyamuni Buddha, the ultimate admonition of the Mahāyāna teaching. He said at midnight of the fifteenth day of the second month, "Monks, you should always endeavor wholeheartedly to search for the way of liberation. All things in the world, whether they are in motion or not, are insecure and bound to decay. Now, all of you be quiet and do not speak. Time is passing and I am going to cross over. This is my last admonition to you." Without expounding dharma any further, the Buddha entered pari-nirvāna.

All disciples of the Buddha should study this teaching. Those who don't learn or know about it are not his disciples. Indeed this is the Tathāgata's treasury of the true dharma eye, the wondrous heart of nirvāna. However, there are many who do not know about this teaching, as there are few who have studied it. Many may have been confused by demons, and those who have few wholesome conditions from the past do not have the opportunity to see or hear about this teaching. In the Ages of True Dharma and Imitation Dharma, all disciples of the Buddha knew about this teaching and practiced it. But nowadays, less than one or two out of a thousand monks seem to know about it. How regrettable! The world has declined since those times. While the true dharma prevails in the billion worlds and the Buddha's pure teaching is still intact, you should immediately practice it without negligence.

It is rare to encounter the buddha-dharma even in the span of countless eons. A human body is difficult to attain. A human body

in the Three Continents of the world is preferable. A human body
in the Southern Continent, Jambudvīpa, is particularly so, as one
can have the chance to see the Buddha, hear the dharma, leave the
household, and attain the way. But those who entered nirvāna and
died before the pari-nirvāna of the Tathāgata could not learn and
practice these eight awakenings of great beings.

Now we can learn and practice these awakenings because of the
merit of our wholesome conditions from the past. By practicing and
nurturing these awakenings, you can certainly arrive at unsurpassable enlightenment and expound them to all beings, just as
Shākyamuni Buddha did.

*On the sixth day, the first month, the fifth year of the Kenchō
Era [1253]. Written at the Eihei Monastery.*

Final Instructions

RECORDED BY GIKAI

ON THE EIGHTH DAY, seventh month, the fifth year of the Kenchō Era, Master Dōgen's disease recurred. I was very alarmed and went to see him.

He said, "Come close to me." I approached his right side and he said, "I believe that my current life is coming to an end with this sickness. In spite of everyone's care I am not recovering. Don't be alarmed by this. Human life is limited, and we should not be overwhelmed by illness. Even though there are ten million things that I have not clarified concerning the buddha-dharma, still I have the joy of not having formed mistaken views and of having genuinely maintained correct faith in the true dharma. The essentials of all these are not any different from what I have spoken of every day.

"This monastery is an excellent place. We may be attached to it, but we should live in accord with temporal and worldly conditions. In the buddha-dharma any place is an excellent place for practice. When the nation is peaceful, the monastery supporters live in peace. When the supporters are peaceful, the monastery will certainly be at ease.

"You have lived here for many years, and you have become a monastery leader. After I die, stay in the monastery, cooperate with the monks and laity, and protect the buddha-dharma I have taught.

If you go traveling, always return to this monastery. If you wish, you can stay in the hermitage."

Shedding tears, I wept and said in gratitude, "I will not neglect in any way your instructions for both the monastery and myself. I will never disobey your wishes."

Then Dōgen, shedding tears and holding his palms together, said, "I am deeply satisfied. For many years I have noticed that you are familiar with worldly matters and that within the buddha-dharma you have a strong way-seeking mind. Everyone knows your deep intention, but you have not yet cultivated a grandmotherly heart. As you grow older I am sure you will develop it."

Restraining my tears, I thanked him. At that time Head Monk Ejō was also present and heard this conversation. I have not forgotten the admonishment that I did not have a grandmotherly heart. However, I don't know why Dōgen said this. Some years earlier when I had returned to the Eihei Monastery and gone to see him he had given me the same admonishment during a private discussion. So it was the second time I was told this.

On the twenty-third day of the seventh month of that year, before I went to visit my hometown, Dōgen told me, "You should return quickly from this trip. There are many things I have to tell you."

On the twenty-eighth day of the same month, I returned to the monastery and paid my respects to him. He said, "While you were gone I thought I was going to die, but I am still alive. I have received several requests from the lord [Yoshishige Hatano] at the Governor's Office in Rokuhara to come to the capital for medical treatment. At this point I have many last instructions, but I am planning to leave for Kyōto on the fifth day of the eighth month. Although you would be very well suited to accompany me on the trip, there is no one else who can attend to all the affairs of the monastery. I want you to stay and take care of the administration. Sincerely take care of the monastery affairs. This time I am certain that my life will be over. Even if my death is slow in coming, I will stay in Kyōto this year. Do not think the monastery belongs to others, but consider it as your own. Presently you have no position, but you have served repeatedly on the senior staff. You should consult with the others on all matters and not make decisions on your own. Since I am very busy now, I cannot tell you the details. Perhaps there are many things that I will have to tell you later from Kyōto.

"If I live to return from Kyōto, then next time we meet I will certainly teach you the secret procedures of dharma transmission. However, when someone starts these procedures, small-minded people become jealous. So, you should not tell other people of this. I know that you have an outstanding spirit for both the mundane and the supermundane worlds. However you still lack a grandmotherly heart." Dōgen had wanted me to return quickly from my trip so that he could tell me these things. I am not recording further details here. Separated by the sliding door, the senior nun Egi heard the conversation.

On the third day of the eighth month, Dōgen gave me the woodblock for printing the eight prohibitory precepts.* On the sixth day of the month, bidding farewell to Dōgen at an inn at Wakimoto, I respectfully asked, "I deeply wish I could accompany you on this trip, but I will return to the monastery according to your instructions. If your return is delayed, I would like to go to Kyōto to see you. Do I have your permission?"

He said, "Of course you do, so you don't need to ask any further about it. I am having you stay behind only in consideration of the monastery. I want you to attentively manage the affairs of the monastery. Because you are a native to this area and because you are a disciple of the late master Ekan, many people in this province know your trustworthiness. I am asking you to stay because you are familiar with matters both inside and outside the monastery."

I accepted this respectfully. It was the last time I saw Dōgen and it was his final instruction to me. Taking it to heart, I have never forgotten it.

Poem

For ten years, I've eaten the rice of the Eihei Monastery.
For ten months, I've lain in bed ill.
Now I must leave these deep mountains to seek a cure in
    the world of mortals—
thus the Buddha of Suchness points my way to the Buddha
    of Healing.

1253, Kyōto

Death Poem

Fifty-four years lighting up the sky.
A quivering leap smashes a billion worlds. Hah!
Entire body looks for nothing.
Living, I plunge into the yellow springs.

Selected Bibliography

JAPANESE

Kawamura, Kōdō, ed. *Eihei Kaisan Dōgen Zenji Gyōjō Kenzei-ki, Shohon Taikō (Kenzei's Biography of the Founder Dōgen of Eihei, Comparative Version)*. Tōkyō: Daishūkan Shoten, 1975.

Masutani, Fumio, trans. *Gendaigo-yaku Shōbōgenzō (Modern Japanese Translation, Treasury of the True Dharma Eye)*, 8 vols. Tōkyō: Kadokawa Shoten, 1973–75.

Nakamura, Sōichi; Sōjun Nakamura; and Kazuaki Tanahashi, trans. *Zen'-yaku Shōbōgenzō (Complete Translation: Treasury of the True Dharma Eye)*, 4 vols. Tokyo: Seishin Shobō, 1971–72.

Ōkubo, Dōshū, ed. *Dōgen Zenji Zenshū (Entire Work of Zen Master Dōgen)*, 2 vols. Tōkyō: Chikuma Shobō, 1970.

Sakai, Tokugen, et al, eds. *Dōgen Zenji Zenshū (Entire Work of Zen Master Dōgen)*, 7 vols. Tōkyō, Shunjūsha. 1988–93.

Takeuchi, Michio. *Dōgen*. Tōkyō: Yoshikawa Kōbunkan, 1962.

ENGLISH

Books about Dōgen

Abe, Masao. *A Study of Dōgen: His Philosophy and Religion*. Albany: State University of New York Press, 1992.

Bielefeldt, Carl. *Dōgen's Manuals of Zen Meditation*. Berkeley: University of California Press, 1988.

Cleary, Thomas, trans. *Rational Zen: The Mind of Dōgen Zenji*. Boston: Shambhala Publications, 1993.

———, trans. *Record of Things Heard: The Shōbōgenzō Zuimonki, Talks of Zen Master Dōgen as Recorded by Zen Master Ejō*. Boulder, Colo.: Prajñā Press, 1980.

————, trans. *Shōbōgenzō: Zen Essays by Dōgen*. Honolulu: University of Hawaii Press, 1986.

Cook, Francis. *How to Raise an Ox: Zen Practice as Taught in Zen Master Dōgen's Shōbōgenzō*. Los Angeles: Center Publications, 1978.

————. *Sounds of Valley Streams: Enlightenment in Dōgen's Zen*. Albany: State University of New York Press, 1989.

Heine, Steven. *A Blade of Grass: Japanese Poetry and Aesthetics in Dōgen Zen*. New York: Peter Lang, 1989.

————. *Dōgen and the Kōan Tradition: A Tale of Two Shōbōgenzō Texts*. Albany: State University of New York Press, 1994.

————. *Existential and Ontological Dimensions of Time in Heidegger and Dōgen*. Albany: State University of New York Press, 1985.

Jaffe, Paul, trans. *Flowers Fall: A Commentary on Zen Master Dōgen's Genjō-kōan, by Hakuun Yasutani*. Boston: Shambhala Publications, 1997.

Kim, Hee-Jin. *Dōgen Kigen: Mystical Realist*. Tucson: University of Arizona Press, 1975.

————, trans. *Flowers of Emptiness: Selections from Dōgen's Shōbōgenzō*. Lewiston, N.Y.: Edwin Mellen Press, 1985.

Kodera, Takashi James. *Dōgen's Formative Years in China: An Historical Study and Annotated Translation of the Hōkyō-ki*. Boulder, Colo.: Prajñā Press, 1980.

LaFleur, William R., ed. *Dōgen Studies*. Honolulu: Kuroda Institute, University of Hawaii Press, 1985.

Leighton, Taigen Daniel, and Shōhaku Okumura, trans. *Dōgen's Pure Standards for the Zen Community: A Translation of Eihei Shingi*. Albany: State University of New York Press, 1996.

Nishijima, Gudō Wafū, and Chodo Cross, trans. *Master Dōgen's Shōbōgenzō*. 4 vols. Woods Hole, Mass.: Windbell Publications, 1994–1998.

Nishiyama, Kōsen, and John Stevens, trans. *Dōgen Zenji's Shōbōgenzō (The Eye and Treasury of the True Law)*. 4 vols. Sendai, Japan: Daihokkaikaku, 1975–1983.

Okumura, Shōhaku, and Taigen Leighton, trans. *The Wholehearted Way: A Translation of Eihei Dōgen's Bendōwa with Commentary by Kōshō Uchiyama Rōshi*. Boston: Charles Tuttle and Co., 1997.

Okumura, Shōhaku, ed. and trans. *Dōgen Zen*. Kyōto: Kyōto Sōtō Zen Center, 1988.

————, trans. *"Shōbōgenzō Zuimonki": Sayings of Eihei Dōgen Zenji, Recorded by Koun Ejō*. Kyōto: Kyōto Sōtō Zen Center, 1987.

Shimano, Eidō, and Charles Vacher, trans. *Shōbōgenzō Uji: Être-temps, Being time.* La Versanne, France: Encre Marine, 1997.

Stambaugh, Joan. *Impermanence Is Buddha-Nature: Dōgen's Understanding of Temporality.* Honolulu: University of Hawaii Press, 1990.

Tanahashi, Kazuaki, ed. and trans. *Moon in a Dewdrop: Writings of Zen Master Dōgen.* San Francisco: North Point Press, a division of Farrar, Straus and Giroux, 1995.

Wright, Thomas, trans. *Refining Your Life: From Zen Kitchen to Enlightenment, by Zen Master Dōgen and Kōshō Uchiyama.* New York: Weatherhill, 1983.

Yokoi, Yūhō, trans. *The Shōbōgenzō.* Tōkyō: Sankibō Buddhist Bookstore, 1986.

Yokoi, Yūhō, with Daizen Victoria. *Zen Master Dōgen: An Introduction with Selected Writings.* New York: Weatherhill, 1976.

Books with Material Concerning Dōgen:

Bodiford, William M. *Sōtō Zen in Medieval Japan.* Honolulu: Kuroda Institute, University of Hawaii Press, 1993.

Cleary, Thomas, ed. and trans. *Minding Mind: A Course in Basic Meditation.* Boston: Shambhala Publications, 1995.

———, ed. and trans. *Timeless Spring: A Sōtō Zen Anthology.* Tōkyō: Weatherhill, 1980.

Kasulis, T. P. *Zen Action/Zen Person.* Honolulu: University of Hawaii Press, 1981.

Leighton, Taigen Daniel. *Bodhisattva Archetypes: Classic Buddhist Guides to Awakening and Their Modern Expressions.* New York: Viking Arkana, 1998.

———, and Yi Wu, trans. *Cultivating the Empty Field: The Silent Illumination of Zen Master Hongzhi.* San Francisco: North Point Press, 1991.

Okumura, Shōhaku, ed. and trans. *Shikantaza: An Introduction to Zazen.* Kyōto: Kyōto Sōtō Zen Center, 1985.

———, and Thomas Wright, trans. *Opening the Hand of Thought: Approach to Zen.* New York: Viking Arkana, 1994.

Snyder, Gary. *The Practice of the Wild.* San Francisco: North Point Press, 1990.

Suzuki, Shunryū. *Zen Mind, Beginner's Mind.* New York: Weatherhill, 1970.

Tanahashi, Kazuaki, and Tensho David Schneider, eds. *Essential Zen.* San Francisco: HarperSanFrancisco, 1994.

Glossary of Terms

In the following entries, C. = Chinese, J. = Japanese, and S. = Sanskrit origins of terms.

abbot: J., *dōchō,* literally meaning "head of the hall." Also, *jūji,* meaning "one who abides in and maintains." The spiritual leader and administrative chief of a Zen monastery. (Later in large Japanese monasteries, the latter function became independent from the abbotship.)

administrator: J., *kan'in, inju,* or *kusu.* The equivalent of director, assistant director, and treasurer combined.

ancestor: An earlier teacher of the dharma lineage.

arhat: (S.) A follower of the Buddha's path who has attained nirvāna; literally, worthy or venerable. See *four fruits of the arhat.*

aspiration: The mind seeking for enlightenment.

assistant: J., *anja.* A personal assistant to the abbot or to a monk in an important position.

assistant to the practice leader: J., *dōan,* or *dōsu anja.*

asura: See *eight types of guardians.*

attendant monk: J., *jisha.* A monk high in seniority who works for the abbot as a secretary, and sometimes also as an assistant teacher.

billion worlds: See *sahā worlds.*

birth: Often means "life," based on the teaching that birth and death occur each moment.

bodhi: (S.) Awakening, enlightenment.

bodhisattva: (S.) One dedicated to enlightenment, who vows to bring others across to the shore of enlightenment before resting there. A future buddha.

bodhisattva precepts: The Mahāyāna precepts. In Dōgen's teaching, these consist of three refuges (in the three treasures), the three pure precepts (vow of following the prohibitory precepts, taking wholesome actions, and awakening sentient beings), and the ten prohibitory precepts.

bodhisattvas of ten stages and three classes: Bodhisattvas are classified into forty-two degrees according to their maturity. The first thirty degrees are called three classes. The more advanced ten degrees are called the ten stages or the ten grounds. That makes forty degrees. There are yet two more stages to go in order to be equal to a buddha.

Buddha: (S.) "The Buddha" often indicates Shākyamuni Buddha, but can apply to any of the other awakened ones described in scripture, such as the Seven Original Buddhas.

buddha: (S.) One who has attained complete awakening.

buddha body: There are three types of buddha bodies: the dharma body (the ultimate reality itself); the bliss body, associated with the fruit of practice; and the manifestation body, which appears in the world and acts for the benefit of beings.

buddha ancestor: An earlier awakened teacher of the dharma lineage.

buddha-dharma: (S.) Truth taught by the Buddha; reality experienced by a buddha.

buddha hall: One of the buildings of a monastery, where the main buddha image is enshrined and ceremonies are held.

buddha seal: Same as buddha mind seal. Unchanging reality experienced by a buddha. Also, recognition of the buddha mind and entrustment of the teaching.

buffalo: A silent, steady practitioner.

clouds and water: Monks who travel freely in search of realization.

combined robe: An upper robe sewn together with a skirt.

desire world: See *three worlds*.

deva: A celestial being, in the highest of the six realms of transmigration. See also *eight types of guardians*.

dhāranī: A repetitive spell or incantation originally in Sanskrit. Later its sounds were converted in other languages' orthographies.

dharma: (S.) A very wide range of meanings, including ultimate reality, the Buddha's teaching of it, and a thing or phenomenon.

dharma hall: One of the main buildings of a monastery, where formal dharma talks are given.

dharma transmission: Passing on of the teaching from teacher to student, certifying succession of the ancestral lineage.

dharma wheel: The full, continuous, and dynamic teaching of the Buddha.

director: J., *kansu*. One of the six main officers of a Zen monastery.

dragon: A guardian deity. Also a metaphor for an excellent practitioner of the way.

dusty world: The ordinary realm of confinement, as opposed to that of freedom through the practice of dharma.

eight prohibitory precepts: Precepts traditionally observed by lay people on the six days of purification in a month: not killing; not stealing; not having sex; not lying; not drinking; not decorating one's hair and not seeing or listening to musical performances; not sleeping on a high, wide bed; and not eating after noon. The six days of purification are: the eighth, fourteenth, fifteenth, twenty-sixth, twenty-ninth, and thirtieth days of each month.

eight types of emancipation: Freedom cultivated by the following types of meditation: to see all things as impure; to reduce attachment; not to give rise to illusion; to see boundless space; to see boundless consciousness; to see nonsubstantiality; to attain the state beyond thought; to attain cessation samādhi in which all mental activity ceases.

eight types of guardians: A deva, dragon, yaksha (flying demon), gandharva (heavenly musician), asura (fighting spirit), garuda (bird god who feeds on dragons), kinnara (heavenly singer), and mahoraga (land dragon).

eightfold noble path: Right understanding, right thought, right speech, right action, right livelihood, right effort, right mindfulness, and right concentration. See also *four noble truths.*

eighty-four thousand dharma gates: The numerous teachings of the Buddha.

eighty-four thousand verses: Also refers to the numerous teachings of the Buddha.

emptiness: Nonindependent and impermanent nature of all things. Interconnectedness. See *twenty types of emptiness.*

enlightenment: Awareness of the ultimate reality, experienced in all stages of practice; conscious realization of the ultimate reality.

five great elements: The five elements of nature according to ancient Indian classification: earth, water, fire, air, and space. See also *five types of matter.*

five hindrances: Literally five "coverings" that conceal the clarity of mind—desire, ill will, laziness, restlessness, and doubt.

Five Schools: See Glossary of Names.

five sense desires: Desires stimulated by form, sound, smell, taste, and the tangible.

five skandhas: The five aggregates or heaps of physical and mental elements in the phenomenal world: matter, feelings, perceptions, impulses, and consciousness.

five types of matter: The five elements of nature according to ancient Chinese classification: wood, fire, earth, metal, and water.

five wrong views: Belief in permanence of the self, belief in permanence or in nonexistence of all things, denial of cause and effect, acceptance of mistaken views, and belief in wrong precepts.

form world: See *three worlds.*

Four Continents: See Glossary of Names.

four forms of birth: All beings are classified into those born from a womb, those born from an egg, those born of moisture, and those born as an effect of past action (such as devas).

four fruits of the arhat: Achievements of a practitioner as: a stream-enterer who has become free from delusions; a once-returner; a never-returner, who have become free from desires; and one who has no more need to study.

four great elements: Earth, water, fire, and air.

four groups of practitioners: Monks, nuns, laymen, and laywomen.

four noble truths: One of the first teachings of the Buddha after attaining enlightenment: suffering is pervasive in life; the cause of suffering is craving; nirvāna is the realm free from suffering; the means for attaining nirvāna is the practice of the eightfold noble path.

four types of confusion: That which goes against the teaching of: impermanence, no bliss, no self, and no purity.

four types of offerings to monks: Food and drink, clothes, shelter, and medicine.

four unwholesome realms: The first four of the six realms: worlds of hell beings, hungry ghosts, animals, and fighting spirits.

gandharva: See *eight types of guardians.*

garuda: See *eight types of guardians.*

han: (J.) A hanging wooden board struck by a wooden mallet as a signal in a monastery.

head cook: J., *tenzo.* One of the six main officers of a Zen monastery.

head monk: J. *shuso.* Literally meaning "head seat." One who assists the abbot in teaching during the practice period.

Hīnayāna: (S.) See *Three Vehicles.*

home-leaver: A monk or nun—a renunciate.

house: A monastery. Also the buddha way, or the sangha throughout space and time.

hundred grasses: All things.

I am always intimate with this: A monk asked, "Among the three bodies (dharma body, bliss body, and manifestation body of the buddha), which body does not fall into the ordinary realm?" Dongshan said, "I am always intimate with this."

icchantika: (S.) One who lacks the capacity for awakening.

just sitting: J., *shikan taza.* Practice of zazen with no attempt to solve questions. Sometimes referred to in contrast with kōan studies.

kalpa: (S.) Eon, an incalculable span of time.

karma: (S.) Action, or effect of action.

kashāya: (S.) A robe constructed of patches, usually worn over one shoulder by a Buddhist monk or nun.

kinnara: See *eight types of guardians.*

kōan: An exemplary story or words of an ancient master pointing to realization, to be studied and experienced by a Zen student under the guidance of the teacher. Also, for Dōgen, the fundamental point, or truth that is experienced directly.

kumbhāndha (S.) A flying demon who sucks on human spirit.

Lesser Vehicle(s): See *Three Vehicles.*

li: (C.) About one third of a mile.

mahāsattva: A great being.

Mahāyāna: (S.) See *Three Vehicles.*

mahoraga: See *eight types of guardians.*

mind seal: Confirmation of the merging of the minds of teacher and disciple. See also *buddha seal.*

monks' hall: One of the main buildings of a Zen monastery, where monks reside, engage in zazen, and take morning and midday meals.

morning star: After the intense meditation under the bodhi tree, Shākyamuni Buddha experienced enlightenment upon seeing the morning star.

nine realms of sentient beings: The desire world (which includes the six realms); four types of meditation heavens; and four types of heavens of no form.

nirvāna: (S.) Literally, "putting out fire." The state of freedom from desire, dualistic thought, and suffering in the chain of rebirth. Also means pari-nirvāna. See *four noble truths.*

pāramitā: Completion, crossing over to the shore of enlightenment.

pari-nirvāna: (S.) The Buddha's great death.

pishācha: (S.) A blood-sucking demon.

practice: A continuous process of actualizing enlightenment, according to Dōgen.

practice leader: S., *karmadāna.* C., *weino.* J., *ino.* One of the six main officers of a Zen monastery. Also called *dōsu* (J.).

practice period: J., *ango,* literally, peaceful dwelling. A ninety-day period of intensive practice. In Dōgen's time the summer practice period ran from the fifteenth day of the fourth month to the fifteenth day of the seventh month. (The winter practice period, which ran from the fifteenth day of the tenth month to the fifteenth day of the first month, was also traditional. But it seems that for Dōgen practice period meant summer practice period.)

prajnā: (S.) Wisdom that goes beyond dualistic views.

prajnā pāramitā: Arriving at prajnā, or completion of wisdom. Six pāramitās, a commonly used set, are: giving, ethical conduct, perseverance, enthusiasm, meditation, and prajnā.

pratyeka-buddha: (S.) A self-enlightened being who understands causation.

rebirth: See *six realms, nirvāna.*

saha worlds: The cosmos within the reach of Shākyamuni Buddha's teaching. "Sahā" (S.) means endurance, referring to the hardships of the inhabitants, which requires the development of patience. Sūtras say that there are a billion such worlds, each consisting of Mt. Sumeru and the Four Continents that surround it.

samādhi: A one-pointed, stable state of meditation.

sangha: (S.) Community of practitioners of the Buddha's teaching.

sentient beings: Living beings, including humans. Sometimes indicates those who are not awakened.

seven types of treasure: Gold, silver, lazuli, moonstone, agate, coral, and amber.

shramana: (S.) A wanderer, or a monk.

shrāvaka: (S.) Literally, a listener, meaning a disciple of the Buddha whose goal is to become an arhat.

simple robe: A robe worn under the one-shoulder robe (kashāya).

six great elements: Earth, water, fire, air, space, and consciousness.

six hindrances: Five hindrances plus the lack of understanding.

six miracles: Freedom from the six sense desires.

six miraculous powers: The power of celestial or supernormal activity, insight into others' minds, the celestial eye, the celestial ear, knowing the past, and removing misery.

six officers: The main administrators of a Zen monastery, who assist the abbot: director, assistant director, treasurer, practice leader, head cook, and work leader.

six realms: The "paths" in the cycle of birth, death, and rebirth: worlds of hell beings, hungry ghosts, animals, fighting spirits, humans, and devas. The first four are regarded as unwholesome and the last two as wholesome.

Sixteen Arhats: Monk disciples of the Buddha, whose images are often enshrined as guardians of buddha-dharma in a Zen monastery.

sixteen visualizations: Ways of meditation for attaining rebirth in the Pure Land of Amitābha Buddha. Visualization of the sun, water, the earth, a heavenly tree, a heavenly pond, a heavenly tower, a flower seat, a statue, the true body, Avalokiteshvara (an attendant bodhisattva of Amitābha), Mahāsthāmaprāpta (another attendant bodhisattva of Amitābha), general matter, particular matter, a higher person, a middle person, and a lower person.

skin bag: A human.

spreading hair on muddy ground: A boy called Sumedha, Shākyamuni Buddha in a former life, spread his hair on the ground to make a passage for Dīpankara Buddha, who then gave him a prediction of enlightenment.

study hall: A building in the Zen monastery where monks read, drink tea, and have evening meals.

stūpa: A memorial tower often containing sacred relics or texts. A symbol of buddha ancestors.

suchness: Reality as it is. Also, thusness.

Sumeru: See *Four Continents*

sūtra: (S.) Scripture that contains the Buddha's teaching. See *Tripitaka*.

Tathāgata: (S.) An honorific name for the Buddha, meaning the one who comes thus, or who has come from thusness.

ten directions: North, south, east, west, their midpoints, plus up and down.

ten wholesome actions: Not to kill, not to steal, not to misuse sex, not to lie, not to use unethical language, not to slander, not to equivocate, not to covet, not to harbor anger, and not to hold false views.

thirty blows: A teacher's encouragement and awakening with the use of a flat wooden stick.

Thirty-three Heavens: See Glossary of Names.

Three Continents: See *Four Continents.*

three insights: The Tiantai way of meditating on emptiness, impermanence, and the absolute value of all things.

three poisons: Greed, hatred, and delusion.

three pounds of flax: Dongshan Shouchu was asked by a monk, "What is buddha?" Dongshan replied, "Three pounds of flax." ("Flax" can also be translated as "sesame seeds.")

three stoppings: The Tiantai way of calming mind with: freedom from attachment; determination to benefit sentient beings; freedom from one-sided views.

Three Teachings: Buddhism, Confucianism, and Daoism.

three times from now: The present lifetime, the next lifetime, and subsequent lifetimes.

three treasures: Buddha, dharma, and sangha.

three types of knowledge: The celestial eye, insight into the future, and knowing how to remove misery.

Three Vehicles: According to the traditional Mahāyāna Buddhist view, the Buddha's teaching is classified into the three ways to bring people across the ocean of birth and death to the shore of enlightenment: the Shrāvaka Vehicle, the Pratyeka-buddha Vehicle, and the Great Vehicle. The first two are called the Hīnayāna or Lesser (Small) Vehicles. The Great Vehicle (Mahāyāna) is also called the Bodhisattva Vehicle.

three worlds: The desire world, which includes the six realms; the form world of those who are free from desire; and the formless world of those who have attained the highest freedom in meditation.

thusness: See *suchness.*

treasurer: J., *fūsu.* One of the six main officers of a Zen monastery.

Tripitaka: (S.) The "three baskets", or groupings, of Buddhist teaching that constitute the entire canon: sūtras, precepts, and commentaries.

turning the dharma wheel: Expounding the teaching of awakening.

turning word: A statement that leads a student to realization.

twelve divisions of scripture: Discourses in prose, discourses in prose and verse, verse, stories about the causes and conditions of events, stories about previous worlds, Jātaka tales (about previous lives of the Buddha), stories about unprecedented events, parables, treaties, teachings offered without request, broadly extended writings, and stories about predictions of enlightenment.

twelve hours: A day, according to the traditional East Asian way of counting.

twenty types of emptiness: Nonindependent nature of: inside, outside, inside and outside together, emptiness itself, major teachings, minor teachings, truth, what is created, what is not created, all things, limitless things, what is dispersed, what is unchanging, original nature, self, co-existence, all dharmas, what cannot be grasped, no nature, and self nature.

twining vines: Being caught up in words. Also in Dōgen's usage, being fully immersed in and free from words.

udumbara flower: A mythic flower that blooms once every three thousand years.

unconditioned body: The buddha body, which is the ultimate reality itself.

views of water by four types of beings: Avabhāva, an Indian Buddhist teacher, said, "Celestial beings see water as jewels, humans see it as water, hungry ghosts see it as pus and blood, and fish see it as a palace."

visitors' room: J., *tangaryō.* A place for visiting monks to stay, where those who request admission to the monastery engage in zazen for a period of some days.

water buffalo: A silent practitioner.

wheel-turning king: One who rules with a heavenly wheel to keep order in society.

work leader: J., *shissui.* One of the six main officers of a Zen monastery.

world beyond conditions: The realm of home-leavers.

World-honored One: A respectful name for the Buddha.

yaksha: See *eight types of guardians.*

yellow springs: The world of the dead.

zazen: (J.) Meditation in a seated posture.

Zen: (J.). S., *dhyāna.* C., *chan.* Meditation in Buddhist ways, or in particular ways developed by teachers in ancient China. Also meaning the Zen School and the Zen Buddhist way of understanding, as well as Zen Buddhist practice centered around zazen.

Glossary of Names

Names of persons, deities, books, Buddhist schools, and some places mentioned in the main text are briefly explained here. The Japanese versions of the Chinese names are shown in brackets. Chinese provinces are parenthesized. The dates are CE(AD) unless specified otherwise.

Ajātashatru, King: Son of King Bimbisāra of Magadha, one of the sixteen kingdoms of India, during the time of Shākyamuni Buddha. Ajātashatru became king by imprisoning his father, who later died in prison. He agonized over his crime but reached peace of mind by taking refuge in the Buddha's teaching. He became a supporter of the first assembling of the sūtras soon after the Buddha's pari-nirvāna.

Amoghavajra: 705–774. A monk from North India who went to China and received the Esoteric Teaching from Longzhi. Translated many Sanskrit texts into Chinese. National teacher for emperors Xuan, Su, and Dai.

Ānanda: A close disciple and attendant of Shākyamuni Buddha. Known for his memory, Ānanda is regarded as the one who recalled and recited sūtras at the first assembling of the Buddha's teaching soon after the pari-nirvāna of the Buddha. Regarded as the Second Ancestor after Mahākāshyapa in the Zen tradition.

Avalokiteshvara: Bodhisattva of Compassion, sometimes described as having one thousand hands and eyes. C., Guanyin (J., Kannon) means one who hears the sounds (of the sufferings of the world).

Baizhang Huaihai: [Hyakujō Ekai] 749–814, China. Dharma heir of Mazu Daoyi. Founder of Dazhi Shousheng Monastery, Mt. Baizhang, Hong Region (Jiangxi). Known as the initiator of monastic regulations for Chinese Zen.

Bao, Lord: [Hōkō] 999–1062, China. Bao Zheng. A politician in the Song Dynasty, renowned as a fair judge.

Baoen Xuanze: [Hō'on Gensoku] Ca. ninth-tenth centuries, China. Dharma heir of Fayan Wenyi, Fayan School. Taught at Baoen Monastery, Jinling (Jiangsu).

Baofu Benquan: [Hofuku Hongon] Ca. twelfth century, China. A dharma heir of Huitang Zuxin, Linji School. Taught at Mt. Baofu, Zhang Region (Fujian).

Baojing: See *Xiang Baojing.*

Bei, Ascetic: See *Xuansha Shibei.*

Bhadrapāla, Bodhisattva: Regarded as a dharma descendant of Prajnātāra, Bodhidharma's teacher.

Biandan Xiaoliao: [Hentan Gyōryō] Ca. seventh-eighth centuries, China. A dharma heir of the Sixth Ancestor Huineng. Biography unknown.

Bimbisāra, King: See *Ajātashatru, King.*

Bodhidharma: [Bodaidaruma] Ca. sixth century. A dharma heir of Prajnātāra in India. Brought the Zen teaching from India to China. Taught at the Shaolin Temple, Mt. Song, Luo Region (Henan). Regarded as the First Ancestor in China of the Zen School.

Bodhiruchi, Scripture Master: Ca. fifth-sixth centuries. An Indian monk who arrived in Luoyang (Henan), China, in 508 and engaged in the translation of sūtras into Chinese. Purportedly one of the monks who accused and attempted to oppress Bodhidharma.

Brahma, King: Also called Mahābrahman. Regarded as king of gods, also as a guardian deity of Buddhism.

Budai: [Hotei] Ca. tenth-century, China. Originally called Qici. As he practiced begging while carrying all his belongings in a cloth bag, he was called Priest Budai (Cloth Bag). Later portrayed as a laughing monk, with a protruding belly. Considered an incarnation of Maitreya Bodhisattva.

Buddha of Healing: Bhaishajyaguru Buddha, depicted holding a medicine pot.

Butsuju Myōzen: 1184–1225, Japan. A dharma heir of Myōan Eisai. As abbot of Kennin Monastery, Kyōto, he taught Rinzai Zen to Dōgen. He took Dōgen to China but died at Tiantong Monastery during his study.

Caodong School: The dharma lineage derived from Dongshan Liangjie. One of the Five Schools of Zen in China.

Caoshan Benji: [Sōzan Honjaku] 840–901, China. A dharma heir of Dong-shan Liangjie. Sometimes regarded as a cofounder of the Caodong School along with Dongshan. Taught at Mt. Cao, Fu Region (Jiangxi). Posthumous name: Great Master Yuanzheng.

Changqing Daan: [Chokei Daian] 793–883, China. A dharma heir of Bai-zhang Huaihai, in the Nanyue line. Also called Lazy An. Taught at Mt. Gui, Tan Region (Hunan), after Guishan Lingyou's death, and then at Changqing Monastery, Fu Region (Fujian). Posthumous name: Great Master Yuanzhi.

Changqing Huileng: [Chōkei Eryō] 854–932, China. A dharma heir of Xuefeng Yicun, Qingyuan line. Taught at Changqing Monastery, Fu Region (Fujian). Posthumous name: Great Master Chaojue.

Changsha Jingcen: [Chōsha Keishin] Ca. ninth century, China. A dharma heir of Nanquan Puyuan, Nanyue line. Taught at Luyuan Monastery, Changsha (Hunan). Also called Tiger Cen. Posthumous name: Great Master Zhaoxian.

Changshui Zhixuan: [Chōsui Shisen] d. 1038, China. A dharma heir of Langye Huijue, Linji School. Taught in Changshui, Shen Region (Zhejiang).

Changzong: See *Zhaojue Changzong.*

Chanmen Baoxun: See *Xihu Guangji.*

Chen, Emperor: [Seitei] The eleventh emperor of the Former Han Dynasty, China. Reigned 33–7 BCE.

Chen, Venerable: See Muzhou Daoming.

Chen Xiuwen: [Chin Kyūbun] 441–513, China. A poet in the Kingdom of Liang.

Chenjin: [Seishin] Ca. third century. Lord of Nanyang (Hunan) in the Later Han Dynasty, China.

Chi, Sister: Ca. thirteenth century, Japan. A nun disciple of Butsuju Myō-zen. Biography unknown.

Chuanzi Decheng: [Sensu Tokujō] Ca. eighth-ninth centuries, China. A dharma heir of Yaoshan Weiyan, Qingyuan line. Taught while disguised as a boatman in Huating (Jiangsu).

Chuyuan: See *Shishuang Chuyuan.*

Cigan: See *Fuyan Cigan.*

Ciming: See *Shishuang Chuyuan.*

Confucious: C., Kongji. 552–479, BCE, China. A thinker and educator on ethics and social order. Regarded as author of *Chonqiu* and founder of Confucianism.

Cuiwei Wuxue: [Suibi Mugaku] Ca. eighth-ninth centuries, China. A dharma heir of Danxia Tianran, Qingyuan line. Taught at Cuiwei Monastery, Mt. Zhongnan (Shanxi). Given the title of Great Master Guangzhao by the Emperor.

Daci Huanzhong: [Daiji Kanchū] 780–862, China. A dharma heir of Baizhang Huaihai, Nanyue line. Taught at Mt. Daci, Hang Region (Zhejiang). Posthumous name: Great Master Xingkong.

Dadian Baotong: [Daiten Hōtsū] 732–824, China. A dharma heir of Shitou Xiqian, Qingyuan line. Taught at Mt. Ling, Chao Region (Guangdong).

Daguang: [Daikō] Ca. twelfth-thirteenth centuries, China. Abbot of Mt. Ayuwang, when Dōgen visited. Biography unknown.

Dai, Emperor: The eighth emperor of the Tang Dynasty, China. Reigned 762–779.

Dajian Huineng: [Daikan Enō] 638–713. The Sixth Ancestor in China of the Zen School. A dharma heir of the Fifth Ancestor Daman Hongren. Also called Laborer Lu. Taught at Baolin Monastery, Mt. Caoxi, Shao Region (Guangdong). Regarded as founder of the Southern School of Zen. Posthumous name: Zen Master Dajian. Some of his dharma discourses are included in *The Sixth Ancestor's Platform Sūtra.*

Damei Fachang: [Daibai Hōjō] 752–839, China. A dharma heir of Mazu Daoyi, Nanyue line. Taught at Mt. Damei (Zhejiang).

Daokai: See *Furong Daokai.*

Daosheng: [Dōsen] Ca. thirteenth century, China. A Daoist studying Zen with Rujing at Tiantong Monastery while Dōgen was there. Biography unknown.

Daowu: See *Tianhuang Daowu.*

Daowu Yuanzhi: [Dōgo Enchi] 769–835, China. A dharma heir of Yaoshan Weiyan, Qingyuan line. Also called Daowu Zongzhi. Taught at Mt. Daowu, Tan Region (Hunan).

Daoxuan, Precept Master: [Dōsen] 596–667. Regarded as founder of the Precept School in China. Taught at Mt. Zhongnan, also called Mt. Nan (Shanxi). Also called Nanshan Daoxuan.

Dayi Daoxin: [Daii Dōshin] 580–651. The Fourth Ancestor of Chinese Zen. A dharma heir of the Third Ancestor Jianzhi Sengcan. Taught at Huangmei, Qi Region (Hubei). Also called Shuangfeng. Zen Master Dayi is his posthumous name.

Dayu: See *Gaoan Dayu.*

Dazu Huike: [Taiso Eka] 487–593. A dharma heir of Bodhidharma. The Second Ancestor of Chinese Zen. Taught in the northern capital of Ye (Henan). Posthumous name: Great Master Zhengzong Pujue.

Deguang: See *Fuzhao Deguang.*

Deshan Xuanjian: [Tokusan Senkan] 780–865, China. A dharma heir of Longtan Chongxin, Qingyuan line. Taught at Mt. De, Ding Region (Hunan). Posthumous name: Great Master Jianxing.

Devadatta: A cousin and a student of Shākyamuni Buddha, who was expelled from the sangha and attempted to kill the Buddha.

Dongshan Liangjie: [Tōzan Ryōkai] 807–869, China. A dharma heir of Yunyan Tansheng, Qingyuan line. Taught at Mt. Dong, Rui Region (Jiangxi). Author of "Song of Precious Mirror Samādhi." Regarded as the founder of the Caodong School, one of the Five Schools of Chinese Zen. Posthumous name: Great Master Wuben.

Dongshan Shouchu: [Tōzan Shusho] 910–990, China. A dharma heir of Yunmen Wenyan, Yunmen School. Taught at Mt. Dong, Rui Region (Jiangxi). Posthumous name: Great Master Zonghui.

Egi: Ca. thirteenth century, Japan. A nun disciple of Butchi Kakuan of the Japan Daruma School. She later studied with Dōgen.

Eisai: See *Myōan Eisai.*

Ejō: See *Koun Ejō.*

Ekan: d. 1251? Japan. A student of Butchi Kakuan of the Japan Daruma School. Taught at Hajaku Monastery, Echizen. Following his student Ejō, Ekan brought other students, Gikai, Giin, Gien, and Giun and joined Dōgen's community in 1241. He later became head monk in Eihei Monastery.

Eun: Ca. thirteenth century, Japan. A student of Dōgen at Kōshō Hōrin Monastery. Biography unknown.

Expansive Lamp Record of the Tiansheng Era: Tiansheng Guangdenglu, compiled by Li Zunxu in 1029. A thirty-fascicle record of Zen masters. Named by a Song Dynasty emperor, China.

Fachang: See *Damei Fachang.*

Fashen: See *Yuantong Fashen.*

Fayan Wenyi: [Hōgen Mon'eki] 885–958. A dharma heir of Dizang Guichen. Taught at Baoen Monastery, Jinling (Jiangsu), also at Qingliang Monastery, Sheng Region (Jiangsu). Posthumous name: Zen Master Great Fayan. Regarded as the founder of the Fayan School, one of the five schools of Chinese Zen.

Fenyang Shanzhao: [Fun'yō Zenshō] 947–1024, China. A dharma heir of Shoushan Xingnian, Linji School. Taught at Mt. Fenyang, Fen Region (Shanxi). Posthumous name: Zen Master Wude.

Five Schools: The major schools of Chinese Zen after the late Tang Dynasty: the Guiyang, Linji, Caodong, Yunmen, and Fayan Schools.

Four Continents: According to sūtras, the world consists of the four continents that lie around Mt. Sumeru. The Northern Continent, Uttarakuru, is where inhabitants live for one thousand years and don't know suffering. Therefore they indulge in the pleasure of the present moment. The Southern Continent, Jambudvīpa, is where we humans live with suffering, but where we have the potential for awakening.

Furi Xiesong: [Butsunichi Kaisū] 1007–1072, China. A dharma heir of Dongshan Xiaocong, Yunmen School. Taught at Mt. Furi, Hong Region (Jiangxi). Given title Great Master Mingjiao by the Emperor.

Furong Daokai: [Fuyō Dōkai] 1043–1118, China. A dharma heir of Touzi Yiqing, Caodong School. Also called Dayang. Taught at Mt. Dayang, Ying Region (Hubei), and later at Lake Furong (Shandong).

Furong Lingxun: [Fuyō Reikun] Ca. ninth century, China. A dharma heir of Guizong Zhichang, Nanyue line. Taught at Mt. Furong, Fu Region (Fujian). Posthumous name: Great Master Hongzhao.

Fuxing Fatai: [Bisshō Hōtai] Ca. eleventh-twelfth centuries, China. A dharma heir of Yuanwu Keqin, Linji School. Taught at Mt. Gui, Tan Region (Hunan). Given the title of Zen Master Fuxing by the Emperor.

Fuyan Cigan: [Fukugen Jikan] Ca. eleventh century, China. A dharma heir of Huanglong Huinan, Linji School. Taught at Fuyan Monastery, Nanyue (Hunan). Because of his stern look, he was called Iron Face Gan.

Fuyan Qingyuan: [Butsugen Seion] 1067–1120, China. A dharma heir of Wuzu Fayan, Linji School. Taught at Baoshan Monastery, He Region (Anhui). Also called Gushan. Given the title of Zen Master Fuyan by the Emperor.

Fuyin Liaoyuan: [Butsuin Ryōgen] 1032–1098, China. A dharma heir of Kaixian Shanxian, Yunmen School. Taught at Kaixian Monastery, Mt. Lu (Jiangxi). Given the title of Zen Master Fuyin by the Emperor.

Fuzhao Deguang: [Busshō Tokkō] 1121–1203, China. A dharma heir of Dahui Zonggao, Linji School. Taught at Mt. Jing (Zhejiang). Given the title of Zen Master Fuzhao.

Gao, Emperor: [Kōsō] 256–195 BCE, China. Liubang. The founding emperor of the Former Han Dynasty. Reigned 296–195 BCE.

Gaoan Dayu: [Kōan Daigu] Ca. ninth century, China. A dharma heir of Guizong Zhichang, Nanyue line. Taught in Gaoan, Rui Region (Jiangxi).

Gikai: See *Tettsū Gikai.*

Guangtong Huiguang, Precept Master: [Kōzu Ekō] 468–537, China. Advocated the precepts that are classified in four divisions. Purportedly one of the monks who accused and attempted to oppress Bodhidharma.

Guanping: [Kōhei] Ca. thirteenth century, China. Attendant monk to Tiantong Rujing while Dōgen studied with Rujing.

Guanxi Zhixian: [Kankei Shikan] d. 895, China. A dharma heir of Linji Yixuan, Linji School. Also studied with Nun Moshan Liaoran. Taught in Guanxi, Changsha (Hunan).

Guidelines for Zen Monasteries: C., *Chanyuan Qinggui.* Ten volumes. Compiled by Changlu Zongze (eleventh-twelfth century, China). The oldest extant collection of monastic guidelines, as most of the earlier guidelines by Baizhang are lost.

Guishan Huaixiu: [Isan Eshū] Ca. eleventh century, China. A dharma heir of Huanglong Huinan, Linji School. Taught at Mt. Gui, Tan Region (Hunan).

Guishan Lingyou: [Isan Reiyū]. 771–853. A dharma heir of Baizhang Huaihai, Nanyue line. Taught at Mt. Gui, Tan Region (Hunan). Guishan and his heir Yangshan are regarded as the cofounders of the Guiyang School, one of the Five Schools of Chinese Zen. He was also called Dagui (Great Gui). Posthumous name: Zen Master Dayuan.

Gushan: See *Fuyan Qingyuan.*

Haihui Shouduan: [Kaie Shutan] 1025–1072, China. A dharma heir of Yangqi Fanghui, Linji School. Also called Boyun. Taught at Haihui Monastery, Mt. Boyun, Shu Region (Anhui).

Haoyue, Secretary: [Kōgetsu] Ca. eighth century, China. A secretary to a high official, and lay student of Changsha Jingcen, Nanyue line.

Hatano, Hironaga: Ca. thirteenth century, Japan. A lay disciple of Dōgen. Possibly related to Yoshishige Hatano. Biography unknown.

Hatano, Yoshishige: Ca. thirteenth century, Japan. A warrior of the Kamakura government, whose title was Governor of Izumo Province, a councilor at the Governor's Office in Rokuhara, Kyōto. As a lord in Echizen Province, he was Dōgen's main lay student and benefactor.

Himālayas: Described in sūtras as where Shākyamuni Buddha practiced in his former life.

History of the Han Dynasty: C., *Hanshu.* A 120-fascicle official history of the Former Han Dynasty, completed by Bangu (32–92) of the Later Han Dynasty.

Hōjō, Tokiyori: 1227–1263. Became the head of the Kamakura government as Regent of Japan in 1246. His Buddhist name is Dōsū of Saimyōji.

Hongzhi Zhengjue: [Wanshi Shōgaku] 1091–1157, China. A dharma heir of Danxia Zichun, Caodong School. Taught at Jingde Monastery, Mt. Tiantong, Ming Region (Zhejiang). Known as leader of "silent illumination Zen." Author of *Hongzhi's Capping Verses,* which became the basis of *The Book of Serenity.* Zen Master Hongzhi is his posthumous name.

Hua, Attendant: See *Shuanglin Hua.*

Huaixiu: See *Guishan Huaixiu.*

Hualin Shanjue: [Karin Zenkaku] Ca. eighth century, China. A dharma heir of Mazu Daoyi, Nanyue line. Taught at Hualin, Tan Region, Fujian. It is said that he kept two tigers as his attendants.

Huang Shangu: [Kō Sankoku] 1045–1105, China. A poet and calligrapher of the Northern Song Dynasty. A government official and lay student of Huitang Zuxin, Linji School.

Huangbo Xiyun: [Ōbaku Kiun] Ca. ninth century, China. A dharma heir of Baizhang Huaihai, Nanyue line. Taught at Mt. Huangbo, Ning Region (Jiangxi). His teachings are collected in Essential Teaching of Transmission of Mind. Posthumous name: Zen Master Duanji.

Huanglong Huinan: [Ōryū Enan] 1002–1069, China. A dharma heir of Shishuang Chuyuan, Linji School. Taught at Mt. Huanglong (Jiangxi). Regarded as founder of the Huanglong branch of the Linji School. Posthumous name: Zen Master Pujue.

Huating: See *Chuanzi Decheng.*

Huayan Xiujing: [Kegon Kyūjō] Ca. ninth century, China. A dharma heir of Dongshan Liangjie, Caodong School. Taught at Huayan Monastery, Jingzhao (Shanxi). Also called Jingzhao. Posthumous name: Great Master Baozhi.

Huike: See *Dazu Huike.*

Huineng: See *Dajian Huineng.*

Huitang Zuxin: [Kaidō Soshin] 1025–1100, China. A dharma heir of Huanglong Huinan. Taught at Mt. Huanglong (Jiangxi). Posthumous name: Zen Master Baojue.

Huiwen: [Emon] Ca. sixth century, China. Lived in the northern kingdom of Qi. Initiated a teaching based on Nāgārjuna's treatise on emptiness. Regarded as the founder of the Tiantai School.

Indra: Originally a Hindu deity. Regarded in Buddhism as a main guardian deity of dharma. Resides in the Thirty-three Heavens above Mt. Sumeru.

Iron Face Cigan: See *Fuyan Cigan.*

Jambudvīpa: See *Four Continents.*

Jeta Grove: The place in the south of the city of Shrāvastī, in Kaushala Kingdom, Central India. According to sūtras, this is where Shākyamuni Buddha's community practiced together in the monastery during the rainy season.

Jeta, Prince: The son of King Prasenajit of Kaushala Kingdom, India. He donated the Jeta Grove to Shākyamuni for creating a monastery.

Jianyuan Zhongxing: [Zengen Chūkō] Ca. eighth–ninth centuries, China. A dharma heir of Daowu Yuanzhi, Qingyuan line. Taught at Mt. Jianyuan, Tan Region (Hunan).

Jianzhi Sengcan: [Kanchi Sōsan] d. 606, China. A dharma heir of Dazu Huike. The Third Ancestor of Chinese Zen. Taught at Mt. Sikong, Shu Region (Anhui). Regarded as the author of "Song of Faith in Mind." Posthumous name: Zen Master Jianzhi.

Jiashan Shanhui: [Kassan Zenne] 805–881, China. First taught at Zhulin Monastery, Jingkou, Run Region (Jiangsu). Then he became a dharma heir of Chuanzi Decheng and taught at Mt. Jia, Feng Region (Hunan). Posthumous name: Great Master Chuanming.

Jing, Emperor: [Keisō] The thirteenth emperor of the Tang Dynasty, China. Reigned 824–826.

Jingjie Yanjun: [Jōkai Ganshun] 882–966, China. A dharma heir of Touzi Datong, Qingyuan line. Taught at Guanyin Monastery in Dongjing (Henan). Given the title of Great Master Jingjie.

Jingqing Daofu: [Kyōsei Dōfu] 864–937, China. A dharma heir of Xuefeng Yicun, Qingyuan line. Taught at Jingqing Monastery, Yue Region (Zhejiang).

Jingyun: Ca. thirteenth century, Korea. A monk who was studying at Tiantong Monastery while Dōgen was there. Biography unknown.

Jingzhao Mihu: [Kyōchō Beiko] Ca. ninth century, China. A dharma heir of Guishan Lingyou, Guiyang School. Biography not known.

Jinhua Juzhi: [Kinka Gutei] Ca. ninth century, China. A dharma heir of Hangzhou Tianlong. Juzhi always responded to dharma questions by simply raising his finger.

Jnānaprabha, Monk: A student of Shākyamuni Buddha, formerly a wealthy man in a small country far from where the Buddha taught.

Juefan Huihong: [Kakuhan Ekō] 1071–1128, China. Also called Simen. A dharma heir of Yunan Kewen, Linji School. Compiler of *The Record within the Forest.* Taught in Simen, Rui Region (Jiangxi).

Juzhi: See *Jinhua Juzhi.*

Kaji: C., Jiazhi. Ca. eighth-ninth centuries, Korea. A dharma heir of Damei Fachang. Biography unknown. Dōgen describes him as an ancestor of Zen in Korea.

Kanetomo, Middle Commander, Minister: Ca. thirteenth century, Japan. Accompanied Kasan'in on a visit to Dōgen at Eihei Monastery in 1251. Biography unknown.

Kao: Ca. ninth century, China. A student of Yaoshan Weiyan. Biography unknown.

Kasan'in, Prime Minister: Ca. thirteenth century, Japan. Sometimes considered to be Norimasa Fujiwara. "Kasan'in" is a Buddhist name. He visited Dōgen at Eihei Monastery in 1251.

Kāshyapa Mātanga: One of the two monks who brought Buddhism from India to China in 67. See also *Zhu Falan.*

Kenne: Ca. thirteenth century, Japan. Studied with Dōgen at Kōsho Monastery. Biography unknown.

King of the Empty Eon. The buddha who emerges in the last of the four stages of a world cycle: eons of becoming, abiding, decaying, and empty.

Koun Ejō: 1198–1280, Japan. After studying Zen with Kakuan of the Japan Daruma School, he became a student of Dōgen in 1234 and became the first head monk at Kōshō Hōrin Monastery. As the most advanced student, he assisted Dōgen and became his dharma heir. He was appointed the second abbot of Eihei Monastery by Dōgen in 1253.

Kumāralabdha: A legendary monk regarded as the Nineteenth Ancestor of the Zen tradition in India.

Langye Huijue: [Rōya Ekaku] Ca. eleventh century, China. A dharma heir of Fenyang Shanzhao, Linji School. Taught at Mt. Langye, Chu Region (Anhui). Posthumous name: Zen Master Guangzhao.

Laozi: [Rōshi] A semilegendary thinker in the Zhou Period (770–256 BCE), China. Regarded as the founder of Daoist philosophy and religion, and as author of *Daodejing.*

Li Jingrang: [Ri Keijō] Ca. ninth century, China. A government official who served Emperor Xian. Biography unknown.

Liang, Lecturer: [Ryō Zasu] Ca. eighth century, China. A student of Mazu Daoyi, Nanyue line. After having realization he secluded himself on Mt. Xi, Hong Region (Jiangxi).

Lingyuan Weiqing [Reigen Isei] d. 1117, China. A dharma heir of Huitang Zuxin, Linji School. Taught at Taiping Monastery, Shu Region (Anhui). Posthumous name: Zen Master Fushou.

Lingyun Zhiqin: [Reiun Shigon] Ca. ninth century, China. A dharma heir of Guishan Lingyou, Guiyang School. Taught at Mt. Lingyun, Fu Region (Hunan).

Linji School: The dharma lineage derived from Linji Yixuan. One of the Five Schools of Chinese Zen.

Linji Yixuan: [Rinzai Gigen] d. 867. A dharma heir of Huangbo Xiyun, Nanyue line. Taught at Linji Monastery, Zhen Region (Hebei). Regarded as founder of the Linji School, one of the Five Schools of Chinese Zen. Posthumous name: Great Master Huizhao.

Longshan: See *Tanzhou Longshan.*

Longya Judun: [Ryūge Kodon] 835–923, China. A dharma heir of Dongshan Liangjie, Caodong School. Taught at Mt. Longya, Tan Region (Hunan). Posthumous name: Great Master Zhangkong.

Luopu Yuanan: [Rakuho Gen'an] 834–898, China. A dharma heir of Jiashan Shanhui, Qingyuan line. Taught in Luopu, Feng Region [Hunan].

Lushi Chunqi: A collection of essays edited by guests of Lu Buwei (d. 235 BCE) of the Former Han Dynasty.

Mahākarunā Bodhisattva: Great Compassion Bodhisattva. Regarded as one of the former lives of Shākyamuni Buddha.

Mahākāshyapa: A senior disciple of Shākyamuni Buddha who was engaged in ascetic practice. Regarded as the First Ancestor of the Zen School.

Manjushrī: Bodhisattva of Wisdom, whose figure is enshrined as the holy monk inside the monks' hall in the Zen tradition.

Maudgalyāyana: One of the ten major disciples of Shākyamuni Buddha. Known for his outstanding miraculous powers.

Mayu Baoche: [Mayoku Hōtetsu] Ca. eighth-ninth centuries, China. A dharma heir of Mazu Daoyi, Nanyue line. Taught at Mt. Mayu, Pu Region (Shanxi).

Mazu Daoyi: [Baso Dōitsu] 709–788, China. A dharma heir of Nanyue Huairang, Nanyue line. Taught at Kaiyuan Monastery, Zhongling (Jiangxi). Also called Jiangxi. Posthumous name: Zen Master Daji.

Mihu: See *Jingzhao Mihu.*

Mingjiao: See *Furi Xiesong.*

Mingjue: See *Xuedou Chongxian.*

Moshan Liaoran, Nun: [Massan Ryōnen] Ca. ninth century, China. A dharma heir of Gaoan Dayu, Nanyue line. Taught at Mt. Mo, Yun Region (Jiangxi).

Mt. Sumeru. See *Four Continents.*

Muzou Daoming: [Bokushū Dōmyō] Ca. ninth century, China. Also called Venerable Chen, by his family name. A dharma heir of Huangbo Xiyun, Nanyue line. Taught at Longxing Monastery, Mu Region (Zhejiang).

Myōan Eisai: 1141–1225, Japan. Studied Tendai and Esoteric (Tantric) practice at Mt. Hiei. On his second visit to China, he became a dharma heir of Xuan Huaichang of the Linji School. Founded and taught Tendai studies, Esoteric Buddhism, and Zen at Jufuku Monastery, Kamakura, and Kennin Monastery, Kyōto. Regarded as founder of the Rinzai School.

Myōzen: See *Butsuju Myōzen.*

Nāgārjuna: Ca. second–third centuries, India. Author of many books including *Mādhyamika Shāstra.* He established the Mahāyāna philosophy based on understanding emptiness. Regarded as an ancestor by Mahāyāna schools including Zen.

Nanda: A younger stepbrother and disciple of Shākyamuni Buddha.

Nanquan Puyuan: [Nansen Fugan] 748–834, China. A dharma heir of Mazu Daoyi, Nanyue line. Taught at Mt. Nanquan, Chi Region (Anhui). He called himself Old Master Wang.

Nanshan Daoxuan: See *Daoxuan, Precept Master.*

Nanyang Huizhong: [Nan'yō Echū]. d. 775. A dharma heir of the Sixth Ancestor Huineng. Taught at Nanyang (Hunan). Posthumous name: National Teacher Dazheng.

Nanyue Huairang: [Nangaku Ejō] 677–744, China. A dharma heir of the Sixth Ancestor Huineng. Taught at Bore Monastery, Nanyue (Mt. Heng), Heng Region (Hunan). Regarded as founder of the Nanyue line. Posthumous name: Zen Master Dahui.

Nanyue Huisi: [Nangaku Eshi] 515–577, China. Studied lotus samādhi with Huiwen of the Kingdom of Qi, China. Taught at Nanyue (Mt. Heng), Heng Region (Hunan). Teacher of Zhiyi, founder of the Tiantai School.

Nanyue Xuantai: [Nangaku Gentai] Ca. ninth century, China. A dharma heir of Shishuang Qingzhu. Known as a poet and called Cotton Robe Tai. Lived on Nanyue (Mt. Heng), Heng Region (Hunan).

Ning, Emperor: [Neisō] d. 1224, China. The fourth emperor of the Southern Song Dynasty, China. Reigned 1194–1224.

Niutou Farong: [Gozu Hōyū] 594–657, China. A dharma heir of the Fourth Ancestor Daoxin. Taught at Mt. Niutou, Jiankang (Jiangsu). Regarded as founder of the Niutou School of Zen.

Pangyun, Layman: [Hōon Koji] d. 808. Also known as Layman Pang. A lay student of Mazu Daoyi, Nanyue line. He lived in Xiang Region (Hubei) and made his living by making baskets and having his daughter Lingzhao [Reishō] sell them in town. His teachings are found in *The Recorded Sayings of Layman Pang.*

Pāpiman: The demon who tried to tempt and obstruct the practice of Shākyamuni Buddha and his disciples.

Pārshva: A legendary monk regarded as the Tenth Ancestor of the Zen tradition in India. His name means Undefiled Sides.

Peixiu, Minister: [Haikyū Shōkoku] 797–870. An officer of the Tang-dynasty government. As a lay student of Huangbo Xiyun, Nanyue line, he edited Huangbo's *Essential Teaching of Transmission of Mind.*

Ping, Attendant Monk: See *Guanping.*

Prajnātāra: Ca., fifth–sixth centuries, India. Bodhidharma's teacher. Regarded as the Twenty-seventh Ancestor in the Zen tradition.

Precepts School: One of the Thirteen Schools of Buddhism in China, based on the Mahāyāna system of precepts. Daoyuan is regarded as founder.

Pu, Old Man: Ca. thirteenth century, China. A monk from Shu who practiced in Tiantong Rujing's monastery.

Pundarīka, Nun: Regarded to have been born wearing a Buddhist robe, (kashāya), birth after birth, as a result of offering a carpet to the Buddha. Her name means White Lotus.

Qingfeng Chuanchu: [Seihō Denso] Ca. ninth century, China. A dharma heir of Luopu Yuanan, Qingyuan line. Taught at Mt. Qingfeng, Fengxiang (Shanxi).

Qingyuan Xingsi: [Seigen Gyōshi] d. 740, China. A dharma heir of the Sixth Ancestor Huineng. Abbot of Jingju Monastery, Mt. Qingyuan, Ji Region (Jiangxi). Regarded as founder of the Qingyuan line. Posthumous name: Great Master Hongji.

Qingzhu: See *Shishuang Qingzhu.*

Rātnakosha Buddha: A mythic buddha regarded as a former life of Shākyamuni Buddha.

Record within the Forest: C., *Linjianlu.* A collection of Zen teachings and stories compiled by Juefan Huigong of the Linji School, China. Published in 1107.

Rujing: See *Tiantong Rujing.*

Ryūzen: Ca. thirteenth century, Japan. Originally a student of Myōan Eisai. He was studying with Rujing at Tiantong Monastery while Dōgen was there.

Sanghanandi: A legendary monk who is regarded as the Seventeenth Ancestor of the Zen tradition in India.

Sanping Yizhong: [Sampei Gichū] 781–872, China. A dharma heir of Dadian Baotong, Nanyue line. Taught at Mt. Sanping, Zhang Region (Fujian).

Sengzhao: [Sōjō] 384–414, China. A disciple of Kumārajīva, the great translator of Sanskrit Buddhist texts into Chinese. Author of *Zhao's Treatise (Zhaolun).*

Senne: Ca. thirteenth century, Japan. An advanced student of Dōgen. Author of *Shōbōgenzō Okikigaki (Notes of the Teachings I Heard, Treasury of the True Dharma Eye),* the first commentary on Dōgen's essays.

Seven Original Buddhas: Six legendary buddhas from the immeasurable past plus Shākyamuni Buddha. Also called Seven Buddhas of the Past.

Shākyamuni Buddha: Around sixth-fifth centuries BCE. Prince Siddhārtha of the Shakya clan who taught in Northern India and was the founding teacher of Buddhism. Also called Gautama Buddha. His honorary titles include Tathāgata and World-honored One. According to the Zen tradition he transmitted dharma to Mahākāshyapa, the First Ancestor. See *Seven Original Buddhas.*

Shānavāsa: Regarded as a dharma heir of Ānanda and as the Third Ancestor of the Zen Tradition.

Shanru: [Zennyo] Ca. thirteenth century, China. A monk practicing with Rujing at Tiantong Monastery while Dōgen was there. Biography unknown.

Shāriputra: Regarded as the most brilliant disciple of the Buddha.

Shenxiu: See *Yuquan Shenxiu.*

Shexian Guixing: [Sekken Kisei] Ca. tenth century, China. A dharma heir of Shoushan Xingnian, Linji School. Taught at Guangjiao Monastery, She Prefecture, Ru Region (Henan).

Shigong Huizang: [Shakkyō Ezō] Ca. eighth century, China. A dharma heir of Mazu Daoyi, Nanyue line. Taught at Mt. Shigong, Fu Region (Jiangxi).

Shigui: See *Zhuan Shigui.*

Shimen: See *Juefan Huihong.*

Shishuang Chuyuan: [Sekisō Soen] 987–1040, China. Also called Zen Master Ciming. A dharma heir of Fenyang Shanzhao, Linji School. Taught at Mt. Shishuang, Tan Region (Hunan).

Shishuang Qingzhu: [Sekisō Keisho] 807–886, China. A dharma heir of Daowu Yuanzhi, Qingyuan line. Taught at Mt. Shishuang, Tan Region (Hunan). Posthumous name: Great Master Puhui.

Shitou Xiqian: [Sekitō Kisen] 700–790, China. Ordained by the Sixth Ancestor Huineng and a dharma heir of Qingyuan Xingsi, Qingyuan line. He taught at Nan Monastery, Mt. Heng, also called Nanyue or Mt. Nan (Hunan). Author of poems "Harmonizing of Sameness and Difference" and "Song of the Grass Hut." Posthumous name: Great Master Wuji.

Shizhi: A two-volume book written by Shijiao of China during the Warring period (the fifth–third centuries BCE).

Shōmu, Emperor: 701–756, Japan. Reigned 724–749. A great supporter of Buddhism.

Shōtoku, Prince: 574–622, Japan. As Regent of Emperor Suiko he established a constitution and sent an envoy to China. A practitioner and pioneering supporter of Buddhism in Japan.

Shoushan Xingnian. [Shuzan Shōnen] 926–993, China. A dharma heir of Fengxue Yanzhao, Linji School. Founded the monastery of Mt. Shou, Ru Region (Henan).

Shuanglin Hua: [Sōrei Ke] Ca. twelfth century, China. A dharma heir of Huitang Zuxin, Linji School. Biography unknown.

Shuguang: [Sokō] Ca. third century, BCE, China. Councilor to the Emperor in the Former Han Dynasty. Known for his pure character.

Shun, Emperor: [Shun] A legendary virtuous ruler of ancient China. Regarded as the successor of Emperor Yao.

Sima, Ascetic: See *Sima Chengzheng.*

Sima Chengzheng: [Shiba Shōtei] Ca. eighth–ninth centuries, China. A lay disciple of Mazu Daoyi, Nanyue line. Residing in Hunan, he was noted for his physiognomic and geomantic skills.

Su Dongpo: [So Tōba] 1036–1101. A renowned poet and essayist of the Song Dynasty, China. Also called Su Shi. A lay student of Zhaojue Changzong, Linji School.

Su, Emperor: [Shukusō] The seventh emperor of the Tang Dynasty, China. Reigned 756–762.

Sudatta, Elder: A wealthy man who lived in the city of Shrāvastī, Kaushala Kingdom, India. He was moved by Shākyamuni Buddha's dharma talk and built and donated a monastery in Jeta Grove with the help of Prince Jeta, the owner of the grove.

Tai, Emperor: [Taisō] 154–220, China. Also called Emperor Wu. The founding emperor of the northern kingdom of Wei. Reigned 216–220. He was called Caocao before ascending to the throne.

Tai, Emperor: [Taisō] 598–649, China. The second emperor of the Tang Dynasty. Reigned 626–649.

Tanzhou Longshan: [Tanshū Ryūzan] Ca. ninth century, China. A dharma heir of Mazu Daoyi, Nanyue line. Secluded on a mountain till the end of his life. Also called Yunshan. Biography unknown.

Tettsū Gikai: 1219–1309, Japan. Ordained by Ekan of Daruma School and later became one of the most senior students of Dōgen. Received dharma transmission from Ejō, studied in China, and became the third abbot of Eihei Monastery.

Thirty-three Heavens: Heavens above Mt. Sumeru, consisting of four in each of the eight directions, and one in the center where Indra resides.

Tianhuang Daowu: [Tennō Dōgo] 748–807, China. A dharma heir of Shitou Xiqian, Qingyuan line. Taught at Tianhuang Monastery, Jing Region (Hubei).

Tianping Congyi: [Tempyō Jūi] Date unknown, China. A dharma heir of Qingxi Hongjin, Qingyuan line. Taught at Mt. Tianping, Xiang Region (Henan).

Tiantai School: One of the Thirteen Schools of Buddhism in China, founded by Zhiyi and based in Mt. Tiantai, Tai region (Zhejiang). Also called the Doctrinal School.

Tiantong Rujing: [Tendō Nyojō] 1163–1228, China. A dharma heir of Xuedou Zhijian, Caodong School. Taught at Qingliang Monastery, Jiankang (Jiangsu), at Ruiyan Monastery, Tai Region (Zhejiang) and at Jingci Monastery, Hang Region (Zhejiang). In 1225 he became abbot of Jingde Monastery, Mt. Tiantong, Ming Region (Zhejiang), where he transmitted dharma to Dōgen.

Tianyi Yihuai: [Tenne Gikai] 993–1064, China. A dharma heir of Xuedou Chongxian, Yunmen School. Taught at Mt. Tianyi, Yue Region (Zhejiang). Posthumous name: Great Master Zhenzong.

Touzi Datong: [Tōsu Daidō] 819–914, China. A dharma heir of Cuiwei Wuxue, Qingyuan line. Taught at Mt. Touzi, Shu Region (Anhui). Posthumous name: Great Master Ciji.

Touzi Yiqing: [Tōsu Gisei] 1032–1083, China. A dharma heir of Dayang Jingxuan, Caodong School. Taught at Mt. Touzi, Shu Region (Anhui). Restored the Caodong School.

Treasure Teaching of the Zen Gate: Chanmen Baoxun, or *Chanlin Baoxun,* compiled by Dahui Zonggao and Zhuan Shigui in the twelfth century, in China.

Upāli, Senior Monk: An advanced student of Shākyamuni Buddha. Known for understanding and maintaining precepts. He recited precepts at the first compilation of the Buddha's teaching soon after the pari-nirvāna of the Buddha.

Utpalavarnā, Nun: The foremost woman disciple of Shākyamuni Buddha. Known for attaining the six miraculous powers and becoming an arhat.

Uttarakuru: See *Four Continents.*

Vairochana Buddha: The luminous buddha who embodies the reality of the universe.

Vasubandhu: The Twenty-first Ancestor of the Zen tradition in India. A legendary figure, possibly named after the famous Mahāyāna commentator of the fifth-century India.

Vimalakīrti, Layman: The main figure of *The Vimalakīrti Sūtra.*

Wang Boxiang: [Ō Hakushō] 1106–1173, China. A writer and government official. Author of *Biography of Zen Master Hongzhi.*

Wen, Emperor: [Bunsō] d. 840, China. The fourteenth emperor of the Tang Dynasty. Reigned 826–840.

Wu, Emperor: [Busō] d. 846, China. The fifteenth emperor of the Tang Dynasty. Reigned 840–846. Oppressor of Buddhism during his reign.

Wu, Emperor: [Butei] 464–549, China. The founding emperor of the southern kingdom of Liang. Reigned 503–549. Regarded as the one who had a dialogue with Bodhidharma.

Wuzhuo Wenxi: [Mujaku Bunki] 821–900, China. A dharma heir of Yangshan Huiji, Guiyang School. Taught at Longquan Monastery, Hang Region (Zhejiang). Wuzhuo is his posthumous name.

Wuzu Fayan: [Goso Hōen] 1024–1104, China. A dharma heir of Haihui Shouduan, Linji School. Taught at Mt. Wuzu, Qi Region (Hubei).

Xiang Baojing: [Kōzan Hōjō] Ca. sixth century, China. Taught at Mt. Xiang, Luoyang (Henan). Sent Dazu Huike to study with Bodhidharma.

Xiang, Emperor: [Kensō] d. 820, China. The eleventh emperor of the Tang Dynasty. Reigned 805–820.

Xiangyan Zhixian: [Kyōgen Chikan] d. 898, China. A dharma heir of Gui-shan Lingyou, Guiyang School. Taught at Xiangyan Monastery, Deng Region (Henan). Posthumous name: Great Master Xideng.

Xiaoang: [Shōgō] Ca. sixth century, Liang Kingdom, China. Known as the Governor of Guang Province who welcomed Bodhidharma when he arrived from India.

Xiaoming, Emperor: [Kōmei Kotei] d. 75, China. The second emperor of the Later Han Dynasty. Reigned 57–75. He sent a messenger to India to invite monks, which resulted in the first official introduction of Buddhism to China in 67.

Xihu Guangji: [Seiko Kōki] A collection of Zen stories from the Xihu or West Lake area (Zhejiang). Details unknown.

Xitang Zhizang: [Seidō Chizō] 735–814, China. A dharma heir of Mazu Daoyi, Nanyue line. Posthumous name: Zen Master Dajue.

Xuan, Emperor: [Sensō] d. 859, China. The sixteenth emperor of the Tang Dynasty. Reigned 846–849. Before ascension, as Monk Dazong, he was a student of Xiangyan Zhixian, Guiyang School.

Xuansha Shibei: [Gensha Shibi] 835–908, China. A dharma heir of Xuefeng Yicun, Qingyuan line. Also called Ascetic Bei. Taught at Xuansha Monastery, Fu Region (Fujian). Given title Great Master Zongyi by the Emperor.

Xuantai, Senior Monk: See *Nanyue Xuantai.*

Xuedou Chongxian: [Setchō Jūken] 980–1052, China. A dharma heir of Zhimen Guangzuo, Yunmen School. Taught at Mt. Xuedou, Ming Region (Zhejiang). His selection of kōans became the basis of *The Blue Cliff Record.* Posthumous name: Zen Master Mingjue.

Xuedou Zhijian: [Setchō Chikan] 1105–1192, China. A dharma heir of Tiantong Zongjue, Caodong School. Taught at Mt. Xuedou, Ming region (Zhejiang). Tiantong Rujing's dharma teacher.

Xuefeng Yicun: [Seppō Gison] 822–908, China. A dharma heir of Deshan Xuanjian, Qingyuan line. Taught at Mt. Xuefeng, Fu Region (Fujian). Posthumous name: Great Master Zhenjue.

Xuyou: [Kyoyū]. A legendary hermit of ancient China, who declined Emperor Yao's offer of the throne.

Yang, Emperor: [Yōdai] d. 618. The second emperor of the Sui Dynasty. Reigned 604–618.

Yangqi Fanghui: [Yōgi Hōe] 993–1046, China. A dharma heir of Shishuang Chuyuan, Linji School. Taught at Mt. Yangqi, Yuan Region (Jiangxi). Regarded as founder of the Yangqi branch of the Linji School.

Yangshan Huiji: [Kyōzan Ejaku] 803–887, China. A dharma heir of Gui-
shan Lingyou. Taught at Mt. Yang, Yuan Region (Jiangxi). Guishan and
Yangshan are regarded as cofounders of the Guiyang School, one of the
Five Schools of Chinese Zen. Posthumous name: Zen Master Zhitong.

Yanguan Qian: [Engan Saian] d. 842, China. A dharma heir of Mazu Daoyi,
Nanyue line. Taught at Haichang Monastery, Yanguan, Hang Region
(Zhejiang). Posthumous name: Great Master Wukong.

Yanjun: See *Jingjie Yanjun.*

Yao, Emperor: [Gyō] A legendary virtuous ruler of ancient China.

Yaoshan Weiyan: [Yakusan Igen] 745–828, China. A dharma heir of Shitou
Xiqian, Qingyuan line. Taught at Mt. Yao, Feng Region (Hunan). Posthumous name: Great Master Hongdao.

Yellow Emperor: A legendary ruler of ancient China. Regarded as creator
of the calendar, music, literature, and medicine.

Yihuai: See *Tianyi Yihuai.*

Yongjia Xuanjue: [Yōka Genkaku] d. 713, China. A dharma heir of the Sixth
Ancestor Huineng. Taught in Yongjia, Wen Region (Zhejiang). Author
of the poem "Enlightenment of the Way." Also called Zen Master
Zhenjue.

Yuanan: See *Luopu Yuanan.*

Yuantong Fashen: [Entsū Hōshū] 1027–1090, China. A dharma heir of
Tianyi Yihuai, Yunmen School. Founded Fayun Monastery, Dongjing
(Henan). Given the title of Zen Master Yantong by the Emperor.

Yuanwu Keqin: [Engo Kokugon] 1063–1135, China. A dharma heir of
Wuzu Fayan, Linji School. Also called Jiashan. Compiler of *The Blue
Cliff Record.* Taught at Mt. Jia, Feng Region (Hunan). Given the titles
of Zen Master Yuanwu and Zen Master Fuguo by Emperors.

Yunmen Wenyan: [Ummon Bun'en] 864–949, China. A dharma heir of
Xuefeng Yicun, Qingyuan line. Established a monastery at Mt. Yunmen, Shao Region (Guangdong). Given the title Great Master Kuang-
zhen by the Emperor. Regarded as the founder of the Yunmen School,
one of the Five Schools of Chinese Zen.

Yunyan Tansheng: [Ungan Donjō] 782–841, China. A dharma heir of Yaoshan Weiyan, Qingyuan line. Taught at Mt. Yunyan, Tan Region
(Hunan). Posthumous name: Great Master Wuzhu.

Yuquan Shenxiu: [Gyokusen Jinshū] d. 706, China. A dharma heir of the
Fifth Ancestor Daman Hongren. Taught at Mt. Dangyang, Jing Region
(Hubei). Regarded as founder of the Northern School of Zen.

Zhao, Superintendent: [Chō Teikyo] Ca. thirteenth century, China. A government officer, grandson of Emperor Ning of the Southern Song Dynasty. A lay student of Tiantong Rujing.

Zhaojue Changzong: [Shōgaku Jōsō] 1025–1091, China. A dharma heir of Huanglong Huinan, Linji School. Taught at Donglin Monastery, Jiang Region (Jiangxi). Zen Master Zhaojue is his posthumous name.

Zhaozhou Congshen: [Jōshū Jūshin] 778–897, China. A dharma heir of Nanquan Puyuan, Qingyuan line. Taught at Guanyin Monastery, Zhao Region (Hebei). Posthumous name: Great Master Zhenji.

Zhixuan: Ca. thirteenth century, Korea. A monk who visited Tiantong Monastery while Dōgen was studying there. Biography unknown.

Zhixuan, lecturer: See *Changshui Zhixuan.*

Zhiyi: [Chigi] 538–597, China. Studied meditation with Huisi and later established the Tiantai doctrine at Mt. Tiantai, Tai Region (Zhejiang). Called Great Master Tiantai and Great Master Zhizhe.

Zhiyi, Ascetic: See *Zhuozhou Kefu.*

Zhizang: See *Xitang Zhizang.*

Zhu Falan: [Jiku Hōran] Ca. first century. An Indian monk who brought Buddhism to China for the first time in 67. Zhu Falan is a Chinese name. His Indian name is unknown. See also *Kāshyapa Mātanga.*

Zhuan Shigui: [Chikuan Shikei] 1083–1146, China. A dharma heir of Fayan Qingyuan, Linji School. Taught at Longxiang Monastery, Wen Region (Zhejiang). Compiled *Treasure Teaching of the Zen Gate* with Dahui Zonggao.

Zhuangzi: [Sōshi] Ca. fourth century, BCE, China. A Daoist thinker of the Warring Period. Author of *Zhuangzi.*

Zhuozhou Kefu: [Takushū Kokufu] Ca. ninth century, China. A dharma heir of Linji Yixuan, Linji School. As he always wore robes made of paper, he was called Ascetic Zhiyi (Paper Robe). He was from Zhuo Region (Henan).

Zong, Emperor: [Chūsō] 656–710, China. The fourth emperor of the Tang Dynasty. Reigned 683–684 and 705–710.

Zuoxi Xianlang: [Sakei Genrō] 673–754, China. Regarded as the Eighth Ancestor of the Tiantai School. He advised his dharma brother Yongjia Xuanjue to go study with Huineng, the Sixth Ancestor of Chinese Zen.